# Teaching Marx & Critical Theory in the 21st Century

# Studies in Critical Social Sciences Book Series

Haymarket Books is proud to be working with Brill Academic Publishers (www.brill.nl) to republish the *Studies in Critical Social Sciences* book series in paperback editions. This peer-reviewed book series offers insights into our current reality by exploring the content and consequences of power relationships under capitalism, and by considering the spaces of opposition and resistance to these changes that have been defining our new age. Our full catalog of *SCSS* volumes can be viewed at https://www.haymarketbooks.org/series_collections/4-studies-in-critical-social-sciences.

*Series Editor*
**David Fasenfest** (SOAS University of London)

*Editorial Board*
**Eduardo Bonilla-Silva** (Duke University)
**Chris Chase-Dunn** (University of California–Riverside)
**William Carroll** (University of Victoria)
**Raewyn Connell** (University of Sydney)
**Kimberlé W. Crenshaw** (University of California–LA and Columbia University)
**Heidi Gottfried** (Wayne State University)
**Karin Gottschall** (University of Bremen)
**Alfredo Saad Filho** (King's College London)
**Chizuko Ueno** (University of Tokyo)
**Sylvia Walby** (Lancaster University)
**Raju Das** (York University)

# Teaching Marx & Critical Theory in the 21st Century

Edited by
Bryant William Sculos
Mary Caputi

Haymarket Books
Chicago, IL

First published in 2019 by Brill Academic Publishers, The Netherlands.
© 2019 Koninklijke Brill NV, Leiden, The Netherlands

Published in paperback in 2020 by
Haymarket Books
P.O. Box 180165
Chicago, IL 60618
773-583-7884
www.haymarketbooks.org

ISBN: 978-1-64259-195-8

Distributed to the trade in the US through Consortium Book Sales and Distribution (www.cbsd.com) and internationally through Ingram Publisher Services International (www.ingramcontent.com).

This book was published with the generous support of Lannan Foundation and Wallace Action Fund.

Special discounts are available for bulk purchases by organizations and institutions. Please call 773-583-7884 or email info@haymarketbooks.org for more information.

Cover design by Jamie Kerry and Ragina Johnson.

Printed in United States.

10 9 8 7 6 5 4 3 2 1

Library of Congress Cataloging-in-Publication Data is available.

# Contents

Acknowledgements    VII
List of Illustrations    IX
Notes on Contributors    X

Introduction    1

### PART 1
### *Issues in Teaching Marx(ism)*

1  The Specter That Haunts Political Science: the Neglect and Misreading of Marx in International Relations and Comparative Politics    15
   *Sebastián Sclofsky and Kevin Funk*

2  Marxism and IPE    48
   *Ronald W. Cox*

3  Marx in Miami: Reflections on Teaching and the Confrontation with Ideology    66
   *Bryant William Sculos and Sean Noah Walsh*

4  Marxferatu: Introducing Marx through the Vampire Metaphor    89
   *Jess Morrissette*

5  Neoliberal Feminist Monsters: Where to Find Them and How to Slay Them    102
   *Maylin M. Hernandez*

### PART 2
### *Rethinking Critical Theory & Critical Pedagogy*

6  The "Great Refusal" Redux: Antidote to Mindless Syncopation    127
   *Mary Caputi*

7  Deep Critique: Critical Pedagogy, Marxism, and Feminist Standpoint Theory in the Corporate Classroom    143
   *Allan Ardill*

8   Pedagogies of Freedom: Exile, Courage, and Reflexivity in the Life of Paulo
    Freire     164
      *Mauro J. Caraccioli*

9   The Materiality of Proletarian Subjectivity: Anticapitalist Antiracist
    Pedagogies for the 21st Century     187
      *Zachary A. Casey*

10  Teaching Marx, Critical Theory, and Philosophy: Some Personal
    Reflections     203
      *Douglas Kellner*

    Coda: Inspiring Action: Rethinking the Public Function of
    Pedagogy     224

    Index     235

# Acknowledgements

The editors would like to extend their deepest appreciation to the various contributors to this volume, both the authors who have been with us from the very beginning and equally to those who joined on later when the project was very much in doubt. This project would, quite literally, be nothing without their hard work and patience. We would also like to acknowledge Dr. Sean Noah Walsh, who, despite having to drop off the project for personal and professional reasons, was a vital catalyst to this volume getting off the ground—and for the initial pedagogical inspiration that led to the writing of the initial article for *Class, Race and Corporate Power* from which the idea for this collection blossomed. We would also like to thank Maylin Hernandez for not only coming up with arguably the best chapter title in this collection (perhaps in any edited volume ever), but also for her diligent and unremunerated supplementary copy-editing of many of the chapters.

Specifically, Bryant would like to thank Mary Caputi for enthusiastically taking up co-editorship of the volume after Sean needed to step away. Her perpetual positivity and light-heartedness combined with her ceaselessly thoughtful and seemingly effortless work making my often-thorny writing more coherent and her sophisticated contributions to our co-written pieces that bookend the collection, are simply beyond words. All of that, combined with her capacities for compassionate, optimistic mentorship, have made this volume incalculably better.

In turn, Mary would like to thank Bryant for offering the possibility to work with him on this volume. I am deeply grateful to Bryant for allowing me to be a part of this important collection of essays that he and Sean initiated, and Bryant has been the central mover and shaker behind it from the beginning. It has been a pleasure working with Bryant whose energy, dedication, and uncompromising political convictions are an inspiration to us all, since the critical edge that informs his vision is precisely what is needed at this historical moment. Bryant's commitment to scholarly excellence coupled with engaged political activism runs throughout this volume, and his sensibilities offer an exemplary model for the classrooms of the twenty-first century. Working with Bryant gives me hope for the future, since it is truly inspiring to see such drive, integrity, and perseverance in a young intellectual.

The editors would like to thank Cambridge University Press, Oxford University Press, and the editors of *Class, Race and Corporate Power* for their permissions to republish versions of articles as Chapters 1, 3, 4, and 8.

Lastly, we would like to thank all those who are engaged in active struggle against capitalism, authoritarianism, racism, sexism, cisheterosexism, settler colonialism, ableism, ecocide, and any number of other anti-democratic forces that circulate across our dying planet. Thanks are hardly enough. A dedication is nary any better, but alas, we dedicate this project and our future pedagogy to them. We hope to have contributed in some small way to our variously and differentially shared project: the total emancipation of planet Earth.

# Illustrations

### Figure

3.1  "Feral Baby" (by Dr. Sean Noah Walsh)     76

### Tables

1.1  Syllabi requiring or recommending Marx's writing     19
1.2  Total required or recommended readings of Marx     19
1.3  Syllabi requiring or recommending "Marxist" readings     21
1.4  Total "Marxist" required or recommended readings     22

# Notes on Contributors

*Allan Ardill*
is Lecturer at Griffith Law School, Griffith University, Australia. Allan has taught property law every year since 2002 and during this time has received several teaching commendations and grants. Allan is a standpoint theorist with research interests in law and its nexus with class, gender, First Australian sovereignties, ideology, social theory, and sociobiology. He holds an Associate Diploma of Business (Industrial Relations) (Queensland University of Technology 1992), Bachelor Degrees in Accounting (Griffith 1998), Business Management (University of Southern Queensland 1998), and Law (Griffith 1998), and a PhD in Law and Sociobiology (Griffith 2008). Allan served as an Editor on the *Griffith Law Review* (2008 – 2012), serves as an Editor on the *Alternative Law Journal* (2009 - present), and is the Founding Editor, Executive and Consulting Editor of the *Griffith Journal of Law & Human Dignity* (2012 – present).

*Mary Caputi*
is Professor of Political Theory at California State University, Long Beach. She publishes in the areas of feminist and critical theories, post colonialism, and psychoanalysis. Her books include *Feminism and Power: the Need for Critical Theory* (Lexington, 2013), *Jacques Derrida and the Future of the Liberal Arts*, co-edited with Vincent Del Casino, Jr. (Bloomsbury, 2013), *A Kinder, Gentler America: Melancholia and the Mythical 1950s* (University of Minnesota Press, 2005), and *Voluptuous Yearnings: A Feminist Theory of the Obscene* (Rowman & Littlefield, 1994). She is currently at work on a book about the Slow Food movement.

*Mauro J. Caraccioli*
is Assistant Professor of Political Science and Core Faculty in the Alliance for Social, Political, Ethical, and Cultural Thought (ASPECT) at Virginia Tech. He teaches Political Theory, Critical International Relations, and Interpretive Approaches to Politics, receiving a PhD in Political Science from the University of Florida in 2015. He writes on the interplay of faith, nature, and empire in Colonial Spanish America, highlighting texts and encounters that broaden the cultural boundaries of New World intellectual production. Currently he is working on a book manuscript titled, *Of Nature & Other Demons: The Politics of Natural History in the Spanish Empire*, which examines the connections between works of naturalist inquiry composed by Catholic missionaries in the sixteenth century and the role of Latin American thought in the Western political canon.

### Zachary A. Casey

is Assistant Professor of Educational Studies at Rhodes College in Memphis, TN, USA. His research focuses on the intersections of critical pedagogy and critical whiteness studies, as well as multicultural education, practitioner research, and teacher education. Dr. Casey received his PhD in 2013 from the University of Minnesota in Culture and Teaching: Curriculum and Instruction. Focusing in particular on the ways in which neoliberal capitalism undermines antiracist praxis and pedagogies, his scholarship seeks to better understand the ways that white racial identity impacts possibilities for a more humanizing, liberatory, education. His work has been featured in *The Harvard Educational Review, Journal of Critical Educational Policy Studies, Journal of Curriculum Theorizing, Race Ethnicity and Education*, as well as other books, presses, and journals. He co-edited *Whiteness at the Table: Antiracism, Racism, and Identity in Education* for Lexington Press in 2018, and his first book, *A Pedagogy of Anticapitalist Antiracism: Whiteness, Neoliberalism, and Resistance in Education*, published by SUNY Press, was awarded the Society of Professors of Education Outstanding Book Award in 2018.

### Ronald W. Cox

is Professor of Politics and International Relations at Florida International University in Miami, where he teaches American Foreign Policy and International Political Economy. He has written or edited six books, which include *Corporate Power, Class Conflict and the Crisis of the New Globalization* (Lexington Books, 2019); *Corporate Power and Globalization in U.S. Foreign Policy* (ed.) (Routledge Press, 2012); and *US Politics and the Global Economy*, co-authored with Dan Skidmore-Hess (Lynne Rienner Press, 1999). In 2013, Professor Cox became the editor-in-chief of an open access journal that he founded, titled *Class, Race and Corporate Power*.

### Kevin Funk

is Assistant Professor of Political Science at the University of the District of Columbia. His research and teaching interests are at the intersection of global political economy, the politics of Latin America and the Southern Cone, and qualitative and interpretive methods. His current research analyzes the sociospatial changes generated by neoliberal urban mega-projects in Rio de Janeiro, Santiago de Chile, and beyond. His writing has appeared in such venues as *Journal of Cultural Economy, International Studies Perspectives, New Political Science*, and *The Latin Americanist*. He received his PhD in 2016 from the Department of Political Science and the Center for Latin American Studies at the University of Florida.

*Maylin M. Hernandez*
is a Ph.D. candidate in the Dept. of Political Science at the University of Massachusetts Amherst and fellow in The Amherst Program in Critical Theory. Her research interests include: critical theory, feminism, fashion studies, political and social theory, cultural studies, and their intersections. As a teaching assistant, she has taught students in the four major subfields within Political Science and was a finalist for the university Distinguished Teaching Award at UMass Amherst. She was also an invited panelist for the Graduate School Teaching Assistant Orientation to discuss pedagogy, classroom strategies, and related challenges with newly admitted graduate students in the Schools of Social and Behavioral Sciences, Management, and Public Health.

*Douglas Kellner*
is George F. Kneller Philosophy of Education Chair in the Division of Social Sciences & Comparative Education of the Graduate School of Education & Information Studies at UCLA. Prof. Kellner also holds a Ph.D. in philosophy from Columbia University, and is the author and/or editor of well over a dozen books and collections, including the collected works of Herbert Marcuse. He is a pioneer in the field of critical media literacies and an internationally recognized expert on Marxism, The Frankfurt School, poststructuralism, and postmodernism.

*Jess Morrissette*
is a Professor of Political Science at Marshall University, where he studies politics and popular culture. His recent research includes work on using fictional depictions of the living dead to teach political thought, analyzing the video game *Papers, Please* through the lens of Max Weber's work on modern bureaucracies, and examining the similarities between the narratives surrounding fictional zombies and "real world" discourses concerning terrorism and nuclear proliferation. Dr. Morrissette earned his Ph.D. in Political Science from the University of Georgia in 2007, after completing his MA at Virginia Tech and his BA at King University. His research has appeared in *PS: Political Science & Politics, Game Studies, Studies in Popular Culture, European Political Science Review*, and elsewhere.

*Sebastián Sclofsky*
is Assistant Professor in the Department of Criminal Justice at California State University, Stanislaus. His research and teaching interests include: Law & Society, Policing, Class and Race. His most recent publication is: "Our North is the

South: Lessons from researching police-community encounters in São Paulo and Los Angeles," *Handbook of Public Criminology* (Forthcoming).

*Bryant William Sculos*
holds a Ph.D. (2017) from Florida International University, where he also taught political theory. Currently, he is Visiting Assistant Professor in the Dept. of History and Political Science at Worcester State University teaching in the areas of global politics and critical political economy. He is also a Mellon-Sawyer Postdoctoral Fellow at the University of Massachusetts Amherst and The Amherst Program in Critical Theory, conducting research on the theoretical and practical relationships between universal basic income proposals and the possibilities of a democratic, egalitarian postcapitalist transition. Dr. Sculos is a member of Socialist Alternative/CWI, Politics of Culture editor for *Class, Race and Corporate Power*, and a regular contributor for The Hampton Institute and *New Politics*.

*Sean Noah Walsh*
is formerly Assistant Professor of Political Science at Capital University and Lecturer in political theory at Florida International University. Dr. Walsh earned his Ph.D. in Political Science from the University of Florida, and he is the author of *Perversion and the Art of Persecution* (Lexington, 2012), *Counterrevolution and Repression in the Politics of Education* (Lexington, 2013), and co-editor (with Prof. Clement Fatovic) of *Interpretation in Political Theory* (Routledge, 2016).

# Introduction

Teaching Marx and critical theory in the twenty-first century can be challenging. For many, the reigning neoliberal paradigm and prevalence of globalized capital have made a leftist critique appear outdated, a throwback to the ideological divisions between East and West that disappeared with the collapse of the Soviet Union. Indeed, the writings of Marx and critical theorists are sometimes looked upon as little more than meaningful contributions to the canon of intellectual history to be read for their historical insights rather than for their pertinence to the contemporary setting. At the extreme, the widespread normalization of markets, unhindered flow of global capital, and rise in populist movements have created an ideological backdrop to the twenty-first century that casts an anachronistic pall over serious leftist analysis, causing scholars of Marx and critical theory to seem notably out of step with the times.

The normalization of markets and attendant ideology of *homo economicus* might thus appear to have triumphed as the Reagan-Thatcher legacy lives on. At this writing, privatization and deregulation seem to have once again declared victory over a more collectivist approach to politics and economics. Yet recent developments also suggest otherwise and point either to an ongoing or a newly established leftist sensibility. In the United States, for instance, the emergence of Occupy in 2011 and more recent groundswell of support for Bernie Sanders, along with the massive growth in membership and political influence of socialist organizations like the Democratic Socialists of America and Socialist Alternative, surely reveals a growing dissatisfaction. Together these developments point to a clearly defined disaffection with unfettered markets, populist rhetoric, and the subsequent dwindling of the middle class and corollary growth of the working class and un(der)employed poor. A robust private sector and concentration of wealth on behalf of the privileged one percent has ushered in changes in American civic life that many find disturbing and that Sanders openly, aggressively opposed during his campaign. Among these are a stalwart defense of loosened economic regulations and the autonomy of financial institutions, the ideology that treats corporations as persons with protected constitutional rights, the unmanageable cost of American higher education coupled with rampant corporate intrusions into the university, our continued abuse of the environment, and the prevailing "rigged" tax structure that delivers a plutocracy. Clearly, there is pushback against undisguised capitalist greed and the many forms of corruption that unchecked power and wealth often deliver. Hence the Occupy Movement, the Fight for $15, and the push for single payer health care all display a determination to unsettle if not dismantle the ingrained bastions of power that have impoverished the once-thriving middle class. Ideologically, too, there is resistance to the ingrained networks that protect the privileged: #MeToo, Black Lives Matter, and the tenacious insistence on the part of America's youth that our gun laws be changed reveal a similar sensibility; while not uniformly leftist, it disdains the ability of ingrained power and wealth to ignore the obvious need for change.

The widespread support for Sanders in the US, Jeremy Corbyn in the UK, Podemos in Spain, and even the early successes of SYRIZA in Greece, together with the grassroots nature of these social movements, thus indicates a desire to seriously engage in a leftist critique of the ubiquitous neoliberal paradigm and rising populist tide. It suggests an openness to reevaluate the harm done by unrestricted markets, and an even more consistent and widespread skepticism and opposition to capitalism itself. It illustrates a pervasive effort to rethink the human cost of an exaggerated individualism that unwaveringly puts personal choice and responsibility above any commitment to social welfare or collective concerns. Echoes of Marx, the Frankfurt School, and other revisionist thinkers clearly infuse this sensibility whose political and economic analyses draw upon the critical categories of class, race, gender, sexual preference, ethnicity, etc. The struggles of these categories highlight the profound malaise and deep dissatisfaction with politics that keynote our time, calling out for intervention and serious reform. Indeed, the pronounced mistrust of politics that inheres in the United States as elsewhere signals a strong desire for change, change that confronts the satisfied one percent and broadened reach of markets as it seeks to either restore or initiate a politics openly committed to egalitarianism and socio-economic justice.

In response to this current political and economic climate, this volume defends the crucial importance of Marx and critical theory[1] to the academic curriculum and to the classroom. It offers a number of reflections on ways to teach and reach students who are dissatisfied with the status quo but who lack the intellectual tools or strategic savvy to initiate change. As educators, we interpret the teaching profession as a serious and unique undertaking with consequences that potentially reach well beyond the classroom.[2] We believe

---

[1] Here we use the term "critical theory" to refer to the Critical Theory of the Frankfurt School (which is typically noted by capitalizing the C and the T) as well as to the broader notion of critical theory that encompasses poststructuralism, postmodernism, feminism, critical race theory, critical pedagogy, and threads of political ecology.

[2] While this volume is written by scholar-teachers at colleges and universities, focusing on and working from the perspectives of higher education, the collective goal of this project is to provide useful—if not always explicit—insights for teachers at all levels, from pre-K through graduate school, and even beyond the classroom entirely.

that teachers hold a privileged position in society: the classroom represents a forum for generating creative political strategies and fostering intellectual ferment designed to change the social sphere. As educators we can inform, challenge, and encourage our students to not only think about the world but, quoting Marx, to change it. We can stretch them beyond their comfort zone of Marcuse's one dimensionality and urge them to take important, life—and world—changing risks.

While there is a troubling lack of writing on the specifics of teaching Marx, Marxism, and critical theoretical traditions, there is a long and well-respected tradition of pedagogy inspired by Marxism and critical theories, most notably being the pathbreaking work of Paulo Freire (1987; [1970] 1996), built on by a number of prominent scholar-teachers such as bell hooks (1994), Ira Shor ([1980] 1987a; 1987b), Henry Giroux (1997, 2011, 2014), and less well known but equally superb radical thinkers Wayne Au (2011, 2018) and Derek Ford (2016, 2018), among many others. Whether explicitly stated or not, the chapters in this volume are inspired by the pioneering work of many scholars of the various traditions of critical pedagogy. Freire opened our minds to the (re)production of imperial-capitalist forms of knowledge production and consumption in the classroom. hooks elucidated, in originally beautiful and deeply sophisticated prose, the challenging intersectional concerns that any critical or liberatory pedagogy must take seriously, specifically race and gender. Building on the earlier works of Freire, Shor, and others, Giroux expanded our thinking about the relationship between traditional (i.e., authoritarian) pedagogies and the broader antidemocratic structures in our society, specifically about the connection between the powerful neoliberal worldview that increasingly governs the university and the consumeristic-productive model of education that now trains students for the capitalist economy; forget about producing thoughtful, critical, or politically-engaged citizens. Ford's and Wu's recent, less widely-known works bring the developments in critical pedagogy closer to the contribution of this volume. For Wu and Ford respectively, pedagogy must (and in manifold, regressive ways, already does!) reach beyond the classroom. The classroom may be the typical site of pedagogy, yet if pedagogy remains isolated from the deeper trends in society and the broader structural forces at work outside the walls of the classroom (or even the virtual space of the increasing common digital classroom), the positive effects of any (critical) pedagogy will be self-undermining.

While access to education should certainly be made more equitable, it is not a silver bullet as such, at least as long as education is ensconced in a society that is structurally exploitative and unequal and remains tied towards producing adaptable, tamed future workers (Bowels and Gints 1977; Marsh 2011).

The form *and* content of education need to be made emancipatory, and only through enhancing our approaches to teaching the most historically powerful intellectual tools for critique—Marx, Marxism, and critical theory—can education play a crucial role in the radical expansion of the freedom of all people, especially the most vulnerable and oppressed in contemporary society: working class people, the unemployed, women, people of color, the non-cisgender or heteronormative, immigrants, and the mentally and physically disabled.

The contributors to this volume thus do not understand the term "academic" to be synonymous with what is effete, arcane, or strategically ineffective, but as a realm in which serious theory-cum-praxis takes place. Thus our essays appeal not to the widespread cynicism that so often parades as sophistication, but to Walter Benjamin's dialectical reading that allows us to read the current catastrophe as the portent of an altered vision: "Only for the sake of the hopeless ones have we been given hope" (Benjamin 1996, 356). The strong disaffection voiced by the ongoing social movements suggests, if not a changed sensibility, then at least the desire for one: it reveals the conviction that the pronounced injustices wrought by the current neoliberal establishment—and the whole of the historical and contemporary capitalist system—must yield to a new understanding of politics.

The essays presented here offer unique perspectives on why Marxism and critical theory embody a much-needed corrective to the dangers and damages of the contemporary practices and structures of the viral capitalist system. Collectively, they advance the value of teaching leftist and revisionist ideology in various contexts, sub-fields, and geographies, and underscore the need for students of the modern world to be versed in a critique of capitalism. The volume's ten chapters thus focus on questions such as the following: what difficulties, prejudices, or disciplinary roadblocks do professors experience when teaching Marx, critical theory, or other disparagements of neoliberalism? What experiences of everyday life can prove pedagogically useful in convincing students that they can transform the social sphere rather than merely acquiesce in its dysfunction? How can professors disabuse students of the pervasive notion that the free market or exploitative labor relations exist as natural phenomena, and convince them that they can act as political agents for change rather than as passive consumers? It is precisely the challenging, probing nature of these questions that allows the classroom to unleash political passion in students. By inviting them into conversations that they might never had had, it introduces them to a sensibility which otherwise might have remained forever foreign.

This project emerged out of an article titled "Marx in Miami: Reflections on Teaching and the Confrontation with Ideology," co-authored by Bryant William Sculos and Sean Noah Walsh, which appeared in the peer-reviewed, open-access journal *Class, Race and Corporate Power* in 2014 (and republished here as Chapter 3). This article, based on the experiences of a then-graduate student instructor and his more experienced mentor, offered reflections on the authors' respective experiences teaching Marx and Marxism to their primarily Cuban and Hispanic students at Florida International University. That piece was well-received and upon finding that there were notably few books covering this timely topic, the editors decided that an important and much-needed project would undertake a drastic and thoughtful expansion of the initial conversation. The dearth of scholarship on the topic was itself an indication that the initial discussion was in need of expansion, elaboration, dissemination, and sharing. Moreover, Mary Caputi's academic career in Southern California serves as further evidence of the need for such a volume. She teaches at a largely Hispanic institution that notably serves undocumented immigrants and first generation degree seekers whose first language is not English. The political consciousness of these students – who are Mexican, Latin American, Cambodian, Vietnamese, and often socio-economically disadvantaged – typically borrows from the expansionist American Dream, the glamour of Hollywood, and the optimistic belief in self-reinvention that permeates the greater Los Angeles area. Yet the lived experience of so many of her students does not bear out their expectations of what America can offer. This undoubtedly explains their often unexpected and surprised receptivity to a leftist critique that, prior to studying it systematically, they had dismissed as without merit. The array of scholar-teachers who comprise the contributors of this volume themselves bring their own diverse experiences and insights to bear on their respective arguments here, many of which are explicitly discussed in their respective chapters—further challenging the dominant scholarly norms of undervaluing personal experiences, explicit reflexivity, and narrative in social science scholarship.

Upon initially contacting a number of the eventual contributors, we received overwhelming enthusiasm for this project from scholars and students eager to fill the existing gap in the literature—and in the public sphere more generally. While this volume will certainly expand the conversation, the editors and contributors hope that this will only be the beginning to an even wider conversation of the intellectual and political importance of Marxist-inspired pedagogy, even as neoliberal trustees and administrators continue to commodify, corporatize, and colonize schools and universities, thereby undermining their important social function as a bastion of creative, oppositional thought. When the normalizing of markets and passive acceptance of socio-economic stratification spills over into places of learning, the need for informed, thoughtful, strategically effective push back augments. This volume takes part in that push back, and seeks to stem commodified education, safeguard critical thinking, and defend intellectual work as something other than a quantifiable undertaking. It enjoins voices from a number of disciplines in an effort to underscore the need for oppositional thought that directly and purposefully takes aim at the existing social sphere wherever neoliberal practices have taken root.

The corpus of writings that Marx and Engels have left us operates as a launching pad for conversations aimed at teaching students to gain distance on the status quo and organize politically against the commercial, profit-oriented interests that invade our space while (often imperceptibly) destroying our quality of life. How to utilize Marx, Marxian, and critical theory praxis in the classroom is the strategic question that our collection explores. These include teaching Marxism to mostly Cuban undergraduates in Miami; the dearth of genuine engagement with the Marxist canon in IR and Comparative Politics graduate programs; three distinct contributions connecting Paulo Freire's critical pedagogy to contemporary liberatory educational practices; the metaphor of vampires and pop culture as cultural critique; updating Herbert Marcuse's Great Refusal in order to disrupt the consumeristic tendencies pervasive in higher education and society more broadly; clarifying the usefulness of Marxism to International Political Economy given its dearth of class-based analysis; reinvigorating a feminist pedagogy against the neoliberal turn in feminism; developing an overtly anticapitalist, antiracist pedagogy rooted in a reconceptualized notion of proletarian subjectivity (also in conversation with Freire's critical pedagogy), and, finally, charting the contributions of "third generation" Frankfurt School critical theorists.

Chapter One is titled "The Specter That Haunts Political Science: the Neglect and Misreading of Marx in International Relations and Comparative Politics." In writing this chapter, co-authors Sebastián Sclofsky and Kevin Funk assess the extent to which elite international relations and comparative politics scholars engage with Marx in the classroom today, and find that even a superficial engagement with the Marxist tradition is exceedingly rare. Subsequently, the authors argue that this striking absence of the leftist tradition signals the embrace of the defeatist, neoliberal logic that characterizes the "end of history." While mainstream disengagement from Marx is perhaps unsurprising, many "critical" political scientists either ignore or misread Marx, often because of his purported Eurocentrism. Yet, as Sclofsky and Funk demonstrate, thinkers around the globe have found value in and made theoretical contributions to the universalist Marxist story. The authors analyze two such cases: the African anticolonial leader Amilcar Cabral and the Peruvian Marxist theorist and activist Jose´ Carlos Mariategui. In engaging with these thinkers, they show two academic disciplines' ability to address important real world problems and to thus bring about meaningful change.

In Chapter Two, "Marxism and IPE," Ronald W. Cox engages the discipline of international political economy as it has been taught in American universities. Cox insists that there has never been more of a need for a serious Marxist pedagogy within the subfield of IPE than there is today. The major textbooks in the field have all but abandoned the Marxist tradition in favor of an eclectic hodgepodge of mini-approaches that tackle specific oppressions, deconstruct other mainstream theories, or advance a particular strand of Marxist thought such as World Systems or Dependency Theory. In other words, the detailed, oppositional critique that informed Marx's *Capital* is completely ignored. Subsequently, many students do not know how to analyze the structural features of class power within a Marxian framework; consequently, student activists today are naïve about how power operates in global capitalism. This chapter documents the virtual disappearance of Marxism as a theoretical competitor to Realism and Liberalism within the subfield of IPE. It advocates bringing Marxism, and a careful reading of *Capital*, back to the classroom in framing a critical class-based analysis of modern capitalism. This approach provides students with the creative and intellectual tools that are needed in investigating, dissecting, and interpreting the systemic power relationships in modern global capitalism.

In Chapter Three, "Marx in Miami: Reflections on Teaching and the Confrontation with Ideology," Bryant William Sculos and Sean Noah Walsh chronicle their experience of teaching Marx to a community of students predisposed to dislike him. When teaching Marx in the United States, one often confronts emotional and intellectual obstacles; in Miami, those obstacles are greatly amplified. Perhaps like no other place in this country is teaching a particular theorist or theoretical tradition as resisted and as taxing on a teacher's patience and even self-esteem as is teaching Marx and Marxism in Miami. Likewise, the experience of learning Marx can be acutely distressing for students who have been raised to accept him as the personification of evil. Miami is the hub of the Cuban exile community in the United States, and thus semester after semester, year after year, the authors encountered groups of students who have basically formed their identities against the name "Marx." In composing this piece, the authors hope to detail some of their pedagogical strategies for combatting the intense ideological fervor against the left; moreover, we believe the lessons learned in this specific environment can be generalized for instructors regardless of geography.

Chapter Four's witty title, "Marxferatu: Introducing Marx through the Vampire Metaphor," reflects Jess Morrissette's awareness of his students' cultural referents. Although today's undergraduates may not be attuned to the implications of class struggle, they are generally well versed in the intricacies of vampire lore thanks to such widely acclaimed books-turned-film as Stephenie

Meyer's *Twilight*. This article outlines how the vampire metaphor can serve as a valuable pedagogical tool for introducing students to fundamental concepts in Marxist thought. As opposed to the supernatural vampires featured in Bram Stoker's *Dracula* or Meyer's *Twilight* saga, this approach treats capitalism as a form of economic vampirism—with the capitalist taking on the role of the vampire and the worker relegated to its prey. Because this pedagogical approach draws deeply on the imagination and on a well-articulated repertoire of cultural referents, it exemplifies a hands-on best practice that meaningfully engages students while teaching them to take the elements of political economy seriously. It teaches that change *is* possible: we just need to think creatively and act purposefully in bringing it about.

In Chapter Five, titled "Neoliberal Feminist Monsters: Where to Find Them and How to Slay Them," author Maylin M. Hernandez revisits the pedagogical scholarship done by earlier socialist-feminists and critical pedagogical scholars. She highlights how the critique of patriarchy and of capitalism's exploitation of women and sexual minorities has been lost while teaching students. Her aim is to analyze how contemporary capitalism and mainstream, neoliberal feminism have co-opted and undermined these struggles and have thus caused them to disappear from the modern classroom. Neoliberal feminism is used to sell wars, shoes, apartments, and careers, as it is molded to fit into every aspect of our lives. Its consumeristic dimension(s,) applied pedagogically, urges the individuation of students through false empowerment narratives, which tend to reproduce the predominance and privilege of masculine characteristics and (hetero)patriarchal and capitalistic notions of success (which are themselves often treated as "gender-neutral"). Hernandez therefore underscores the pressing need to take a socialist-feminist approach to teaching in order to be intersectionally inclusive while providing an academic space that continues to challenge capitalist conventions regarding feminism. By offering pushback against co-optation, she underscores the emancipatory impetus of feminism and reaffirms the classroom's role in providing a crucial foundation for potential political resistance—and thoughtful, engaged, humane politics at the very least.

This thematic of change, especially as initiated by the young, continues throughout the volume's other chapters. In Chapter Six, "The 'Great Refusal' Redux: Antidote to Mindless Syncopation," Mary Caputi argues that the writings of Herbert Marcuse remain pertinent to the contemporary political landscape and speak meaningfully to students today. While many of Marcuse's revisionist concepts help freshen Marx's orthodox views and make them accessible to students in the twenty-first century, the notion of "repressive desublimation" especially captures their imagination as it unmasks the falseness of commodity culture and the conservative, depoliticizing influence of globalized capital. In this chapter, Caputi argues that repressive desublimation remains a timely analytic tool even today, for following the debacle of 2008 many Americans still believe in free market enterprise and the glamour of the American dream. Marcuse's analysis helps students discern the tendency of commodity culture to imbue shopping with spiritual, supernatural, erotic attributes; it reveals their hidden, deeper longing for a social connection that globalized capitalism thwarts even as it ironically promises the same. The chapter weaves together both critical and affect theories and argues that Marcuse's "Great Refusal" of the 1960s has bearing on the contemporary political landscape, allowing young people to perceive the deadening effect of market ideology that nevertheless promises so much.

Chapter Seven is titled "Deep Critique: Critical Pedagogy, Marxism, and Feminist Standpoint Theory in the Corporate Classroom." In this essay, Allan Ardill recounts his experience of teaching Marxism and Feminist Standpoint Theory in a compulsory law course to produce graduates with a propensity for deep critique. Graduates skilled in deep critique – that is, a critique that evaluates law through the lens of philosophy, political science, economics, sociology, and other fields – are capable of critically assessing law and understanding how a legal system is socially constructed rather than ontologically given. It gives graduates an appreciation of how ideological vantage points coalesce with political economy to shape legal relations, and graduates learn how to be self-critical and reflective. Graduates who have thus attained an appreciation of how the law contributes to the reproduction of hierarchy are more likely to be open to transformational politics. If deep critique is not part of the curriculum then it is inevitable that graduates will simply grease the wheel of existing relations. Still, teaching deep critique is not without its challenges. The key lies in designing the course to engage with these challenges by linking this method to pedagogical best practices in an effort to justify the content and teaching style to potentially skeptical students. Although teaching Marxism and Feminist Standpoint Theory in a compulsory law course presents significant challenges that at times seem overwhelming, course evaluations indicate that students benefit from this pedagogy.

Chapter Eight, "Pedagogies of Freedom: Exile, Courage, and Reflexivity in the Life of Paulo Freire," is written by Mauro J. Caraccioli. This chapter exemplifies a reflexive ethnography of academic life by examining the relationship between exile and courage in the work of Paulo Freire. Caraccioli turns to Freire's experience of exile and the role it plays in his critical pedagogy in order to develop a framework linking scholarly encounters with global politics and different forms of courage. Caraccioli offers a portrait of Freire's life and work, focusing on the distinct elements in his writing that contribute to what is termed an "exilic reflexivity." This includes Freire's writing on conscientization, pedagogy, and the role of ideology in higher education, all of which highlights the missed opportunities especially by international relations scholarship to engage with alternative forms of existential courage. Freire's approach to education offers teachers and scholars an opportunity to rethink exile in light of ongoing structural challenges within the political economy of academic life. Caraccioli maintains that Freire, while not a scholar of international relations as such, conveys through his writing a pedagogy of freedom that remains highly relevant today.

Zachary A. Casey argues at the intersection of antiracist and anticapitalist pedagogy in Chapter Nine, titled "The Materiality of Proletarian Subjectivity: Anticapitalist Antiracist Pedagogies for the 21st Century." Building on a variety of classical and contemporary critical pedagogy scholarship, including Freire, Casey uses Marxian concepts of class positionality and subjectivity to elaborate a powerfully-sophisticated case for a kind of radicalized intersectional pedagogy that is explicitly anticapitalist and revolutionary—at least it aims in that direction. Building on his argument in previous work that the university is an inherently conservative, if not regressive, institution, Casey further argues that the classroom can, at its best, still be a site of radical experimentation and consciousness-raising if pedagogy is understood as inherently political and oriented towards radical, self-critical learning.

In Chapter Ten, "Teaching Marx, Critical Theory, and Philosophy: Some Personal Reflections," Douglas Kellner, one of the foremost experts on Marxism, critical theory, media, and education, presents an autobiographical narrative conveying his various experiences related to the teaching of Marx and Critical Theory over the course of his accomplished and influential academic career. He focuses primarily on how his personal life related to the development of his own thinking in relation to the various subjects on which he has written, emphasizing how teaching Marx and critical theory has changed. Covering the range of time from the raucous late sixties up to the present day, this chapter is filled with entertaining and insightful anecdotes and we are privileged to include it in our volume.

Given the current political climate with its troubling expressions of conservatism (including among far too many ostensibly on the "left"), we know that are many dissatisfied academics who share an interest in learning how to make Marxist and critical theory come alive in the classroom today and ultimately have an impact on the social sphere. Eager for change, we all desire the tools that will help train students to think and act politically in the current neoliberal, populist climate, making them agents of radical—or at least progressive—social change rather than passive consumers or uninvolved observers. We believe that the classroom offers innumerable teachable moments that can generate significant social change and lasting political results. It is therefore our hope that this volume will serve as a starting point for such seminal conversations meant to not only interpret the world, but to change it.

## Bibliography

Au, Wayne (2011) *Critical Curriculum Studies: Education, Consciousness, and the Politics of Knowing*. New York, NY: Routledge.

Au, Wayne (2018) *A Marxist Education: Learning to Change the World*. Chicago, IL: Haymarket Books.

Benjamin, Walter (1996) "Goethe's Elective Affinities." *Walter Benjamin's Selected Writings*. Trans. Stanley Corngold. Cambridge, MA: Belknap Press.

Bowels, Samuel and Gintis, Herbert (1976) *Schooling in Capitalist America: Educational Reform and the Contradictions of Economic Life*. New York, NY: Basic Books.

Ford, Derek R. (2016) *Communist Study: Education for the Commons*. London, UK: Lexington.

Ford, Derek R. (2018) *Politics and Pedagogy in the "Post-Truth" Era: Insurgent Philosophy and Praxis*. London, UK: Bloomsbury.

Freire, Paulo ([1970] 1996) *Pedagogy of the Oppressed*. Trans. Myra Bergman Ramos. London, UK: Penguin.

Giroux, Henry A. (1997) *Pedagogy and the Politics of Hope: Theory, Culture, and Schooling*. Boulder, CO: Westview Press.

Giroux, Henry A. (2011) *On Critical Pedagogy Today*. New York, NY: Continuum.

Giroux, Henry A. (2014) *Neoliberalism's War on Higher Education*. Chicago, IL: Haymarket Books.

hooks, bell (1994) *Teaching to Transgress: Education as the Practice of Freedom*. New York, NY: Routledge.

Marsh, John (2011) *Class Dismissed: Why We Cannot Teach or Learn Our Way Out of Inequality*. New York, NY: Monthly Review Press.

Shor, Ira and Freire, Paulo (1987a) *A Pedagogy for Liberation: Dialogues on Transforming Education*. New York, NY: Bergin & Garvey.

Shor, Ira ([1980] 1987b) *Critical Teaching and Everyday Life*. Chicago, IL: University of Chicago Press.

# PART 1

*Issues in Teaching Marx(ism)*

∴

CHAPTER 1

# The Specter That Haunts Political Science: the Neglect and Misreading of Marx in International Relations and Comparative Politics

*Sebastián Sclofsky and Kevin Funk*

## 1      Introduction

Given his status as one of history's most influential thinkers, one would expect that Karl Marx, along with Marxist thought in general, would garner significant attention within political science. Yet with the partial exception of political theorists (Sculos and Walsh 2015), relatively few US political scientists seriously engage with his work. Many ignore him entirely.

To assess the extent to which this lack of engagement with Marx is reflected in how political science is taught and reproduced, we have compiled an original database of syllabi for introductory, graduate courses in international relations (IR) and comparative politics (CP) from the top-ranked departments in the United States. Analysis of these syllabi provides overwhelming support for the assertion that substantive—or even superficial—engagement with Marx or the Marxist tradition is exceedingly rare within these subfields' mainstreams.[1]

As we argue, Marx's near-total absence from elite, graduate education in these subfields is due to factors that are simultaneously *intellectual* and *political*. These include: a refusal to analytically separate Marxism from the (failed) Soviet Union; the rise of quantitative, hypothesis-testing research and the concomitant decline of social or grand theory (Oren 2016); an ideological commitment to scientific "objectivity" and "neutrality," with a corresponding aversion to scholarship that advances a political agenda that challenges the status quo; and the embrace of the defeatist, neoliberal logic of the "end of history." In

---

[1] The extent to which the same is true outside of the United States is beyond the scope of the current analysis. However, there is prima facie evidence to suggest that engagement with Marx is indeed more common in at least certain other countries. For example, in commenting on the "transatlantic divide" between United States and British international political economy, Cohen (2007, 213) identifies in the latter "a more relaxed attitude toward Marxism or other leftist doctrines, which reinforced a critical disposition toward markets and their consequences."

other words, while there are certainly academic motives behind mainstream political science's disregard for Marx, the discipline is also clearly haunted by the ideological specter of Marx and Marxism (Callinicos 1996, 10).

While mainstream disengagement from Marx is perhaps unsurprising, the failure to seriously engage with Marx or the Marxist tradition is in fact much more widespread. Indeed, both mainstream and many self-avowedly critical political scientists ignore and/or misread Marx. Accordingly, we extend our analysis by examining the argument, common to many mainstream and especially postcolonial thinkers, that Marx was a Eurocentric theorist whose writings are of little to no use to efforts that analyze the non-European world or associated questions relating to race and other axes of identity.

Though Marx's writings are at times infused with ethnocentric biases, such strident accusations of Eurocentrism overlook his analysis of the "intersections" between race, class, gender, and national identity, as well as his attempts to grapple with the specificity of the non-European world. Crucially, in turn, these critics fail to account for how thinkers and movements around the globe have found value in and made theoretical contributions to the universalist Marxist story. Here, we briefly analyze two such cases: the African anticolonial leader Amílcar Cabral and the Peruvian Marxist theorist and activist José Carlos Mariátegui. As their efforts demonstrate, reading Marx vis-à-vis the colonial world produced both theoretical development and modification within the Marxist tradition as well as important insights that were instrumental in national liberation struggles. Overall, we argue that this superficial engagement, misreading, and—in some cases—outright ignoring of Marx hinders political science's ability to address important real-world problems or theoretical debates, let alone make the discipline *matter*.

## 2     Ignorance is Not Bliss: Why We Need Marx

Before analyzing the extent to which and reasons why Marx is largely ignored and/or misread in political science, we must first engage in the straightforward—if rather curious—task of explaining why this is a problem that needs to be addressed. It is a straightforward endeavor because all we wish to establish is that Marx's thought is worthy of sustained engagement (and not that he was necessarily "right"). And it is curious because one does not expect to have to justify the importance of reading one of history's most influential and cited authors. Yet based on the observed tendency to caricaturize and/or ignore Marx, circumstances obligate us to make the case for Marx's continuing relevance.

## 3  Why Marx Was Right—Or, at Least Worth Paying Attention To

Sure, Marx was an important political thinker who wrestled with capitalist modernization and its discontents, but really, *who cares*? From Adam Smith (Hoffman 2013) to Edmund Burke (O'Neill 2016), social scientists often engage in misguided readings of classic thinkers. Why should we be particularly troubled by the tendency to misread Marx, or even ignore him entirely?

Our initial response is, again, straightforward. As Tucker (1978, ix) notes in the preface to the widely used *The Marx-Engels Reader*, "A knowledge of the writings of Marx and Engels is virtually indispensable to an educated person in our time, whatever his political position or social philosophy." Indeed, their thought "has profoundly affected ideas about history, society, economics, ideology, culture, and politics," as well as "the nature of social inquiry itself" (ibid.). Here, one might add that Marx is of course part of the triumvirate of essential classic social theorists, along with Max Weber and Émile Durkheim. Tucker (ibid.) continues: "Not to be well grounded in the writings of Marx and Engels is to be insufficiently attuned to modern thought," and also to be "self-excluded" from the debates that define "most contemporary societies" as well as those that have shaped the trajectories of the aforementioned disciplines. A political scientist who largely overlooks Marx is akin to a specialist in English literature with only passing knowledge of Shakespeare. Accordingly, rather than having to defend the proposition that Marx is worthy of close reading, it should be the turn of those who caricaturize and studiously ignore Marx to justify their own lack of thorough engagement with a thinker who has done more than nearly any other to influence both our social world and how it is studied.

Yet there is also a more sophisticated response: that Marx, far from fading into irrelevance, is *especially* relevant for our current times. Various reasons make this so. First, his analysis—though of course not without its flaws—was remarkably prescient. For example, long before "globalization" became an inescapable buzzword, Marx had already encapsulated the core of at least the economic aspects of this fuzzy concept by observing that "[t]he need of a constantly expanding market for its products chases the bourgeoisie over the whole surface of the globe. It must nestle everywhere, settle everywhere, establish connexions everywhere" (Marx and Engels [1888] 1978, 476). Given that we live in hypercapitalist times in which nearly *everything* is seemingly being marketized, capitalist globalization is creating an increasingly global system defined by "time-space compression" (Harvey 1990), and extreme market fundamentalism—neoliberalism—has become orthodoxy, Marx's analysis seems more relevant than ever. As Eagleton (2011, 2) puts it, "as long as capitalism is still in business, Marxism must be as well." Capitalism's global triumph—the so-called end of history and the fact that capitalist logic "has penetrated just about every aspect of human life and nature itself" (Wood 1997)—should thus make us *more* attuned to Marx, not less.

In turn, along with capitalism's global spread, so too have we borne witness to global crises (such as the 2008 global financial meltdown), increased global inequality and the oppositional movements it has spurred (including Occupy Wall Street and the Bernie Sanders campaign in the United States), and globalized repression in the name of capital accumulation (ranging from dispossession of the indigenous Mapuche by loggers in southern Chile to violence against union leaders and striking workers the world over). As Eagleton (2011, 8–9) again observes, such issues are precisely the ones "on which Marxism has acted and reflected for almost two centuries. One would expect, then, that it might have a few lessons to teach the present." Whatever one makes of Marx's *normative* positions concerning how to overcome these maladies, we are at least obligated to engage with his *critique*.

Second, many of the objections launched against Marx are simply *wrong*. As we explore below, while Marx is typically rejected by postcolonial and other thinkers for his supposedly crude universalism and corresponding inability as a Eurocentric theoretician to conceptualize uniquely Global South/Third World realities, Marx indeed has long been a source of inspiration for myriad thinkers and movements *all across the globe*. From the Chilean student movement of the past decade to anti-austerity protests in Greece that began in earnest in 2010, our understanding of today's mass mobilizations would be much richer if we were to understand and grapple with Marx's complex and nuanced critique of the capitalist system.

Further, while we are said to live in intersectional times that should lead us to dismiss Marx and his entire brand of class reductionism, this critique is based on, at best, a partial reading of Marx. As Anderson (2015) argues, while Marx of course did not address all of today's issues, he did understand that "race, class, and gender were concrete categories that intersected in various ways—and sometimes coalesced in a revolutionary fashion—across the historical modes of production that he analyzed." For example, "for Marx, uprooting slavery and racism in America was not only a political question of constitutional amendments and civil rights bills, but also one that concerned the economic structures of society" (Anderson 2015). In times defined by racialized police violence, mass incarceration, and inequality, Marx thus clearly remains a worthy interlocutor.

One may of course reasonably disagree with various aspects of Marx's political program, normative commitments, or social analysis. Yet what is

TABLE 1.1   Syllabi requiring or recommending Marx's writing

|  | Total syllabi | Syllabi: Marx required | Syllabi: Marx recommended |
|---|---|---|---|
| CP | 10 | 1 | 1 |
| IR | 12 | 0 | 0 |
| Total | 22 | 1 | 1 |
| Percentage | 100.00% | 4.55% | 4.55% |

TABLE 1.2   Total required or recommended readings of Marx

|  | Total required readings | Total recommended readings | Total required Marx | Total suggested Marx |
|---|---|---|---|---|
| CP | 664 | 1036 | 1 | 1 |
| IR | 826 | 724 | 0 | 0 |
| Total | 1490 | 1760 | 1 | 1 |
| Percentage | 100.00% | 100.00% | 0.07% | 0.06% |

not intellectually justifiable in our attempts to grapple with contemporary politics, as we argue below, is to neglect to engage with his thought. Such a lack of engagement, as we demonstrate, is based more on neoliberal ideological commitments than on a scientific desire to understand the world around us.

## 4   Haunting the Haunted: the (Dis)Engagement of Political Science with, or from, Marx

To analyze Marx's place in today's political science landscape, we have sought to discover what graduate students in top ten US political science programs read in introductory courses in IR and CP.[2] For consistency's sake, we focus on

---

2  We utilize the *US News and World Report* ranking, available at: http://grad-schools.usnews.rankingsandreviews.com/best-graduate-schools/search?program=top-political-science-schools&specialty=&name=&zip=&program_rank=top_10&sort=&sortdir. The top ten US political science graduate programs are: (1) Harvard University; (2-tie) Princeton University; Stan-

courses taught during the 2015–2016 academic year.[3] We chose to focus on top ten programs as they are representative of and play a disproportionate role in shaping the discipline's "mainstream," both in the United States and around the world.[4] Indeed, there is little reason to expect substantial variation in non-top-ten Ph.D.-granting institutions (Colgan 2016), given that—as our random sample demonstrates—just more than 62 percent of tenurable or tenured faculty in the top fifty departments graduated from these very same top-ten programs.[5]

We collected twenty-two such syllabi: ten for introductory CP courses, and twelve for IR.[6] We counted the total numbers of required and recommended readings and how often Marx's writings appear in either category. We then counted how many works written by Marx were required or suggested in these courses. The results appear in Tables 1.1 and 1.2.

Marx is almost completely absent from both tables. Only in the CP course at MIT was one of Marx's texts required (*The Communist Manifesto*). In a corresponding course at Harvard, it was recommended that students read the *18th Brumaire of Louis Bonaparte* in the week dedicated to research methodologies.[7]

---

ford University; (4-tie) University of Michigan; Yale University; (6) University of California, Berkeley; (7) Columbia University; (8-tie) Massachusetts Institute of Technology; University of California, San Diego; (10-tie) Duke University; University of California, Los Angeles.

3   Three of the syllabi correspond to the 2014–2015 academic year. However, we were informed by the instructors that they would be using the same syllabi for the 2015–2016 academic year.
4   We are aware that the status of Marx may be different outside of the United States, as well as in other disciplines, or in colleges and universities with a teaching as opposed to research focus. Such comparisons provide an interesting basis for future research.
5   To assess the disproportionate influence of top-ten programs, we divided the remainder of the top fifty into four groups (11–20, 21–30, 31–40, 41–50) and randomly chose three institutions from each range. They are: University of Chicago (ranked #12, with 78.9% of tenurable and tenured faculty from top-ten programs); New York University ($15 [tied], 63.8%); University of Wisconsin-Madison (#15 [tied], 51.5%); Northwestern University (#21 [tied], 81.4%); University of Illinois Urbana-Champaign (#23 [tied], 52%); University of Washington (#28 [tied], 51.9%); Rice University (#32 [tied], 25%); University of Virginia (#36 [tied], 67.4%); University of Notre Dame (#36 [tied]; 66.7%); University of Colorado Boulder (#45 [tied], 35.7%); Rutgers University-New Brunswick (#45 [tied], 57.1%); and Brown University (#45 [tied], 81.5%). While there is fairly wide variation in this sample, notably it does not appear to correlate to any significant degree to the program's position within the top fifty.
6   There are twelve IR syllabi (instead of ten) because at Stanford the introductory course was taught twice in the past academic year, while Yale has a sequence of two introductory courses. University California–San Diego does the same in CP; however, as we were unable to obtain one of these syllabi, only ten entered into our analysis.
7   Given that Marx considered dialectics to be his main methodological approach, which he developed in *Capital*, this would be a more fitting text than the *18th Brumaire* to present Marx's methodology, if that were the intention.

We then counted how many Marxist or Marxist-inspired authors/texts were assigned as required or suggested readings. To be included, we determined that the text must fulfill at least one of the following three criteria:[8]

1. The author self-identifies as Marxist or following the Marxist tradition (for instance, Lenin).
2. The author uses a Marxist framework of analysis and/or advocates for a Marxist political project. The former refers to the presumption that the socioeconomic structure and class struggle are the fundamental (though not the only) factors explaining the phenomenon under investigation. Internationally, this means that capitalist expansion and capital accumulation, with their concomitant uneven development, are the core elements that explain international political phenomena (for example, as delineated by dependency theory).[9]
3. The author acknowledges the Marxist tradition with its limitations and attempts to complement it by incorporating other elements not thoroughly considered by Marx without abandoning the centrality of the socioeconomic structure and class relations. A prime example is Anderson's (1991) *Imagined Communities*.[10]

Our results appear in Table 1.3.

From the perspective that Marx deserves to be read, the above numbers are more promising. However, when the amount of Marxist readings is compared to total readings (see Table 1.4), the data again highlight Marx's absence.

TABLE 1.3   Syllabi requiring or recommending "Marxist" readings

|  | Total syllabi | Syllabi with required readings | Syllabi with recommended readings |
|---|---|---|---|
| CP | 10 | 6 | 3 |
| IR | 12 | 1 | 3 |
| Total | 22 | 7 | 6 |
| Percentage | 100.00% | 31.82% | 27.27% |

---

8   It is worth noting that we sought to give the benefit of the doubt to the courses under examination by being generous in our inclusion of texts.
9   Examples in this category include: Esping-Andersen (1990), Cardoso and Faletto (1979), Wallerstein (1974), and Polanyi (1944).
10  Further examples include: Evans (1979), Rueschemeyer, Huber, and Stephens (1992), Ashley (1984), and Wallerstein (1986).

TABLE 1.4  Total "Marxist" required or recommended readings

|  | Total required readings | Total recommended readings | Total required "Marxist" readings | Total recommended "Marxist" readings |
|---|---|---|---|---|
| CP | 664 | 1036 | 13 | 14 |
| IR | 826 | 724 | 1 | 3 |
| Total | 1490 | 1760 | 14 | 17 |
| Percentage | 100.00% | 100.00% | 0.94% | 0.97% |

These data appear to suggest that the discipline's leading lights believe Marx has very little to say to their subfields. This absence becomes even more glaring given that many of these introductory IR courses dedicate a significant amount of time to the study of international political economy. Yet not even these syllabi assign a single text by Marx, despite the fact that he produced some of history's most important analyses of the international political-economic system.

In some cases, Marx's absence is also particularly puzzling. For example, an introductory CP course at University California–Berkeley dedicates an entire week to the study of class *without a single writing by Marx*.[11] Similarly, even though many of these IR and CP syllabi include a substantial focus on structural forces, Marx and Marxist authors are not read in these sessions. Where on the one hand, as we argue here, Marx is often (somewhat unfairly) criticized by mainstream scholars for giving too much explanatory force to economic structures; on the other hand, when students in elite graduate programs study the influence of structures, economic and otherwise, they seemingly do so without sustained engagement with the Marxist tradition. Further, this contradiction passes without comment in the discipline. Instructors assign readings covering topics such as poverty and prosperity, revolutions and regime change, political structures, and the balance between structure

---

11  The instructors assigned Eidlin (2014), which reviews the evolution of class identity, as understood by Marx and Weber, from a central and clear analytical concept to a more complex and nuanced one, as well as the decline of class-based politics. They also assigned Roberts (2002), which analyzes the decline of class cleavages in Latin America despite social inequalities. While Marx lingers in the background of these articles, the absence of writings by Marx himself or those of more Marxist-inclined authors is nevertheless problematic. The instructors also assigned Marshall and Bottomore (1992).

and agency without including Marx or even tenuously Marxist authors. For example, Harvard's introductory IR course features two weeks dedicated to structural explanations. Yet no readings by Marx or Marxist authors are assigned for these sessions, save for the partial exception of Ashley (1984), which is a suggested (but not required) reading and engages with Marx without adopting a Marxist position per se.

The data also reinforce the conclusions of the Teaching, Research, and International Policy (TRIP) Project, which finds that Marxism has lost substantial ground as an IR paradigm since the 1980s and is being taught less and less in this subfield, particularly in the United States (Maliniak et al. 2011). Concomitantly, Katzenstein, Keohane, and Krasner (1998) have shown that constructivism has replaced Marxism as the principal challenger to realism and liberalism. According to the TRIP Project, the perception of Marxism as being read in the discipline has dropped systematically and significantly since the 1990s. In fact, "[i]n 2008, IR scholars thought that Marxism was less prominent than either feminism or the English School" (Maliniak et al. 2011, 444).

Analyzing the time devoted to each paradigm in introductory IR classes from 2004 to 2008, the TRIP data show a decline in Marxism from 14 percent in 2004 to 7 percent in 2006 and then an increase to 10 percent in 2008.[12] This is half the time dedicated to realism or liberalism and 7 percent less than the time dedicated to nonparadigmatic readings. Further, these data reveal that Marxist articles are the least published type of articles in the field. Interestingly, paradigmatic articles are cited more than nonparadigmatic articles, with the exception of articles that adopt a Marxist approach; these are cited less than nonparadigmatic ones. In the TRIP survey, participants were asked to choose the most prominent IR scholars. Not a single scholar named by US respondents identifies with Marxism. Given the preceding, it is no surprise that Maliniak et al. (2011, 450) conclude that, "Marxist theory has all but disappeared."

Based on our own analysis and the data collected by the TRIP Project, we observe two important trends. First, Marxism has suffered a huge decline in elite US graduate training in these fields, to the point of being almost completely abandoned. Second, Marx and Marxists are so infrequently read or assigned that there is a real risk that graduate students are being trained to respond to (if not reject) a caricaturized version of Marx and Marxism without having ever seriously engaged with either.

---

12   This increase does not seem to be significant vis-à-vis the overall perception that Marx is virtually absent from IR. Nonetheless, further research may show that Marx is increasingly being read in certain areas within political science, perhaps as an attempt to grapple with the global economic crisis and its ongoing effects.

## 5 So, Why Has Marx Been Abandoned?

In 1999, Gamble argued that Marxism was widely perceived by academics to be in a terminal crisis. While for most of the twentieth century a critical engagement with Marx and Marxism was an essential part of social science, Gamble (1999, 1) indicated that "a new generation of social scientists is growing up, which has little or no contact with Marxist ideas and Marxist methods of analysis." To its dishonor, political science appears to have been precocious in its abandonment of Marx and Marxism. As leading realist IR scholar Walt (1998, 34) comments, Marxist theories of international politics "were largely discredited before the Cold War even ended" and "succumbed to [their] various failings."[13]

In contrast, we suggest that this abandonment of Marxism in US CP and IR was largely not the product of Marxism's intellectual "failings," but rather can be attributed to: the (troubling) association of Marxism with and the fall of the Soviet Union, an adherence to the end of history ideology with its acceptance of capitalism and liberalism as the only game in town, the desire to avoid a modern 1968-style college uprising, and the triumph of the ideology of so-called scientific neutrality. We will briefly consider these in turn.

Although the characterization of the Soviet Union as Marxist was endlessly rejected by many Marxists, and although its tenets and policies resonated in only the most superficial of ways with Marx's ideas, the Soviet Union's fall provided a useful opportunity for Marx's detractors who promoted the idea that Marx and Marxism were also withering away. It was, in other words, "guilt by association" (Kellner 1995, xi). As we argue, this inability—or refusal—to separate Marx from Soviet authoritarianism continues to inform mainstream political science's rejection of Marx.

Likewise, the perceived need to accept capitalism and full integration into the global market has become the new universal wisdom (Gamble 1999, 3). Fukuyama's (1992) *The End of History* became the mantra for those arguing against Marxism and any possibility of social or economic reform that

---

13  As would-be supporting evidence, Walt (1998, 34) observes that "[t]he extensive history of economic and military cooperation among the advanced industrial powers showed that capitalism did not inevitably lead to conflict. The bitter schisms that divided the communist world showed that socialism did not always promote harmony." Among the errors of analysis and interpretation contained in these pithy lines, it is especially fitting to note that Marxist theory of course does not preclude intercapitalist cooperation (as repeatedly argued by Karl Kautsky and others). Further, as discussed below, it is highly troubling to blindly associate Marx and Marxism with the self-proclaimed socialism of Cold War–era authoritarian regimes. We would like to thank one of the reviewers for directing our attention toward this source and quote.

challenges the existing capitalist and neoliberal structures. Fukuyama proposes that there is no alternative to capitalism and liberal democracy, thus rendering Marx passé. This implies capitalist triumphalism is accompanied by a cultural pessimism that represents a neoconservative version of Baudrillard (1975) and similar authors, who proclaim the existence of a "post-historical" world devoid of meaning, in which private consumerism attempts, unsuccessfully, to fill the emptiness left by the disappearance of the great metaphysical and political struggles of time's past (Callinicos 1989).

It is no coincidence that Fukuyama was a student of Samuel Huntington, who in 1968 expressed concern about the disorder that an increase in mass political participation could cause if not channeled through an adequate institutional framework. As he wrote, "[u]rbanization, increases in literacy, education, and media exposure all give rise to enhanced aspirations and expectations, which, if unsatisfied, galvanize individuals and groups into politics. In the absence of strong and adaptable political institutions, such increases in participation mean instability and violence" (Huntington 1968, 48). Further, in the midst of the civil rights movement and campus revolts across the United States and the world, Huntington argued that the higher the level of education of the unemployed, alienated, or dissatisfied person, the more extreme his/her destabilizing behavior. "Alienated graduate students prepare revolutions," he wrote (Huntington 1968, 48).

This work reveals Huntington's real fear concerning the revolutionary potential of university students. To him, the study of Marx and other thinkers who advocate not only for a critical reading of society's structures and politics, but also call for action, had the potential to create revolutionary elements, bringing disorder and chaos to society. The ideology of scientific neutrality, which posits the separation of facts from values, together with the argument that the main, and almost exclusive, role of social scientists is to contribute to their disciplines (as opposed to the "real world"), is connected with Huntington's fears and suggests the rejection of any body of thought that envisions the unity of theory and praxis. As Gunnell (1993, 7) contends, "in a highly pluralistic society, the authority for knowledge seemed to require speaking with a neutral voice grounded in scientific values and facts."

According to Taylor (1994, 547), positive political science—as embodied by the remaking of political science in the image of economics through the meteoric rise of rational choice theory, formal modeling, and advanced statistical techniques—claimed to have become value-free and in so doing had liberated itself from political philosophy.[14] Indeed, the scientific method is said to

---

14  As a corollary to our analysis, we also examined the frequency with which texts in social and political theory are assigned in the aforementioned courses. Weber is required four

allow for the dispassionate study of the empirical world, without metaphysical presuppositions or value biases (Taylor 1994, 547). Marx, on the other hand, is portrayed as an ideological thinker whose normative commitments introduce bias into his observations.

Yet, when we want to understand the reasons behind social phenomena and answer *why* questions, it is impossible not to *interpret* the evidence we observe (Taylor 1971). And it is here that values, and normative theory, enter. As Harvey (1973, 24) remarks, to regard reality as independent of human perception and action is itself "idiotic and ideological." The problem with arguments to the contrary is that they fail to recognize that "value-free" political science is itself both an ideological position, and, indeed, a myth.

Many critics, such as Popper, argue that there is nothing scientific about Marxism because its propositions cannot be scientifically tested (Mandel 1976, 25). Yet, as Mandel (1976) posits, there are very simple ways to test whether Marx was "wrong." For example, one could discredit Marx by discovering that the more capitalist industry develops, the smaller the average factory becomes, the less it depends upon new technology, the more its capital is supplied by the workers themselves, and the greater the share of surplus value they accumulate. Yet, plainly, none of this has occurred.

Others argue that the lack of working-class revolutions in advanced industrialized countries is a sign of Marx's predictive failure. Yet only an oversimplified reading of Marx—precisely the type that prevails in political science—suggests that revolutions will occur without human agency. Indeed, while Marx of course argues that the inherent contradictions of capitalist society will provoke a revolutionary situation, this requires the development of revolutionary consciousness, for "material forces can only be overthrown by material forces, but theory itself becomes a material force when it has seized the masses" (Marx [1844] 1978, 60). In this vein, Marx and Engels wrote the *Manifesto* precisely to *convince* the masses to rise up and engage in class struggle. Indeed, this radical, political message is precisely what Huntington and his fellow travelers most feared.

---

times (0.3%) and suggested four times (0.2%) in four different syllabi. Other classic theorists, such as Durkheim, Hobbes, Machiavelli, Hume, Aristotle, de Tocqueville, Popper, Kuhn, and Lakatos are required in seven instances (0.5%) and suggested in fifteen (0.9%). On the one hand, it appears that social and political theory *in general* are under attack; yet, our contention is that the abandonment of Marx responds to specific ideological perspectives and is even more critical than these other cases given that the syllabi we have reviewed specifically address capitalism, globalization, and class, all issues about which Marx was a foundational thinker.

Openly normative discussions in political science, and in this sense Marx too, have been pushed toward political theory. And in turn, it is no coincidence that political theory is under attack as the subfield that does not deal with "science." As Cavarero (2002) indicates, the canon of science became the criteria for defining appropriate work. The consequence is that everything else is rejected as metaphysics, "a sort of literary production lacking in scientific rigor" that is seen as "untrustworthy" (Cavarero 2002, 510).[15]

Similarly, Berlin previously argued that political theory would never become a science because it deals with normative questions that are specifically philosophical (Grant 2002, 577). If we further consider the fact that capitalism, according to Brown (2002), has become an almost unchallengeable fact for political theorists, then the future of Marx in political science in general may seem doomed. To summarize, there are numerous reasons—both individual and structural—that have led to the abandonment or rejection of Marx. Yet it appears that they are more political than intellectual. That is, the collective lack of engagement with Marx's writings seems to be based less on their own intellectual merit (or lack thereof) and more on their political ramifications.

Marx poses two problems for political scientists. First, he contradicts current norms in favor of "navel-gazing" by suggesting that our chief ambition should be to contribute to *society*, not *the discipline*. And second, even if one rejects his political arguments, engaging with Marx tells us that we should take political positions, be politically active, and question our role as academics in maintaining or challenging the status quo. Marx wants us not only to *interpret* the world, but to *change* it. For those who proffer the problematic (and ideological) notion that social science can and should be value-free or promote the political pessimism of the end of history, Marx is thus indeed a haunting specter.

## 6 Between Readings and Misreadings: On Marx, Intersectionality, and the Charge of Eurocentrism

Our analysis of graduate syllabi reveals in unequivocal fashion that, at least in pedagogical terms, Marx has largely vanished from the IR and CP main-

---

15  Here, one may be tempted to point to the rise of constructivism in IR in particular as countering the notion that there is a sustained attack in political science on all forms of anti/non/post-positivist research. Yet the version of constructivism that has become a leading IR paradigm is precisely the "thin" form that is far more amenable to value-free, positivist norms (Wendt 1999). We thank one of the reviewers for pushing us to develop our thoughts on this matter.

streams. As we detail above, the reasons for this abandonment are more political than intellectual in nature. That the mainstream has largely dismissed Marx does not necessarily mean that Marx is absent from these subfields as a whole, for indeed both enjoy a significant degree of theoretical diversity at least at the margins. Yet even most "critical" scholars in these areas have abandoned Marx. In this section, we analyze one of the principal reasons behind this lack of engagement: namely, the charge that Marx is a Eurocentric thinker who has little to say about the non-European world.

Below, we document how both mainstream and especially critical thinkers—both within and beyond the aforementioned top-ranked departments—have constructed this "Eurocentric Marx."[16] Subsequently, we turn to Marx's own voluminous, but largely overlooked, writings on colonialism and imperialism, focusing in particular on the cases of China and India. Though Marx of course was at times weighed down by Eurocentric and modernist baggage, he nevertheless made serious and repeated efforts to grapple with non-European realities. And indeed, as noted by Bieler (2016), "[w]hen analyzing concrete struggles, Marx was careful not to generalize his findings from one country to another." Further, as we explore at the end of this section, the fact that so many non-European thinkers would take the baton from Marx and both use and modify the Marxist tradition to analyze their own realities is an additional argument against the attempt to dismiss Marx as simply another modernist, Eurocentric product of the Enlightenment.

## 7   The Construction of a Eurocentric Marx

The finding that Marx is not being taught in the discipline's centers of power is somewhat ironic given that many key thinkers in these subfields readily acknowledge both their own training in Marxist theory and how their reactions to (or against) this literature shaped their thoughts and scholarly trajectories. For example, let us take the case of Drezner (2013), who acknowledges having "read *a lot* of Marx in college and graduate school" and argues that "a return to Marx seems entirely appropriate" for his "critique of capitalist political economy," even though he believes that there are "some Very Big Things that

---

16  In the present context, we understand Eurocentrism as the intellectual tendency to downplay, dismiss, and ignore concerns, ideas, and thinkers from beyond the European world and its offshoots. Eurocentrism also embodies the tendency to regard itself as exceptional and universalize based on the European experience while denying the validity of other ways of thinking, acting, or knowing.

Marx got wrong—badly, world-historically wrong."[17] While he posits his blockbuster *Theories of International Politics and Zombies* as a review of "existing international relations theories," he justifies his lack of engagement with Marx therein using the following tortured logic: "[t]o be blunt, this project is explicitly prohuman, whereas Marxists would likely sympathize more with the zombies" (Drezner 2015, 18). Notably, while Drezner added coverage of feminism to the 2015 "revived" edition—he had previously lumped feminists together with Marxists as "sympathiz[ing] more with the zombies" (2011, 17)—Marx's specter continues to be absent from the text.

Although we were taken aback by the extent to which Marx and Marxist authors are absent from the above courses, the general trend we identify will likely be unsurprising to many readers. Indeed, for years critical voices—such as those of the Caucus for a New Political Science—have alleged that the discipline's mainstream is status-quo-oriented (if not conservative) and uninterested, or perhaps even fearful of, systemic critique (Barrow 2008). Still, it is tempting to believe that profound engagement with Marx and the Marxist tradition have continued to flourish in more hospitable surroundings *outside of the mainstream*. Yet this is largely not the case. While significant numbers of scholars—particularly outside of the United States and in the subfields of comparative and global political economy—continue to keep the Marxist flame alive, it has repeatedly been pointed out that many thinkers from the dominant "critical" intellectual traditions of our time—postmodernism, poststructuralism, and postcolonialism—have joined the mainstream in either neglecting or rejecting Marx (Dirlik 2000; Bartolovich and Lazarus 2002; Chibber 2013). Reasons vary and include a tendency to embrace the aforementioned end of history ideology, the notion that *universalism* (of the Marxist or other varieties) is invariably a dirty word and the presumption that Marx is an irredeemably Eurocentric thinker. Accordingly, while vibrant pockets of Marx-influenced scholars remain in IR and CP, they are small and concentrated outside of political science's US core, and largely isolated from their fields' mainstreams.

Here, we focus on the last of the aforementioned charges against Marx: his purported Eurocentrism. While it is by no means the sole reason for which "critical" scholars choose to dismiss Marx, it is of special interest in the present

---

17  Notably, this is reminiscent of Wolff's (2003) conclusion in *Why Read Marx Today?*: "Marx's grandest theories are not substantiated. But he is not to be abandoned"—for he "remains the most profound and acute critic of capitalism, even as it exists today" (Wolff 2003, 125–26). Again, whether or not Marx was right, there is little intellectual justification for perpetuating obliviousness to his work.

context, for assertions of Marx's ineradicable European character are common to many critical and mainstream scholars. As such, this section proceeds by analyzing Marx's Eurocentric credentials.

Despite Marx's fairly extensive engagement with the non-European world, Avineri (1969, 1)—who compiled such writings in the landmark (but relatively unknown) volume, *Karl Marx on Colonialism and Modernization*—recounted that "Marx is usually considered a European thinker, primarily interested in the impact of industrialization on Western society." In fact, Marx is often identified in such terms in the political science mainstream, even today. Marx "focused on capitalism in Europe," according to a recent IR textbook, which falsely goes on to imply that only "neo-Marxists"—and not Marx himself—have demonstrated any interest in "developing countries" (Jackson and Sørensen 2016, 51). Indeed, Ahmad (2015, 199–200) argues that the accusation of "Marx's Eurocentrism was manufactured mainly in Anglo-American discourses" and exported once the "1960s uprisings had been contained."

To the extent that Marx's non-European writings are acknowledged, we again typically receive only a caricatured version. In Gilpin's (1987, 271) rendering, "Marx believed the external force of Western imperialism" was necessary to move non-Western societies through the predetermined stages of history, and that such capitalist expansion, even if carried out violently, represented "a step forward for humanity." Though Marx indeed made such crude assertions, Gilpin (1987, 271) neglects to mention that Marx's views on these matters evolved and that he would in fact become the first major European thinker to oppose the British imperial project in India. And despite referring to Avineri's text as an "excellent collection," nor does Gilpin (1987, 271) repeat Avineri's (1969, 19) assertion that Marx came to believe that both India *and* the British working class were "being exploited for the benefit of the English ruling classes through British rule in India."

Postcolonial thinkers have often been even less generous in their assessments of Marx's non-European credentials. They have tended to see Marxism as "indelibly Eurocentric, [and] complicit with the dominative master-narratives of modernity (including that of colonialism itself)" (Bartolovich 2002, 1). As such, "it has … become perfectly acceptable" for postcolonial scholars "to make no mention of Marxism, even when the situations described seem to call out for it" (ibid.). And, "[w]hen the subject of Marxism *is* brought up, it is typically with hostility" (Bartolovich 2002, 9).[18] Of course, a critique of Marx's

---

18  There are exceptions. In the magisterial *Postcolonialism: An Historical Introduction*, Young (2001, 6–7) argues—rightly or wrongly—that postcolonialism "operates within the historical legacy of Marxist critique" and "incorporates a Marxism developed outside, and

"Orientalism" has been standard fare at least since Said's (1978) classic homonymous work.[19] For Kayaoglu (2010, 199), Marx was guilty of subscribing to the very same ideology of "European normative exclusivity and supremacy"—which "was constructed in conjunction with the creation of inferiority of the Other"—as his liberal and other contemporaries. For his part, Hobson (2012, 20) refers in *The Eurocentric Conception of World Politics* to "the paternalist Eurocentrism of Marx" and other disparate thinkers. Tellingly, he entitles one of the book's chapters, "Eurocentric Imperialism: Liberalism and Marxism, c. 1830–1914."

Yet without seeking to diminish the importance of the very real oversights, biases, and flaws that undergird Marx's non-European writings (Chowdhry and Nair 2002, 7), it is simply not the case that Marx deserves to be equated in these counts with liberalism, which unabashedly served as imperialism's and colonialism's chief ideological enabler. To be sure, the "broadly Marxist tradition" of anti-imperialist thinkers merits criticism for its "concentration on the histories of Europe and North America" (Saurin 2006, 34). More generally, Gruffydd Jones (2006, 12) is doubtlessly correct to note that "even critical IR" has "turned almost exclusively to Europe's heritage of critical thought" while studiously ignoring (if not deriding the contributions of) non-European thinkers, including those whom we analyze below. But this is not a call for turning our backs on Marx. The problem, as Gruffydd Jones (2011, 48) observes, is not "turn[ing] fruitfully" to European thinkers such as Marx, but "persistently overlook[ing] other sources of critique." Thus, as Chowdhry and Nair (2002, 17) suggest by drawing from Fanon, Marxism needs to be "stretched"—not discarded—"to better accommodate the historical interpellation of race, gender, and class" that characterizes international politics. Though they too refer to "the Eurocentrism of

---

generally neglected in the west, a flexible Marxism responsive to local conditions in" Latin America, Asia, and Africa. In his nuanced estimation, "Marx's specific writings on colonialism ... are productive if problematic" (Young 2001, 105).

19  Anderson criticizes Said for basing many of his complaints against Marx on Marx's use of Goethe's *West-Eastern Divan* poems. In his article on "British Rule in India," Marx quoted the following stanza:
    Should this torture then torment us
    Since it brings us greater pleasure?
    Were not through the rule of Timur
    Souls devoured without measure?
For his part, Anderson posits that there is evidence that Marx is using the poem to characterize the British colonialist perspective rather than his own (Anderson 2010, 17).

Marx" and reject Marxism's "universalist assumptions," theirs is at least a call for *dialogue*, not *rejection* (Chowdhry and Nair 2002, 22–23).[20]

## 8   Our Reading

We read Marx as a thinker who, despite his flaws and oversights, made serious attempts to wrestle with non-Western realities. There is in fact a growing body of revisionist scholarship that supports this assertion and questions the dominant, Eurocentric characterization of Marx (Bartolovich and Lazarus 2002; Achcar 2013; Pradella 2015).

Indeed, for a Eurocentric thinker, Marx had a great deal to say about European exploitation of the rest of the world. Particularly in his oft-overlooked *New York Tribune* articles, Marx frequently addressed Britain's crimes in India, China, and elsewhere. He argued that the West's prosperity depended on the slave and opium trades and that Western powers would hastily use force to impose their continuance (Ledbetter 2007, xxv). As Marx ([1853c] 2007, 3) wrote concerning the British opium trade in China,

> [w]hatever the social causes, whatever religious, dynastic, or national shape they may assume, that have brought about the chronic rebellions subsisting in China ... and now gathered together in one formidable revolution, the occasion of this outbreak has unquestionably been afforded by the English cannon forcing upon China that soporific drug called opium.

And referring to British behavior in China, Marx ([1857] 2007, 23) declared

> ... this most unrighteous war has been waged. The unoffending citizens and peaceful tradesmen of Canton have been slaughtered, their habitations battered to the ground, and the claims of humanity violated, on the flimsy pretense that "English life and property are endangered by the aggressive acts of the Chinese!" The British Government and the British people ... know how false and hollow are such charges.

While Marx may not have been the most outspoken advocate for colonialism's victims, he did not ignore them. He addressed British colonialism (and its

---

20   As Bartolovich (2002, 1) observes, "[t]he neglect (even ignorance) of Marxism in postcolonial studies has often been countered by the reflexive dismissal of the entire field of postcolonial studies by Marxist writers."

crimes) as historical facts and part of the natural development of capital accumulation. Nonetheless, Marx took a strong stand in favor of the abolition of slavery in the United States and the liberation of Fenian (Irish republican) prisoners in England. Marx strove to convince the First International and British working-class leaders to support the Irish rebels, condemning British atrocities in Ireland and praising British workers' opposition to slavery in the US south.[21] Marx saw the US Civil War as a major battle for human emancipation, which would force white labor in the United States and Britain to take a stand against slavery. At the same time, Marx saw in Irish nationalism a source of opposition to British and global capital (Anderson 2010). It is interesting to note how Marx, when addressing the Civil War, and especially in regard to Ireland and Irish workers, connected race and ethnicity as part of the exploitation generated by capitalism, showing how the bourgeoisie benefited from working-class racial divisions and animosities.[22] For example, Marx bitterly complained about how working-class consciousness was debilitated by anti-Irish prejudice (Anderson 2010, 145).[23]

Further, as Avineri (1968, 24) comments, "nothing could be more scathing than [Marx's] exposé of the sheer inhumanity of the British opium trade with China, or the cruelties inflicted by the British on India in the wake of the Mutiny." Avineri (1969, 28) fittingly goes on to observe that, while "one can criticize Marx on many counts," nonetheless "one has to admit that few nineteenth-century thinkers and social theorists grasped as well the long-range implications of European colonial expansion for the socioeconomic structure of non-European society" and that "even fewer had a comparable vision of the degree of world historical change brought about by the corrosive influence of Western commerce."

His writings on India in particular, including the passage below, illustrate precisely the duality of Marx's thought. Deeply disturbed by the barbarity of British colonialism but shedding few tears for the social order it was uprooting, in 1853, in one of his regular contributions to the *Tribune* (Marx [1853a] 2007,

---

21   The British bourgeoisie and political leadership expected the workers to protest the North's embargo against the South and southern cotton in particular. This had a detrimental effect on the British economy and indeed directly affected British labor; however, the workers stood firm in their antislavery position.

22   Taylor (2016) also argues that capitalism has used racism to justify plunder, conquest, and slavery, as well as to generate divisions inside the working class and allow the bourgeoisie to impede the formation of a broader multiracial working-class coalition.

23   Anderson (2010) further shows how Marx and Engels used the oppressive situation of Irish peasants and workers as an example of capitalist social relations and the repressive nature of the British government.

213), he wrote, "I share not the opinion of those who believe in a golden age of Hindostan." He had few qualms about the destruction of precapitalist India,[24] which he saw as a necessary evil for the advancement of capitalism and—sooner or later—a revolution (Jani 2002). In that sense, as Marx ([1853a] 2007, 219) wrote, British imperialism was "an unconscious tool of history."

Yet as Jani (2002) indicates, to arrive from here to the accusation that Marx was Eurocentric and a supporter of British imperialism requires a huge leap of faith. Indeed, several caveats are in order. First, Marx was certainly a product and creature of Europe who suffered from many of the same ethnocentric vices as his contemporaries (Bartolovich 2002). Yet he was also "a trilingual, cosmopolitan intellectual" who lived a life of exile, engaged extensively with the non-European and colonized worlds, and displayed an increasing propensity over the course of his life to wrestle with local particularities (Anderson 2010, 1).[25] Anderson writes:

> In the 1840s, he held to an implicitly unilinear perspective, sometimes tinged with ethnocentrism, according to which non-Western societies would necessarily be absorbed into capitalism and then modernized via colonialism and the world market. But over time, his perspective evolved toward one that was more multilinear, leaving the future development of these societies as an open question. (2010, 2)

While critics are prone to cite Marx's reference to "Oriental despotism" as absolute proof of his Eurocentric tendencies, it is thus important to consider how his thought evolved in a more pluralist direction over time (Tansel 2015). As Achcar has argued, "any comment on Marx's attitude towards India that considers his 1853 articles alone, without exploring the whole history of his statements on India until his last writings, and builds on those articles in order to formulate a general judgment on his 'Orientalist' or 'Eurocentric' bias, is fundamentally flawed and unsound" (quoted in Kumar 2014).

Further, Pradella (2015, 120) indicates that Marx saw capitalism as a globalized system, rooted in colonial exploitation and slavery, and in the early 1850s he changed his "previous unidirectional view of international revolution,

---

24  Ahmad (2015, 203) indicates that Marx's attack on the "obnoxious cruelties of the Brahminical caste system" was very much welcome, and "no Indian Marxist ... has ever taken offense at the abusive language Marx used about the caste system."
25  Pradella sustains that "Marx's investigation into precapitalist societies ... was not due to his journalistic activity but responded to a noncontingent interest, present from the beginning of his elaboration of historical materialism" (2015, 170).

tracing a relation between proletarian struggle in the metropolis and anti-colonial movement in the colonies." Revolts and revolutions in the colonies would deepen the inherent contradictions of capitalism, accelerating the outbreak of the proletarian revolution in Europe. Specifically, he argued that its demise would come from the interaction between non-European liberation movements and European proletariat revolutions, which he noted vis-à-vis the Taiping Revolution in China (Pradella 2015). Second, Marx's analysis indeed appears (relatively) praiseworthy when juxtaposed with the standards of his time. Contrary to other classical thinkers such as John Locke, John Stuart Mill, or Edmund Burke, Marx never directly advocated imperial policies or actions. He had no investments in companies involved in exploiting British colonies, as did Locke (the Royal African Company) (Macpherson 1980, x) and Mill (East India Company) (Collini 1989, ix), nor did he lend ideological support to imperialism, as did Burke (O'Neill 2016). In fact, while liberal heroes such as Mill were arguing for "benevolent despotism" in Britain's handling of the colonies, Marx's 1853 writing on India "constitutes the first instance of a major European thinker supporting India's independence" (Anderson 2010, 238). Again, whatever his biases and flaws, Marx hardly warrants being tarred with the same Eurocentric brush.

If by Eurocentrism we mean a worldview that makes Europe the center of the globe, "then Marx of the India articles is not Eurocentric," according to Jani (2002, 94). Marx was a product of the European Enlightenment, but also among its strongest critics. And he was keenly aware of how colonial exploitation benefited European capitalism, as he expressed in *Capital* (Marx 1976, 931), as well as the broader ills of imperialism. As he wrote concerning British rule in India,

> [t]he profound hypocrisy and inherent barbarism of bourgeois civilization lies unveiled before our eyes, turning from its home, where it assumes respectable forms, to the colonies, where it goes naked ... Did they not, in India, to borrow an expression of that great robber, Lord Clive himself, resort to atrocious extortion, when simple corruption could not keep pace with their rapacity?
> 
> MARX [1853b] 2007, 224

These are strange words for a supposedly Eurocentric, Orientalist thinker who is invested in "European normative exclusivity and supremacy."

Our position is thus in accord with the great Egyptian economist Amin (2009, 89), who acknowledges that Eurocentrism "is strong" among Western Marxists, some of whom have over the years adopted "pro-imperialist" positions.

He further notes that Marxism "inherits a certain evolutionist perspective that prevents it from tearing down the Eurocentric veil of the bourgeois evolutionism against which it revolts" (Amin 2009, 156).

Yet it is also the case that "the tools developed by Marxism have the potential capacity to surpass [these] contradictions," for "Marxism was founded on an awareness of the historical limits of the culture of the Enlightenment in relation to its real social content: namely, the rationalization of the national, European, and global capitalist project" (Amin 2009, 190). Indeed, while Marxism—"vulgar" and otherwise—succumbed to the temptation to extrapolate from Europe to fashion a universal model, this occurred "despite *Marx*'s precautions," for Marx himself "was careful about making hasty generalizations" about the non-European world (Amin 2009, 191; emphasis added). Thus, we must "go beyond the construct proposed by Marx" but without "throwing the baby out with the bath water" or abandoning "universalism" entirely (Amin 2009, 156, 190).

## 9      Marxist Engagements from the Non-European World

In fact, "many [twentieth-century] movements for independence and national development in the colonial and Third Worlds drew," and still draw, "their political inspiration from Marxism" (Matin 2011, 5). As Acharya and Buzan observe,

> … it is not difficult in parts of East Asia to find Marxists who interpret Marx's opposition to liberalism (capitalism) as placing him outside the West. The idea that a thinker so deeply embedded in Western philosophy and sociology as Marx could be seen as non-Western comes as a big surprise to Westerners who encounter it. (2010, 238)

This should *not* "surprise" us. It is indeed notable that while Marx has so often been dismissed in the West as crudely universalist and Eurocentric, countless non-European thinkers, leaders, and activists have found inspiration in Marx (Aguilar 1978; Bartolovich and Lazarus 2002; Prashad 2016). The best and brightest have not been passive readers of Marx or sought to slavishly apply his ideas and concepts to their circumstances (which Marx himself would also not have wanted). Rather, they have adopted certain parts of the Marxist tradition while modifying or discarding others, just as we would expect of any thinker who is seeking to reconcile insights derived from one set of surroundings with their own, local realities.

Here, we briefly examine two such thinkers: Amílcar Cabral and José Carlos Mariátegui. Cabral, the great anticolonial leader of Guinea-Bissau and Cape Verde, in his "Brief Analysis of the Social Structure in Guinea" (1974), nicely embodies this balancing act. Here, he engages in a nuanced analysis of agrarian Guinea's class dynamics, noting that while there are indeed "wage-earners," he is "careful not to call these groups the proletariat or working class" (1974). He observes the existence of another group for whom "we have not yet found the exact term," and in general notes that he is "not trying to stretch alien concepts" (1974). Cabral comments: "we looked for the working class in Guinea and did not find it," though they were able to discover "our little proletariat," particularly among boat- and dockworkers (1974). While it may be "absurd" to consider that there could be "a working class mentality" without "the material conditions of the working class," which Guinea plainly did not have, Cabral mentions that "in fact we managed to inculcate these ideas into a large number of people" (1974).

Crucially, local conditions and particularities are fundamental to his analysis. While Marx had (in)famously argued that precapitalist societies had no history (Avineri 1969, 10–13), per his progressive, modernist view that "history" only began after feudalism had been swept away, Cabral (1974) asserts the opposite:

> There is a preconception held by many people, even on the left, that imperialism made us enter history at the moment when it began its adventure in our countries. This preconception must be denounced: for somebody on the left, and for Marxists in particular, history obviously means the class struggle. Our opinion is exactly the contrary. We consider that when imperialism arrived in Guinea it made us leave history—our history. We agree that history in our country is the result of class struggle, but we have our own class struggles in our own country.

The immediate task facing Guinea, then, is not a European-style class struggle, but the struggle for "national liberation," for which "unity of all the social strata is a prerequisite for success" (Cabral 1974). In this monumental task, the "African petty bourgeoisie" must be the ones to "tak[e] control of the state apparatus when the colonial power is destroyed," since only they "have learned how to manipulate [it]" (Cabral 1974). He—we—cannot mechanically apply Marx to Guinea because "[t]he working class hardly exists as a defined class; it is just an embryo" (Cabral 1974). Further, "[t]here is no *economically viable* bourgeoisie because imperialism prevented it being created" (Cabral 1974).

What we find here are both engagement with and significant departures from Marx's thought—especially in regard to materialism/idealism (and the creation of working-class consciousness), class dynamics and nomenclature, and the notions of the stages of history, or even history itself. Cabral observes: "you must connect all these things up with the history and conditions of Africa" (1974).[26] As we have argued, and contrary to conventional readings, (later) Marx would presumably have agreed with at least the spirit of this endeavor.

A second example can be found in José Carlos Mariátegui, a Peruvian agitator and writer from the early twentieth century who dedicated his short life to political struggle and the development of Marxist thought vis-à-vis the Latin American context and who is said to be responsible for "the most interesting and insightful Marxist writings on Latin America" (La Botz 2012). As the editors of a recent anthology of his writings note, Mariátegui "energetically and actively engaged with European thought, working out new methods to analyze the problems of non-Western societies like his own," and "develop[ed] a creative Marxist analysis that was oriented toward the specific historical reality of Peru and Latin America in the 1920s" (Vanden and Becker 2011, 13).[27]

Particularly notable were Mariátegui's elaboration of an "open," "non-sectarian," and anti-Stalinist Marxism, his focus on the role of "subjective elements" such as "political education," and his argument that rural peasants and indigenous peoples—often seen, at least in the former case, as forming a "reactionary class" in orthodox Marxist analysis—had revolutionary potential (Vanden and Becker 2011, 13). In other words, he argued that even a largely preindustrial, feudal society such as Peru was potentially ripe for socialist revolution.

He thus analyzed "the problem of the Indian from a socialist point of view," which led him to focus on "their right to land" (Vanden and Becker 2011, 69). Though feudalism persisted in Peru, and there was no "true capitalist class" to bring about its "liquidation," Mariátegui argued that Peru should avoid "the liberal solution," which would entail "breaking up the large landholdings to create small properties" (Vanden and Becker 2011, 70). Instead, "our agrarian problem has a fundamental indisputable and concrete factor that gives it a special character" and suggests a different path forward: "the survival of the community and elements of practical socialism in Indigenous agriculture and life" (Vanden

---

26   Notably, "Cabral did not proclaim himself a Marxist nor adhere to rigid and orthodox formulations." Yet, "he was faithful both to the Marxist method and to the proposition that good theory not only may be based on the ideas of others but also must be subject to concrete and historical conditions of real experiences that test theory" (Chilcote 1991, 20).
27   On Marx and Marxism in Latin America, see Liss (1984) and Löwy (1992).

and Becker 2011, 71). This Inca or agrarian socialism thus provided a basis for "collective management of agriculture" (Vanden and Becker 2011, 239). Yet it is not a fundamental upending of Marx's story, warts and all. As he writes in his elaboration of the "Programmatic Principles of the Socialist Party" of Peru,

> [b]ut this, like the stimulation that freely provides for the resurgence of Indigenous peoples, the creative manifestation of its forces and native spirit, does not mean at all a romantic and antihistorical trend of reconstructing or resurrecting Inca socialism, which corresponded to historical conditions completely bypassed, and which remains only as a favorable factor in a perfectly scientific production technique, that is, the habits of cooperation and socialism of Indigenous peasants. Socialism presupposes the technique, the science, the capitalist stage. It cannot permit any setback in the realization of the achievements of modern civilization, but on the contrary it must methodically accelerate the incorporation of these achievements into national life.
> 
> VANDEN and BECKER 2011, 239

Whatever one makes of Mariátegui's conceptualization of Inca socialism, his theory of history, or his reference to "modern civilization," this represents an honest effort to bring a Marxist and socialist analysis to the level of Peruvian reality.

The larger point is that these and many other Third-World thinkers have used Marx as a lens to shed light on their own circumstances and relations, adopting certain concepts, theories, and ideas while dropping or modifying others. It is indeed natural, considering Marx's position regarding colonialism, for non-European thinkers fighting colonialism to engage with Marx. In the process, they have contributed greatly to the richness, vibrancy, and heterogeneity of the Marxist tradition (Bartolovich 2002, 3). They argue alongside of but also *with* Marx, but do not immediately cast him aside as a Eurocentric thinker. In this regard, one may also consider current engagement with Marx by Kurdish rebels and Latin American student activists.

It is indeed unfortunate that so many political scientists (and others) not only tend to overlook such instances of fruitful cross-pollination between Marxist theory and non-European realities, but also largely neglect to engage in more of the same. Per Avineri's (1968, 31) prognosis from almost half a century prior, "[t]he irony of history may thus make Marx into a respectable, even fashionable, subject for academic discourse in a relatively affluent and bourgeois West, while in the non-European world an ideology relating itself to Marxism, yet overlooking most of what he said about the non-European world, may be politically triumphant." Though perhaps overly sanguine concerning Marx's staying power in the "bourgeois West," let alone Marxism's triumph elsewhere, he was correct to perceive the magnitude of Marx's influence in the non-European world. Marx may have been a creature of Europe, but the legacy of his ideas "belong" as much to the non-European world as to anyone (Bartolovich 2002, 10).

## 10  Conclusion

This chapter has sought to answer two basic questions: Is Marx seriously read in IR and CP? And if not, why? Based on analysis of a newly compiled database of graduate syllabi from introductory courses in these subfields from the top-ranked US departments, the answer to the first question is an almost absolute "no." Whereas Marx used to be standard fare even in undergraduate courses (D'Anieri 2014, 100), it is now exceedingly rare for Marx—or any Marxist author, even broadly defined—to be assigned. As we have seen, such writings do not even appear when the thematic areas under consideration—such as "social class"—surely require engaging with Marx's thought. While further analysis is required to assess the extent to which Marx is read in other subfields or disciplines, or within non-US political science programs, the trend we have identified at the heights of the IR and CP US-based mainstream could not be clearer.

Among the reasons for Marx's near-total absence, we focus on the critique—common to many mainstream and especially critical scholars—that Marx is an irredeemably Eurocentric thinker who has little to say to the non-European world.[28] While Marx was a product of Europe who was invested in the notion of universal theory and conceptualizing capitalism at the systemic level, he also "strove to avoid formalistic and abstract universals," as evidenced by his repeated attempts "to work out the specific ways in which the universalizing powers of capital and class were manifesting themselves in particular societies or social groups" (Anderson 2010, 244). As Avineri notes,

> Marx's writings on Asia, though far from flattering to anyone who has cherished a romantic image of pristine Oriental purity reigning supreme before the advent of the Western barbarians, abound with criticisms of European hypocrisy in Asia, its double standards, and the wanton

---

28  For examples of such assertions in mainstream political science, see the above section, "The Construction of a Eurocentric Marx."

cruelty implicit in the introduction of Western commerce in Asian society. (1969, 24)

Accordingly, we should be highly suspicious of efforts to tar Marx with the Eurocentric brush.

In turn, as we explore through briefly analyzing the thought of Cabral and Mariátegui, there is a long tradition of non-European thinkers who have thoughtfully engaged with Marx. Rather than serving as mere conveyor belts for Marx's ideas, or rejecting him as a modernist and universalist product of the European Enlightenment, they have instead *read* Marx and adapted him to their local realities, thus generating new practical and theoretical insights. As Tucker (1978, ix) correctly points out, "[n]o other intellectual has so powerfully shaped the mind of modern left-wing radicalism in most parts of the world." It is of course highly ironic that it has become so fashionable for Western academics to dismiss Marx as Eurocentric even as so many non-European thinkers *on the ground* have sought to claim him as one of their own.

Yet while this and other intellectual challenges to Marx are frequently invoked, we argue that a key factor motivating the rejection of Marx is instead political. It is the discipline's embrace of the ideologies of the end of history—accompanied by what Eagleton (2011, 6) refers to as "a creeping sense of political impotence"—and value-free scientific "neutrality." In other words, Marx has become a haunting specter for contemporary, US political science precisely because he challenges both the discipline's attachment to the liberal-capitalist order and its detachment from open political engagement.

What, then, should be the place of Marx in our discipline? In light of recent economic crises, increasing inequality, and frequent challenges to the neoliberal model, there is much to gain from engaging with Marx. The point, again, is not to thoughtlessly reproduce his arguments or overlook his flaws (Callinicos 1996), but to actually *read* one of history's most important thinkers so that we may glean and generate insights that will advance our understanding of the social world, as well as our ability to act in it. As Eagleton notes,

> [t]he *Communist Manifesto* has been described as ... the single most influential text written in the nineteenth century. Very few thinkers, as opposed to statesmen, scientists, soldiers, religious figures, and the like, have changed the course of actual history as decisively as its author. There are no Cartesian governments, Platonist guerrilla fighters, or Hegelian trade unions. Not even Marx's most implacable critics would deny that he transformed our understanding of human history. (2011, x)

Whatever our normative or intellectual positions, it is thus incumbent upon us to grapple with his contributions. Unfortunately, at present, it appears that most political scientists are willing to do anything to and with Marx—from downplaying his importance, to producing and reproducing blatant mischaracterizations of his arguments, and ignoring him entirely. Except to *read* him.

### Acknowledgements

The authors would like to thank the anonymous reviewers for their especially helpful and thoughtful comments, along with Estefanía Martínez and Jany Méndez for their (unremunerated) research assistance. Finally, the authors are greatly appreciative of the encouragement they received from panel members and attendees after presenting a previous version of this chapter at the 2016 Annual Convention of the International Studies Association

### Bibliography

Acharrya, Amitav and Buzan, Barry (eds.) (2010) *Non-Western International Relations Theory: Perspectives on and Beyond Asia.* New York: Routledge.

Achcar, Gilbert (2013) *Marxism, Orientalism, Cosmopolitanism.* Chicago: Haymarket Books.

Aguilar, Luis E., (ed.) (1978) *Marxism in Latin America.* Philadelphia, PA: Temple University Press.

Ahmad, Aijax (2015) "Karl Marx, 'Global Theorist.'" *Dialectical Anthropology* 39 (2): 199–209.

Amin, Samir (2009) *Eurocentrism: Modernity, Religion, and Democracy: A Critique of Eurocentrism and Culturalism.* 2nd ed. New York: Monthly Review Press.

Anderson, Benedict (1991) *Imagined Communities: Reflections on the Origins and Spread of Nationalism.* London, New York: Verso.

Anderson, Kevin B. (2010) *Marx at the Margins: On Nationalism, Ethnicity, and Non-Western Societies.* Chicago: University of Chicago Press.

Anderson, Kevin B. (2015) "Karl Marx and Intersectionality." *Logos: A Journal of Modern Society & Culture* 14 (1). Accessed March 2, 2016. http://logosjournal.com/2015/anderson-marx/.

Ashley, Richard K. (1984) "The Poverty of Neorealism." *International Organization* 38 (2): 225–86.

Avineri, Shlomo (1968) *The Social and Political Thought of Karl Marx.* Cambridge: Cambridge University Press.

Avineri, Shlomo (ed.) (1969) *Karl Marx on Colonialism and Modernization: His Despatches [sic] and Other Writings on China, India, Mexico, the Middle East and North Africa*. Garden City, NY: Anchor Books.

Barrow, Clyde W. (2008) "The Intellectual Origins of New Political Science." *New Political Science* 30 (2): 215–44.

Bartolovich, Crystal (2002) "Introduction: Marxism, Modernity, and Postcolonial Studies." In *Marxism, Modernity, and Postcolonial Studies*, edited by Crystal Bartolovich and Neil Lazarus, 1–19. New York: Cambridge University Press.

Bartolovich, Crystal and Lazarus, Neil (eds.) (2002) *Marxism, Modernity, and Postcolonial Studies*. New York: Cambridge University Press.

Baudrillard, Jean (1975) *The Mirror of Production*. St. Louis, MO: Telos Press.

Bieler, Andreas (2016) "Karl Marx, Class Struggles in France and the Historical Materialist Method!" *Progress in Political Economy*. Accessed January 15, 2017. http://ppesydney.net/karl-marx-class-struggles-in-france-and-the-historical-materialist-method/.

Brown, Wendy (2002) "At the Edge." *Political Theory* 30 (4): 556–76.

Cabral, Amílcar (1974) "Brief Analysis of the Social Structure in Guinea." Accessed January 15, 2017. https://www.marxists.org/subject/africa/cabral/1964/bassg.htm.

Callinicos, Alex (1989) *Against Postmodernism: A Marxist Critique*. Cambridge: Polity Press.

Callinicos, Alex (1996) "Whither Marxism?" *Economic and Political Weekly* 31 (4): 9–17.

Cardoso, Fernando Henrique and Faletto, Enzo (1979) *Dependency and Development in Latin America*. Berkeley: University of California Press.

Cavarero, Adriana (2002) "Politicizing Theory." *Political Theory* 30 (4): 506–32.

Chibber, Vivek (2013) *Postcolonial Theory and the Specter of Capital*. Brooklyn, NY: Verso.

Chilcote, Ronald H. (1991). *Amilcar Cabral's Revolutionary Theory and Practice: A Critical Guide*. Boulder: Lynne Rienner.

Chomdhry, Geeta and Nair, Sheila (eds.) (2002) *Power, Postcolonialism and International Relations: Reading Race, Gender and Class*. New York: Routledge.

Cohen, Benjamin J. (2007) "The Transatlantic Divide: Why are American and British IPE so Different?" *Review of International Political Economy* 14 (2): 197–219.

Colgan, Jeff D. (2016) "Where Is International Relations Going? Evidence from Graduate Training." *International Studies Quarterly* 60 (3): 486–98.

Collini, Stefan (ed.) (1989) *J.S. Mill: 'On Liberty' and Other Writings*. Cambridge: Cambridge University Press.

D'Anieri, Paul (2014) *International Politics: Power and Purpose in Global Affairs*. 3rd ed. Boston, MA: Cengage Learning.

Dirlik, Arif (2000) *Postmodernity's Histories: The Past as Legacy and Project*. Lanham, MD: Rowman & Littlefield.

Drezner, Daniel W. (2011) *Theories of International Politics and Zombies*. Princeton, NJ: Princeton University Press.

Drezner, Daniel (2013) "The Hipster Global Political Economy of Karl Marx." *Foreign Policy.com*, October 15. Accessed January 15, 2017. http://foreignpolicy.com/2013/10/15/the-hipster-global-political-economy-of-karl-marx/.

Drezner, Daniel W. (2015) *Theories of International Politics and Zombies*. Princeton, NJ: Princeton University Press.

Eagleton, Terry (2011) *Why Marx Was Right*. New Haven, CT: Yale University Press.

Eidlin, Barry (2014) "Class Formation and Class Identity: Birth, Death, and Possibilities for Renewal." *Sociology Compass* 8 (8): 1045–62.

Esping-Andersen, Gosta (1990) *The Three Worlds of Welfare Capitalism*. Princeton, NJ: Princeton University Press.

Evans, Peter (1979) *Dependent Development: The Alliance of Multinational, State, and Local Capital in Brazil*. Princeton, NJ: Princeton University Press.

Fukuyama, Francis (1992) *The End of History and the Last Man*. New York: Avon Books.

Gamble, Andrew (1999) "Why Bother with Marxism?" In *Marxism and Social Science*, edited by Andrew Gamble, David Marsh, and Tony Tant, 1–10. Urbana: University of Illinois Press.

Gilpin, Robert (1987) *The Political Economy of International Relations*. Princeton, NJ: Princeton University Press.

Grant, Ruth (2002) "Political Theory, Political Science, Politics." *Political Theory* 30 (4): 577–95.

Gruffydd Jones, Branwen (ed.) (2006) *Decolonizing International Relations*. Lanham, MD: Rowman & Littlefield.

Gruffydd Jones, Branwen (2011) "Anti-racism and Emancipation in the Thought and Practice of Cabral, Neto, Mondlane and Machel." In *International Relations and Non-Western Thought: Imperialism, Colonialism and Investigations of Global Modernity*, edited by Robbie Shilliam, 47–63. New York: Routledge.

Gunnell, John G. (1993) *The Descent of Political Theory: The Genealogy of an American Vocation*. Chicago, IL: University of Chicago Press.

Harvey, David (1973) *Social Justice and the City*. Oxford: Blackwell.

Harvey, David (1990) *The Condition of Postmodernity: An Enquiry into the Origins of Cultural Change*. Malden, MA: Blackwell.

Hobson, John M. (2012) *The Eurocentric Conception of World Politics: Western International Theory, 1760–2010*. New York: Cambridge University Press.

Hoffman, Tom (2013) "Where Art Thou, Adam Smith?" *Perspectives on Politics* 11 (1): 193–203.

Huntington, Samuel P. (1968) *Political Order in Changing Societies*. New Haven, CT: Yale University Press.

Jackson, Robert and Sørensen, Georg (2016) *Introduction to International Relations: Theories and Approaches*. 6th ed. Oxford: Oxford University Press.

Jani, Pranav (2002) "Karl Marx, Eurocentrism, and the 1857 Revolt in British India." In *Marxism, Modernity, and Postcolonial Studies*, edited by Crystal Bartolovich and Neil Lazarus, 81–99. New York: Cambridge University Press.

Katzenstein, Peter J., Keohane, Robert O., and Krasner, Stephen D. (1989) "International Organization and the Study of World Politics." *International Organization* 52 (4): 645–85.

Kayaoglu, Turan (2010) "Westphalian Eurocentrism in International Relations Theory." *International Studies Review* 12 (2): 193–217.

Kellner, Douglas (1995) "The Obsolescence of Marxism?" In *Whither Marxism?*, edited by Bernd Magnus and Stephen Cullenberg, 3–30. New York: Routledge.

Kumar, Deepa (2014) "Marxism and Orientalism." International Socialist Review 94. Accessed January 15, 2017. http://isreview.org/issue/94/marxism-and-orientalism.

La Botz, Dan (2012) "Latin American Marxist: José Carlos Mariátegui." *New Politics* 14 (1). Accessed January 15, 2017. http://newpol.org/content/latin-american-marxist-jos%C3%A9-carlos-mari%C3%A1tegui.

Ledbetter, James (ed.) (2007) Dispatches for the New York Tribune: Selected Journalism of Karl Marx. New York: Penguin Books.

Liss, Sheldon B. (1984) Marxist Thought in Latin America. Berkeley: University of California Press.

Löwy, Michael (ed.) (1992) Marxism in Latin America from 1909 to the Present: An Anthology. Atlantic Highlands, NJ: Humanities Press International.

Macpherson, C.B. (ed.) (1980) Second Treatise of Government: John Locke. Indianapolis, IN: Hackett Publishing.

Maliniak, Daniel, Oakes, Amy, Peterson, Susan, and Tierney, Michael J. (2011) "International Relations in the US Academy." International Studies Quarterly 55 (2): 437–64.

Mandel, Ernest (ed.) (1976) Karl Marx: Capital. London: Penguin Books.

Marshall, T.H., and Bottomore, Tom (1992) Citizenship and Social Class. London: Pluto Press.

Marx, Karl ([1844] 1978) "Contribution to the Critique of Hegel's Philosophy of Right: Introduction." In Marx-Engels Reader, 2nd ed., edited by Robert C. Tucker. 53–65. New York: W.W. Norton & Co.

Marx, Karl ([1853a] 2007) "The British Rule in India." In Dispatches for the New York Tribune: Selected Journalism of Karl Marx, edited by James Ledbetter. 212–218. New York: Penguin Books.

Marx, Karl ([1853b] 2007) "The Future Results of British Rule in India." In Dispatches for the New York Tribune: Selected Journalism of Karl Marx, edited by James Ledbetter. 219–224. New York: Penguin Books.

Marx, Karl ([1853c] 2007) "Revolution in China and in Europe." In Dispatches for the New York Tribune: Selected Journalism of Karl Marx, edited by James Ledbetter. 3–10. New York: Penguin Books.

Marx, Karl ([1857] 2007) "English Atrocities in China." In Dispatches for the New York Tribune: Selected Journalism of Karl Marx, edited by James Ledbetter. 20–24. New York: Penguin Books.

Marx, Karl and Engels, Friedrich ([1888] 1978) "Manifesto of the Communist Party." In The Marx-Engels Reader, 2nd ed., edited by Robert C. Tucker, 469–500. New York: W. W. Norton & Co.

Marx, Karl (1976) Capital: A Critique of Political Economy Vol. I. London: Penguin Classics.

Matin, Kamran (2011) "Redeeming the Universal: Postcolonialism and the Inner Life of Eurocentrism." European Journal of International Relations 19 (2): 353–77.

O'Neill, Daniel I. (2016) Edmund Burke and the Conservative Logic of Empire. Oakland: University of California Press.

Oren, Ido (2016) "A Sociological Analysis of the Decline of American IR Theory." International Studies Review 18 (4): 571–96.

Polanyi, Karl (1944) The Great Transformation. New York: Farrar & Rinehart.

Pradella, Lucia (2015) Globalisation and the Critique of Political Economy: New Insights from Marx's Writings. New York: Routledge.

Prashad, Vijay (ed.) (2016) Communist Histories, Volume 1. New Delhi: LeftWord Books.

Roberts, Kenneth M. (2002) "Social Inequalities without Class Cleavages in Latin America's Neoliberal Era." Studies in Comparative International Development 36 (4): 3–33.

Rueschemeyer, Dietrich, Huber, Evelyn Stephens, and Stephens, John D. (1992) Capitalist Development and Democracy. Chicago: University of Chicago Press.

Said, Edward W. (1978) Orientalism. New York: Pantheon Books.

Saurin, Julian (2006) "International Relations as the Imperial Illusion; or, the Need to Decolonize IR." In Decolonizing International Relations, edited by Branwen Gruffydd Jones, 23–42. Lanham, MD: Rowman & Littlefield.

Sculos, Bryant W. and Walsh, Sean Noah (2015) "Marx in Miami: Reflections on Teaching and the Confrontation with Ideology." Class, Race and Corporate Power 3 (2): 1–17.

Tansel, Cemal Burak (2015) "Deafening Silence? Marxism, International Historical Sociology and the Spectre of Eurocentrism." European Journal of International Relations 21 (1): 76–100.

Taylor, Charles (1971) "Interpretation and the Sciences of Man." The Review of Metaphysics 25 (1): 3–51.

Taylor, Charles (1994) "Neutrality in Political Science." In Readings in the Philosophy of Social Science, edited by Michael Martin and Lee C. McIntyre, 181–212. Cambridge, MA: MIT Press.

Taylor, Keeanga-Yamahtta (2016) From #BlackLivesMatter to Black Liberation. Chicago: Haymarket Books.

Tucker, Robert C. (ed.) (1978) The Marx-Engels Reader. 2nd ed. New York: W. W. Norton & Co.

US News and World Report (No date) "Graduate School Search—Political Science Programs." Accessed April 12, 2016. http://grad-schools.usnews.rankingsandreviews.com/best-graduate-schools/search?program=top-political-science-schools&specialty=&name=&zip=&program_rank=top_10&sort=&sortdir=.

Vanden, Harry E. and Marc, Becker (eds.) (2011) *José Carlos Mariátegui: An Anthology*. New York: Monthly Review Press.

Wallerstein, Immanuel (1974) "The Rise and Future Demise of the World Capitalist System." *Comparative Studies in Society and History* 16 (4): 387–415.

Wallerstein, Immanuel (1986) "Incorporation of Indian Subcontinent into Capitalist World-Economy." *Economic and Political Weekly* 21 (4): 28–39.

Walt, Stephen M. (1998) "International Relations: One World, Many Theories." *Foreign Policy* 110: 29–32, 34–46.

Wendt, Alexander (1999) *Social Theory of International Politics*. New York: Cambridge University Press.

Wolff, Jonathan (2003) *Why Read Marx Today?* New York: Oxford University Press.

Wood, Ellen Meiksins (1997) "Back to Marx." *Monthly Review* 49 (2). Accessed December 29, 2016. http://monthlyreview.org/1997/06/01/back-to-marx/.

Young, Robert J.C. (2001) *Postcolonialism: An Historical Introduction*. Malden, MA: Blackwell.

CHAPTER 2

# Marxism and IPE

*Ronald W. Cox*

## 1   Introduction

The subfield of international political economy has long relegated Marxism to the margins of political inquiry within the U.S. academy. For a brief period during the 1970s and 1980s, both dependency theory and world systems theory were given some limited attention in IPE textbooks alongside the dominant paradigms of realism and liberalism (Long, Maliniak, Peterson and Tierney 2005, 21). Otherwise Marxism as a serious paradigm of intellectual inquiry and method has been either nonexistent or woefully underrepresented in standard IPE textbooks and in most international relations and political science departments in the U.S. The fact that the study of Marxism increased as the Cold War between the U.S. and the Soviet Union intensified during the late 1970s and early 1980s indicated the reflexive tendency of mainstream scholars to see Marxism as a mere adjunct of geopolitical struggle—legitimized by the very existence of the Soviet Union. When the Cold War ended, Marxism as a "third" paradigm in competition with liberalism and realism was replaced by constructivism and postmodernism as "critical" perspectives within IPE (Cafruny, Talani and Martin 2016, 105).

In this chapter I argue that there has always been a serious Marxism gap within IPE, even when dependency theory and world systems theory were allowed a slightly more prominent place in introductory textbooks and the occasional Marxist was hired in IR and political science departments. The gap has been intensified due to a lack of a serious engagement with class analysis in actually existing Marxism. The most prominent Marxist theorists in IPE have written expertly on the expansion of global production and its affects in helping to create a transnational class structure that had managed to make their ideas hegemonic on a global scale. These Marxian scholars invoked Gramscian concepts of political, economic and cultural hegemony to illustrate the growing power of this bloc of transnational capitalists (Cox 1987; Gill 1992; Sklair 2001; Robinson 2014). This branch of IPE Marxist literature has a very effective track record in providing us the tools to understand how transnational capitalists began to organize politically in the early 1970s to forge a global response to capitalist crises. However, this approach has operated almost exclusively at the level of a "high-range" theory, examining the dynamics of capitalist accumulation on a global scale, but often sacrificing a more fine-grained, mid-range method that would allow for observation of transnational capitalist political coalitions in the context of particular regional or nation-state settings.[1] As a result, the actually existing Gramscian theories of IR often have not paid much attention to how transnational capitalists battle with other sectors of capital, or other competing interests, in the process of business conflict and/or class struggle. At the same time, these theories have rarely been linked to those of Marxian economists who have written extensively about the process of surplus value extraction within the current transnational capitalist system of accumulation (Resnick and Wolff 1987; Roberts 2016).

Meanwhile dependency and world systems theorists have focused heavily on the embedded class relationships within the North-South divide, concentrating their arguments on what they considered to be the intractable power relationships that were constitutive of global capitalism. However, these approaches also have operated at the level of high-range, structural theories, which meant that the categories of "class" were intertwined with the mechanisms that maintained the Northern domination and exploitation of Southern economies through the process of unequal exchange (Frank 1967; Amin 1979; Wallerstein 1984; Smith 2016; U. Patnaik and P. Patnaik 2016). These high-range theories, then, were not equipped to interrogate class relationships at the point of production, a critique that has long been made by Marxist critics of these theoretical frameworks (Brenner 1977; Barone 2015). While dependency and world systems approaches have offered powerful insights about the structural power of transnational capital and how state structures reinforce that power, their theories have typically not included attention to the mid-range exercise of class analysis. Specifically, the political economy of surplus value extraction linked to production has been bypassed by these theories in favor of a focus on large-scale, systemic factors endemic to global capitalism.

In short, class analysis, to the extent that it existed within the dominant strands of Marxism in IPE, has been either narrowly focused on how the bourgeoisie reconstituted itself as a transnational class or how unequal exchange is inherent to a global capitalist system that locks countries in to a narrowly defined path of dependency. Some of the best Marxian scholarship, particularly within the Gramscian IR school, has focused on structures of capitalist production from the top-down: how transnational capitalists had used their political, economic and cultural power to facilitate a move toward a new

---

[1] There are clear exceptions to this, especially the work of William Robinson, *Transnational Conflicts: Central America, Social Change and Globalization*, London: Verso 2003.

transnational production system. Or, how, from a world systems perspective, despite the changes in how production was organized, the old system of North-South domination had proven remarkably impervious to structural change. The focus on transnational capitalist power, as well as the structural power relationships embedded within global capitalism, often left little room for a more serious interrogation of business conflict and/or class struggle within the changing dynamics of global (and national) production. What was being left out of the majority of Marxian or Marxian-inspired work is the extent to which the increasingly transnational system of production was exerting profound effects on the global constitution of the working class (Ness 2016). The extent to which capitalism is a set of specific exploitive relationships between capitalist and worker were often minimized in favor of frameworks that invoked culture, ideology and state power with more frequency than extraction of surplus value or the labor theory of value (Chibber 2013).

Indeed, as the Marxian-inspired critiques of capitalism took root in recent decades, the very category of surplus value and the labor theory of value have been called into question. Among Marxists who seriously engage with class analysis, such as Erik Olin Wright, class relationships are defined by relations of power and domination, more so than by the political economy of surplus value extraction (Wright 2015). Wright dismisses the labor theory of value, namely due to what he perceives to be the problem in equating the hours expended by workers in production to something that can be tangibly measured (via price) as a finished product within capitalism. So instead Wright develops his class analytic framework around primarily Weberian categories of power and domination, which becomes an exercise in trying to ascertain how much (or how little) control workers or middle managers have over their economic lives versus owners of production and those who serve their interests. This definition of class is detached from one of the most important developments in modern capitalism: the growing divergence between worker productivity and worker compensation in the form of wages. The fact that worker productivity has been rising in global manufacturing and that wages have been lagging behind productivity, is a key feature of contemporary capitalism. Another key feature is the increasing flow of profits and value to transnational owners of production, and away from workers who are experiencing a greater gap between stagnating or declining wages and rising productivity in neoliberal capitalism (Karanassou and Sala 2014).

The fact that the expansion of transnational production has depended on an expansive exploitation of an enlarged global working class should have been a central insight of Marxian scholars during the age of neoliberalism. And for some Marxian scholars, such as William Robinson, David Harvey and World

Systems theorists such as Beverley Silver, it certainly has been an important focus (Robinson 2014; Harvey 2007; Silver 2003). However, for students trained in International Relations or the subfield of IPE, they are just as likely to encounter Marxian scholars who treat class and especially concepts such as the working class, as being less important than how workers understand their subjective position within global capitalism. It is here that cultural signifiers and manifestations of ideological power have often displaced class as the focal point of scholarly concerns. In the book *Empire*, Michael Hardt and Antonio Negri reject the term working class in favor of "multitude," encompassing diverse occupations and overlapping identities, to describe those that might be capable of mounting a challenge to the foundational structure of global capitalism (Hardt and Negri 2001). In other works, such as that of self-described post-Marxists such as Ernesto Laclau and Chantal Mouffe, the authors deny the central importance and even the utility of the term "working class" given what they see as the profound changes in the way that workers and consumers define their identity in the new global capitalism. Discarding the term "working class," Laclau and Mouffe have developed the concept of "people power" (Laclau and Mouffe 2014). They advocate a left populism that is based on using a coherent cultural signifier to weave a narrative of unity that they believe is capable of displacing the hegemonic domination of capital. These approaches share an important characteristic in common: a rejection of efforts to frame "class-in-itself" in favor of a more subjective, cultural, ideological definition of identities as they are shaped by the manifestations of capitalism in our current age.

The result is a move away from attempts to analyze where profits are being produced, where they are being directed and accumulated, and the political economy of exploitation that is so central to the politics of capitalism. What is absent from much of contemporary Marxian and Marxian-inspired scholarship is a sufficiently mid-range theory that provides a class-centered focus on the political economy of production. This is especially noteworthy given that Western capitalist states and institutions are declining in legitimacy, unable to maintain the cultural and ideological domination that has long been the focal point of contemporary "Marxian" critiques of capitalism. Had Marxists been focused more on a class-centered Marxism that emphasized the politics of surplus value and value extraction, the eroding legitimacy of capitalist institutions at the national and global levels would have been easier to anticipate and to understand. The fact that working class people have been the first to become disillusioned with their own capitalist states during this period of neoliberalism is inextricably linked to deepening levels of exploitation within the structures of capitalist production and exclusion from political representation (Mair 2013).

## 2  International Relations and the Obliteration of Class

The subfield of international political economy has moved away from a Marxist scholarship that provides tools for understanding the exploitation of workers under capitalism. As I have discussed, this tendency has been reinforced by a Marxist scholarship that has reduced the centrality of class analysis in its theoretical frameworks. At the same time, mainstream IR approaches have long excised class analysis from their foundational assumptions, creating a vacuum within the field that has remained intact even as capitalism has entered one of its most crisis-prone periods. This has had serious implications for how scholars teach International Relations in their classes, as well as how scholars utilize IR theoretical frameworks in their research and writing. The two dominant theories in International Relations, which have also dominated the subfield of IPE, are realism and liberalism. According to the most recent detailed study of teaching and research in IR across a range of public universities and colleges in the U.S., there has been remarkable consistency in the domination of realist and liberal theoretical approaches in the field during the 1980s and 1990s (Long et al. 2005). This continues to be true today as liberalism and realism continue to dominate both teaching and research in IR (Sclofsky and Funk 2017).

Of the two main paradigms, liberal approaches had overtaken realist approaches as the preferred orientation in scholarly articles starting in the 1990s and continuing to the present—reversing the earlier preference for realism. On the other hand, in the IR curriculum, realist approaches continue to be used alongside liberal approaches in almost equal measure, accounting for almost 50% of the paradigms that are used in classroom teaching (Long et al. 2005). IR and IPE textbooks that used to showcase Marxism as an alternative theoretical framework have mostly dropped Marxism altogether in favor of constructivism. In other cases, such as several leading IPE texts, theoretical debates have been replaced by thematic discussions of issues that utilize a combination of liberal and realist-inspired frameworks with a dose of constructivism mixed in for good measure. In other words, the broader theoretical debates that once had a place, albeit limited, for a class analysis that critiqued the limited assumptions of realism and liberalism, were now viewed as outdated. Realism and liberalism had somehow "won" the ideological Cold War of ideas, and constructivism was the new entry point for critical work (Cafruny, et al. 2016).

Liberalism and Realism continue to dominate the IR field and the IPE subfield, sharing inherent biases that filter out a class analysis of the market and the state. Liberalism, dominated by the longstanding and much assigned works of Joseph Nye and Robert Keohane as prime examples, treats the history of IR as one of contested "issue areas" with power being determined by institutional histories, state leverage, and the nature of the issue area itself (Nye and Keohane 2011). Such an approach minimizes or excludes altogether a focus on broader socioeconomic power structures embedded within capitalism. In effect, linkages between capitalism as a socioeconomic system and the policy preferences of capitalist states is severed in favor of a more narrow set of assumptions that frames "issue areas" in relative isolation from broader class relationships. This tendency is inherent, of course, in the set of assumptions that have long animated liberalism: a separation of the capitalist state from the capitalist socioeconomic system, as assumption of pluralism as a mechanism for determining outcomes in issue area bargaining, and an overriding concern with how disparate "interests" express themselves in diverse agenda-setting environments.

Realism approaches these topics from a seemingly different vantage point, yet the results in excluding class analytical frameworks are remarkably similar. Neoclassical realist approaches, at their best, have acknowledged that the ideas of the ruling class are by definition the ideas that animate the state (Gilpin 1983). However, this insight has rarely been used by realists to interrogate the assumption that states act autonomously in pursuit of their "national interests." The assumption of state autonomy has been so ingrained within the realist paradigm that the "black box" of the state is often shielded from the implications of linkages to powerful societal actors. That is, states actors are assumed to act with a broader set of purposes necessary to advance state power or to safeguard territorial sovereignty from immediate or long-term threats (Ripsman and Taliaferro 2016). As such, realism is supposed to be better equipped than other theories to explain state behavior within an anarchic world system that forces structural imperatives upon state actions.

However, realism as a paradigm or an eclectic set of approaches has spent much of its history trying to uncomfortably explain why state actors do not behave in ways that realism would predict. Christopher Layne's recent *Peace of Illusions* is a case-in-point. Layne, writing with conviction from a set of neoclassical realist assumptions, devotes most of his book to explaining why the foreign policies of the most dominant state in the world system, the U.S., failed to conform to realist expectations (Layne 2007). For Layne, U.S. state elites, contrary to what realism would both predict and recommend, practiced policies of military overextension, during the Cold War and beyond, based more on ideology than an informed assessment of "interests." This military overextension, according to Layne, was a product of an ideological conviction that (mistakenly, for Layne) equated a global U.S. military presence as necessary for maintaining an "open door" for global capitalist markets. That this was a false ideological conviction, for Layne, that bore little resemblance to what realist scholars would predict or recommend regarding U.S. strategic policy and/or objectives, was not enough to make him discard realism. He instead combines the "open door" school of left revisionists with realism to critique the gap between U.S. foreign policy practice and actually existing U.S. "national interests."

If such a gap can exist at the commanding heights of imperial power between what realists would actually expect policy to be and what in fact policy is, perhaps it's time to acknowledge the inherent problems of using realism to glean meaningful insights about the behavior of contemporary states. For Layne, it's the adoption of a mistaken ideology that has steered U.S. elites in a wrongheaded direction of over-commitments and over-extension, creating a gap between commitments and genuine interests. Yet, there is an alternative, Marxian view, which locates this tension between state policy and interests within the realm of socioeconomic class relationships, not ideology. In this view, U.S. foreign policy is not an ideological "mistake" but a product of the vested interests of a narrowly powerful socioeconomic capitalist class (or contested battles between competing factions of that class) that are attempting to use the state to advance their own material interests, even if at the expense of the domestic population (van der Pijl 2012; Cox 2012; Appeldoorn and de Graaff 2016). This critique thereby connects state action directly to the imperatives of powerful capitalist interests within the marketplace.

This Marxian critique of the capitalist state does have a place within the Gramscian school of IR, most notably associated with well-known pioneers and adherents such as Robert Cox and Stephen Gill. This framework has a lot to offer students of IR interested in a materialist critique of mainstream liberal and realist approaches. The advantages include an explicit connection between the broader socioeconomic power structure and the capitalist state, critiquing the severing of this relationship in both liberalism and realism. Indeed, this school of IPE has influenced my own recent scholarship to a great extent, and has been picked up, developed and refined by sociologists most closely associated with the development of the term, "transnational capitalist class," to describe what they see as the emergence of a powerful, cross-border set of political organizations that have achieved hegemonic power within capitalist states today. For scholars like Leslie Sklair and William Robinson, the TCC is the key to understanding the politics of class hegemony that has transformed state structures in modern neoliberal capitalism. If accurate, this view of IR demolishes the liberal and realist fiction that we can separate issue areas and state action from powerful socioeconomic class structures.

While this Gramscian perspective has many insights, it has been primarily the sociological literature where these insights have been most developed, as this perspective is still often either minimized or excluded altogether in introductory IR or IPE textbooks in the U.S. and rarely appears in mainstream U.S. research journals and, in many cases, is either left out of the IR curriculum or included only marginally. And even outside the U.S., the dominant approaches in recent decades have been realism and liberalism. Constructivism and other ideational approaches, including within strands of Marxism itself, often have been more prevalent than the Gramscian school (Cafrany et al. 2016).

In addition, although the Gramscian approach has, in my view, made tremendous advances in critical theory, practitioners have typically focused on the organizational, socioeconomic, and cultural/ideational power of the TCC rather than a more encompassing class analysis that is capable of integrating the power of the TCC within the socioeconomic class dynamics of accumulation and surplus value extraction. As a result, the TCC too often is applied in a schematic fashion, attributing power to the TCC without focusing enough on the political process of class exploitation that has played itself out differently depending on the class-specific context in which such exploitation occurs.

As I will argue in the remainder of this paper, those of us committed to developing a full-blown Marxian political economy within IPE and elsewhere need to help build a mid-range class analytic framework to spearhead a renewed focus on critical materialism. This is necessary to fully resuscitate a Marxian political economy and a research agenda that can offer contributions in scholarship and in teaching. The final section explores the outlines of what such an approach would entail, and the advantages offered by such an approach compared to the limited engagement with class analysis in much contemporary Marxist and critical scholarship.

## 3  Marxist Economists to the Rescue

For those of us interested in making sure our students have the tools to engage in empirically grounded analysis of the political economy of capitalism, there is no better place to start than in mapping a class structure of capitalist production. The advantages of starting with a focus on production, as opposed to patterns of cultural or ideological domination, are numerous and will be developed in this section of the paper. I will also compare this approach to the post-Marxist detachment from class that has emerged as a counterpart within some quarters of critical IPE. Finally, I will discuss how the Gramscian school of IPE is firmly compatible with a more mid-range orientation that, if adopted, would make its insights more immediately relevant to scholars and activists pursuing critical work.

The focus on production should strike everyone reading this as an intuitively obvious starting point for a Marxist analysis. Yet, perhaps surprisingly, most actually existing Marxist frameworks in political science, international relations and sociology, have moved away from a serious engagement with the political economy of production in recent decades. It is past time to move back, and here we can draw on a wide range of Marxist economists whose work never left the realm of critical analyses of the politics of production. At the same time, there has been a rich history of the sectoral analyses of production, most (but not all) written from a non-Marxist orientation and closely associated with the earliest work of Peter Gourevitch, Jeffrey Frieden, David Gibbs and Thomas Ferguson, among others, that can contribute to efforts to build a more production-oriented critical agenda within IPE (Gourevitch 1986; Frieden 1992; Gibbs 1991, 2009; Ferguson 1995).

Marxian economists, led by the co-authored books of Stephen Resnick and Richard Wolff, have developed a rigorous class analysis of production centered on the political economy of surplus value. This work has given us the tools to analyze the relationship between an increasingly complex transnational system of production and the distribution of value added in the exploitative relationships between capitalists, middle-tier contractors and managers and workers. Given that transnational capitalists use a wide range of mechanisms, including political power, market power and offshore tax havens to maximize their value extraction from other actors in the system, this sort of mid-range class analytic framework is necessary to fully address crucial questions for Marxist scholars: how value is distributed and the extent of worker exploitation within the system (Palan, Murphy and Chavagneux 2013; Roberts 2016, Smith 2016).

The shift to a mid-range class analytic framework would give Marxist and aspiring Marxist-scholars, as well as other scholars interested in critical research methods from a power elite perspective, the tools to more effectively address the distribution of revenues and profits under capitalism. And, in the process, would provide ways to further explore the mechanisms that the most powerful capitalist firms utilize to maximize value extraction. The Gramscian Marxist school in IPE, along with the dependency and world systems schools, have long understood that transnational capitalists, due to their market size and power and their privileged position within policymaking circles, occupy a hegemonic or dominant role in the capitalist world system. However, without a mid-range theory of the political economy of production, a more precisely developed theory of transnational corporate power is often sacrificed on the altar of generalization. For example, the category of the "transnational capitalist class" is useful at the level of abstraction to illustrate the growing hegemony of this bloc of capitalists on a global scale. But the use of the TCC as an analytic category often obscures or minimizes the extent to which this powerful faction of capitalist interests has to maneuver within distinct and varied regional and national economies to advance their political and economic objectives (Cox 2012, 189–190). It is within the circumstances of varied political and economic contestation, within regions and within nations, that we can more fully understand the battle between transnational capital and rival capitalist interests that are less globally interconnected, more nationally or regionally oriented, and divided based on sectoral characteristics that often matter in political and business conflict.

In summary, what is needed is a mid-range Marxism that is centered on the politics of surplus value extraction at the point of production. The advantages of such a mid-range approach are significant and here I specify the analytical clarity and rigor that this approach would bring, as well as the utility of such an approach in aiding class-based social movements. First, the focus on production would turn our attention to the ways that capitalist owners use their political and economic power to maximize the accumulation of surplus value in the production process. This means a concrete examination of wealthy investors, corporations, corporate-state linkages, and conflicts with competing interests within society and within the state that impact on investment decisions, and revenue distribution in the market.

The intellectual and foundational origins of such an approach can be found in the writings of Karl Marx, especially volumes 2 and 3 of *Capital*, which deepens our analyses of class processes to allow for a multilayered, overdetermined approach to class analysis. Here I also borrow from the work of economists Stephen A. Resnick and Richard Wolff to develop the outlines of a class analysis framework (Resnick and Wolff 1987). The first aspect of class analysis, developed first by Marx, separates the "foundational" aspects of the class process from the "subsumed" aspects. The foundational aspect of class analysis refers to the relationship between capitalist and worker that involves the extraction of surplus value. Marx understood that not all capitalists were the same, and not all workers were the same. Some capitalists, which he labeled "industrial capitalists" and refined the definition in Volume 3 of *Capital*, were foundational to the system because of their role in ownership of capital and labor power that generated surplus value, defined as the new value created by workers in excess of their labor cost. The extraction of surplus value is thus confined to the exploitation of labor power by capitalists and occurs by definition at the point of production (Marx *Capital*, Vol. 3, Part 2, Chapter VIII 1894).

The subsumed class processes involve a wide range of activities by other capitalists and non-capitalist actors. Subsumed class processes include all activities involved with the management and distribution of surplus value. In other words, surplus value is not to be equated with capitalist profit. This is because portions of the surplus value go toward maintaining a set of relationships necessary to carry out the extraction of surplus value at the point of production. These relationships include managerial functions, marketing, advertising, retail functions, taxes and regulatory obligations to governments, and various "middle-man" functions that are required to facilitate and enable the exploitative processes connected to the extraction of surplus value. In this formulation, which is most developed in *Capital, Vol. 3*, neither capitalists nor workers are a homogenous class. Capitalists are distinguished by their relationship to surplus value extraction; whether they are foundational (directly involved in ownership of labor power used to produce surplus value) or subsumed to this process (merchants, moneylenders and landlords would fit in this category, for example). The productive working class are those workers whose labor power produces surplus value for the capitalists. The subsumed or nonproductive working class includes those who are self-employed and those who exchange their labor power for the selling of a commodity (rather than its production) (Resnick and Wolff 1987, 117–124).

This analysis does not attach any primary importance to industrial capitalists or to productive workers over other capitalists or workers. In other words, these are analytical categories that allow Marxian scholars to better understand the politics of surplus value extraction. The power relationships embedded in exploitative relationships are not just a function of "profit" but a contested struggle among competing groups of capitalists and workers. Capitalists are divided by sectoral position and location within the productive/distributive system. Capitalists also confront working class organizations (or lack thereof) which affects the distribution of surplus value along the chain of distribution. Similarly, capitalists may dominate the state, but also may cede a level of institutional control for the sake of profit-making stability, depending on the historical-structural context of capitalist organization, competition, and relationship to an organized or disorganized working class, as well as other institutionally powerful competitors. A Marxian analysis argues that the political economy of surplus value extraction is a crucial arena for understanding the broader political economy of capitalism. But rather than establish rigid categories, whereby classes act as "agents" embodying inherent interests based on their designation as "class-in-itself," a non-deterministic framework allows for more subjectivity within the process of how classes become aware (or blind) of their class position.

In providing an outline of class analysis as a "process," I am following the tradition of Resnick and Wolff, who take the view that Marxism is not a deterministic theory, with class "determining" all other relationships (Resnick and Wolff 1987, 49–52). These authors, rightly I believe, argue that class should always be understood as an adjective, not a noun, in that the analysis of class processes reveal the power relationships involved in capitalist production. These relationships do have central importance in understanding the politics of capitalist production. They also are central to providing an emancipatory framework to pursue a politics of redistributive justice, most crucially a socialist praxis. But class does not determine identity by itself, as the identity of workers and capitalists are overdetermined by a variety of complementary and contradictory relationships.

This reality of overdetermination has justified the move of some Marxists and some post-Marxists to abandon the terminology of the working class. But such a step is wrongheaded and counterproductive for three reasons. The first is that, as a class-in-itself, an analysis of capitalists and working class identities in the process of capitalist exploitation is central to understanding who profits from the system. Second, how the surplus value is distributed within the capitalist system produces insights regarding the politics of capitalist production, especially through investigation of competing claims on surplus value distribution. The third factor is the importance of an analysis of surplus value extraction and distribution for forging a politics of emancipation or socialist liberation.

Today, the increasing concentration of capitalist firms on a global scale is manifest by the growing importance of the transnational corporation. The relationship of the corporation to the extraction of surplus value and the distribution of surplus value is understudied (and often ignored) in contemporary Marxist scholarship that engages in "high-level" abstraction. That is much, although not all, of the dependency and world systems tradition has operated at the level of the world system to focus on the systemic exploitation that locks entire countries and regions into a socioeconomic structure of exploitation. There are many insights to be gleaned from these approaches. However, they often miss a mid-level understanding of the class process, which is heavily mediated by capitalist competition, sectoral differences among competing capitalists, and the history of working class struggle that is differentiated by geographic, regional and nation-state histories—producing a politics of surplus value extraction and distribution that is affected by these conflicts. A thorough analysis of the transnational corporation, its dominance, its historiography and its ties to states, as well as its cooperation and conflicts with other actors—both capitalist and non-capitalists—provides a more nuanced geography to an understanding of surplus value extraction and distribution (Cox 2012).

For example, the centrality of global supply chains in contemporary neoliberal capitalism is an obvious arena that needs further clarification, analysis and exposure from a Marxian analytical framework. A focus on transnational corporations at the top of the global supply chains, their linkages to a myriad of investment partners positioned at various levels within these supply chains, and the growing importance of workers in production and logistics is crucial for a Marxism that seeks to understand the conditions of exploitation. Fortunately, a recent book from the dependency theory tradition has given us the tools to undertake this process.

John Smith in *Imperialism in the 21st Century*, successfully applies dependency theory to analyze the shift in manufacturing production from developed to developing states. For Smith, transnational corporations concentrated at the top of global supply chains have been able to expand profits through a system of super-exploitation that depends on pushing costs of production downward to independent contractors and especially to vulnerable workers. Transnational corporations at the top of global supply chains profit overwhelmingly from their concentration of ownership of patents, branding, and their favorable market position relative to powerful retailers and distribution networks. In turn, these firms are able to rely on contract manufacturers to produce products in a range of foreign locations, contracting in many cases at "arms-length" with independent producers whose cost margins are extremely tight. Ultimately, the political economy of global supply chains rests on dramatically increasing the supply of workers locked into precarious conditions of part-time employment, the threat of long-term unemployment and vigorous competition within a reserve army of laborers who are trapped by lack of mobility and a relatively closed immigration system.

The genius of Smith's approach is that he is very precise in documenting the political economy of surplus value extraction within the conditions of the global supply chain. In the process of his analysis, we get a reinvigorated dependency theory that takes the politics of production seriously, using the latest and best economic data from scholars who have been on the cutting edge of analyzing value extraction in global supply chains. This process of analytical clarification is necessary for providing potential answers for working class political organizations regarding the following: how transnational firms are able to make super-profits from a system of labor exploitation that dramatically increases labor productivity while keeping wages low or stagnant. For Smith, the consequences of this system of exploitation is most starkly revealed by the following observation: "Commodities produced mostly or entirely in low-wage countries and consumed mostly or entirely in imperialist countries expand the GDP of the nations where they are consumed by far more than the GDP of the nations they are produced" (Smith 2016, 37–38). This creates the optical illusion of value-added in the developed states, which in reality is the ability of transnational corporations at the top of the global supply chain to use their market power to capture more revenue as "profit" as a result of their privileged position.

From Smith's framework, we start to get an appreciation of what a Marxian political economy of production would look like. However, even this approach, as good as it is, needs to be deepened to give us more effective analytical tools. Transnational corporations are not all the same; they arise from particular domestic and regional histories. Transnational firms have particular characteristics embodied within their corporate structure. Their power is contested by rivalries with other domestic actors, including rival firms, sectoral conflicts, and mobilized sectors of the population that have competing interests, such as workers, environmental movements and consumer movements. According to a recent IMF study, it is the power of workers movements, measured through trade unions (an imperfect measure to be sure) that explains, more than any other single variable, the extent to which inequality decreases or increases over time (Jaumotte and Buitron 2015). Of course, the relative strength of working class movements cannot alter the crisis-prone nature of a capitalist system that rests on the extraction of surplus value as its underlying feature. But it can redirect the tools used by capitalists to try to regain a better position within the capitalist marketplace, a process that generates ongoing crisis tendencies within the system.

The fact that workers movements have been declining in strength across the capitalist world explains the dramatic rises in inequality better than any other single factor. At the same time, workers movements have not been declining at the same speed. Therefore there is still some variation based on the nation-state, and the relative importance of the nation-state and its workforce to the transnational accumulation structure. At the same time, contrary to the myth of the reduced importance of the "working class" in contemporary capitalism, the objective position of workers within the global capitalist system is at an all-time high numerically. Capitalism has never had a period where so much of humanity depends on selling their labor power for survival. And workers are increasingly concentrated in large numbers within logistical nodes of global supply chains, meaning that the actions of thousands of strategically placed workers in logistics and distribution centers have power that is disproportionate to their numbers.

Despite their increased importance to the system, the support infrastructure that exists to reproduce workers from one generation to the next is in the process of breaking down. That is, the benefits that workers historically fought for in countries that have a social democratic history: health insurance, unemployment compensation, retirement benefits, and welfare assistance, are all being reduced in most advanced capitalist countries, and in countries where these benefits are still relatively extensive, prognostications for latter decline have become the norm (Streeck 2017). Meanwhile, transnational corporations are replacing the labor of domestic workers with foreign workers who are trapped in a precariously competitive set of circumstances without any significant social safety net. The key for any emancipatory project is to forge unity between these groups of workers across the borders of countries. A critique of the political economy of supply chains, where profits are overwhelmingly concentrated at the top of the production hierarchy due to capitalist power within the market and within political systems, is an important place to start (Nolan and Zhang 2010; Milberg and Winkler 2013).

What is apparent is that most workers cannot easily see these relationships by themselves, in isolation from other workers who are increasingly concentrated in distant locations. It therefore is up to those within the working class movement who can see these linkages, along with their allies in academia and in existing socialist movements, to make this information available to them. This is the best antidote to the rise of the far right in Europe and in the United States. Instead, we often get a leftist response, dominated by identity politics discourse bereft of class analysis, which simply writes off supporters of Brexit or of Trump as hopelessly irredeemable, outside the confines of a cosmopolitan sensibility that champions diversity and immigrant rights (Lapavitsas 2016). The problem, however, is that the liberal cosmopolitan ideology that defends diversity and immigrant rights rarely has anything to say about the contemporary conditions of workers under really existing capitalism (Sculos 2017). The ability of neoliberal capitalism to capture and utilize appeals to diversity and inclusion on its own terms has exposed the failures of identity politics as disconnected from class.

The task, then, of Marxist theory, is to bring back a mid-range Marxism that takes class seriously as the starting point for engagement in meaningful social transformation. If we overlook the fact that capitalism continues to rely on the same central techniques of labor exploitation, extraction of surplus value and concentration of profits through capitalist power over markets and over states, we are not providing ammunition for those that are central to changing the system. If we focus narrowly on "cultural signifiers" or the "multitude" in an attempt to develop an emancipatory struggle against capitalism, then we are not getting at the central dynamic of the system. In fact, we will merely be using ideological language that can easily be turned against us to defend the exploitative processes of the capitalist system that needs to be challenged and overturned.

## Bibliography

Amin, Samir (1979) *Imperialism and Unequal Development*. Monthly Review Press.
Apeldoorn, Bastiaan and de Graaff, Nana (2016) *American Grand Strategy and Corporate Elite Networks*. London: Routledge.
Barone, Charles (2015) *Marxist Thought on Imperialism*. New York: Routledge Press.
Brenner, Robert (1977) "The Origins of Capitalist Development: A Critique of Neo-Smithian Marxism," *New Left Review*, I/104, July-August 1977.
Cafruny, Alan, Talani, Simona, and Pozo Martin, Gonzalo (2016) *Palgrave Handbook of Critical International Political Economy*. New York: Palgrave Macmillan.
Chibber, Vivek (2013) *Postcolonial Theory and the Specter of Capital*. London: Verso.
Cox, Robert W. (1987) *Production, Power and World Order: Social Forces in the Making of History*. New York: Columbia University Press.
Cox, Ronald W. (ed.) (2012) *Corporate Power and Globalization in U.S. Foreign Policy*. New York: Routledge.
Ferguson, Thomas (1995) *Golden Rule: The Investment Theory of Party Competition and the Logic of Money-Driven Political Systems*. Chicago: University of Chicago Press.
Frank, Andre Gunder (1967) *Capitalism and Underdevelopment in Latin America*. New York: Monthly Review Press.
Frieden, Jeffrey (1992) *Debt, Development and Democracy: Modern Political Economy and Latin America*. New Jersey: Princeton University Press.
Gibbs, David (2009) *First Do No Harm: Humanitarian Intervention and the Destruction of Yugoslavia*. Nashville: Vanderbilt University Press.
Gibbs, David (1991) *The Political Economy of Third World Intervention: Mines, Money and U.S. Policy in the Congo Crisis*. Chicago: University of Chicago Press.
Gill, Stephen (1992) *American Hegemony and the Trilateral Commission*. London: Cambridge University Press.
Gilpin, Robert (1983) *War and Change in World Politics*. London: Cambridge University Press.
Gourevitch, Peter (1986) *Politics in Hard Times: Comparative Responses to International Economic Crises*. Ithaca: Cornell University Press.
Hardt, Michael and Negri, Antonio (2001) *Empire*. Boston: Harvard University Press.
Harvey, David (2007) *A Brief History of Neoliberalism*. London: Oxford University Press.
Jaumotte, Florence and Buitron, Carolina Osorio (2015) "Inequality and Labor Market Institutions," IMF Staff Discussion Note, SDN/15/14, July 2015.

Karanassou, Marika, and Sala, Hector (2014) "The Role of the Wage-Productivity Gap in Economic Activity," *International Review of Applied Economics*, Vol. 28, Issue 4, Feb. 21, 2014.

Keohane, Robert and Nye, Joseph (2011) *Power and Interdependence*, 4th Edition. New York: Pearson.

Laclau, Ernesto and Mouffe, Chantal (2014) *Hegemony and Socialist Strategy: Towards a Radical Democratic Politics*. London: Verso.

Lapavitsas, Costas (2016) "Why They Left." *Jacobin*, July 7, 2016.

Layne, Christopher (2007) *Peace of Illusions: American Grand Strategy from 1940 to the Present*. Ithaca: Cornell University Press.

Long, James, Maliniak, Daniel, Peterson, Susan, and Tierney, Michael (2005) "Teaching and Research in International Politics: Surveying Trends in Faculty Opinion and Publishing," ISA Paper, March 1–5, 2005.

Mair, Peter (2013) *Ruling the Void: The Hollowing Out of Western Democracy*. London: Verso.

Marx, Karl (1993) *Capital: A Critique of Political Economy, Volume 3*. New York: Penguin Classics.

Milberg, William and Winkler, Deborah (2013) *Outsourcing Economics: Global Value Chains in Capitalist Development*. London: Cambridge University Press.

Ness, Immanuel (2015) *Southern Insurgency: The Coming of the Global Working Class*. New York: Pluto Press.

Nolan, Peter and Zhang, Jin (2010) "Global Competition After the Financial Crisis." *New Left Review*, Vol. 64: 97–108.

Palan, Ronen, Murphy, Richard, and Chavagneux, Christian (2009). *Tax Havens: How Globalization Really Works*. Ithaca: Cornell University Press.

Patnaik, Utsa and Patnaik, Prabhat (2016) *A Theory of Imperialism*. New York: Columbia University Press.

Resnick, Stephen and Wolff, Richard (1987) *Knowledge and Class: A Marxian Critique of Political Economy*. Chicago: University of Chicago Press.

Ripsman, Norrin M. and Taliaferro, Jeffrey W. (2016) *Neoclassical Realist Theory of International Politics*. London: Oxford University Press.

Roberts, Michael (2016) *The Long Depression: Marxism and the Global Crisis of Capitalism*. Haymarket Books.

Robinson, William (2014). *Global Capitalism and the Crisis of Humanity*. London: Cambridge University Press.

Sclofsky, Sebastian and Funk, Kevin (2017) "The Specter That Haunts Political Science: The Neglect and Misreading of Marx in International Relations and Comparative Politics." *International Studies Perspectives*.

Sculos, Bryant W. (2017) *Worlds Ahead: On the Dialectics of Cosmopolitanism and Postcapitalism*. PhD Dissertation, Florida International University.

Silver, Beverly (2003) *Forces of Labor: Workers' Movements and Globalization since 1870*. London: Cambridge University Press.
Sklair, Leslie (2000) *The Transnational Capitalist Class*. New York: Wiley-Blackwell.
Smith, John (2016) *Imperialism in the Twenty-First Century: Globalization, Super-Exploitation and Capitalism's Final Crisis*, Monthly Review Press.
Streeck, Wolfgang (2017). *Buying Time: The Delayed Crisis of Democratic Capitalism*. London: Verso, 2nd Edition.
Van der Pijl, Kees (2012) *The Making of an Atlantic Ruling Class*. London: Verso.
Wallerstein, Immanuel (2004). *World Systems Analysis: An Introduction*. Durham: Duke University Press.
Wright, Erik Olin (2015) *Understanding Class*. London: Verso.

CHAPTER 3

# Marx in Miami: Reflections on Teaching and the Confrontation with Ideology

*Bryant William Sculos and Sean Noah Walsh*

## 1   Exile and Dislocation

In composing this piece we hope to detail some of our strategies and pedagogical experiences teaching Marx and Marxism in Miami, Florida.[1] Although Miami is certainly a special case regarding the intensity and character of ideological fervor against leftist political and social theory, we believe the lessons adapted to this specific environment can be generalized for instructors regardless of geography. Teaching Marx in the United States often poses unique challenges. In Miami, those obstacles feel frequently amplified.[2]

Perhaps like no other place in this country is teaching a particular theorist or theoretical tradition as resisted and as taxing on a teacher's patience and even self-esteem as is teaching Marx and Marxism in Miami. Likewise, the experience of learning Marx can be acutely distressing for students who have been raised to accept him as the personification of evil. Miami is the hub of the Cuban exile community in the United States, and thus semester after semester, year after year, we encounter groups of students who have basically formed their identities against the name "Marx." A sizeable fraction of our students were either born in Cuba or were raised by parents who fled the authoritarian regime of Fidel Castro. An even larger part of the population, though not ethnic Cubans, were raised in a fiercely anti-Castro and anti-Marxist environment. Though we have found the younger generation of Cuban-Americans are sometimes more socially liberal than their parents and grandparents, there is still vociferous, yet uninformed and thus unfounded opposition to just about anything associated with Marx or Marxism.[3]

---

1   These reflections are drawn from political theory courses in which we teach Marx and Marxism. They include Modern Political Theory, Political Ideologies, Contemporary Political Theory, Humanist Marxism, Structural Marxism, and Critical Aesthetic Theory.
2   One student casually informed me that his cousin wanted to physically attack Sean for teaching Marx, specifically saying, "He said he's going to kick your ass."
3   Indeed, there is often intense opposition to anything that even remotely resembles socialism (or the color red, unless it indicates the hue of Marco Rubio's tie that day).

From our experiences, the resistances we have faced as instructors can be categorized into three groups: (1) those that conflate Marx's ideas with the actions and policies of Fidel Castro, Che, Mao, or figures from the Soviet Union (2) those that dismiss Marxism by reference to vague notions of human nature, and (3) those that argue Marx's conception of communism looks great on paper, but is impractical and unworkable in real political practice. We describe each of these, along with our pedagogical strategies, developed through dialogue in the classroom.

It may be useful to note that we teach Marx according to an orthodox (but still self-critical) Marxian assumption: some historical ideas are accurate and others false. This principle is also applicable to ideas about Marxism, especially preconceived ideas. As Friedrich Engels (1978, 766) remarked, the adversaries of Marxism used every opportunity to generate "misunderstandings and distortions." Accordingly, in order to teach Marx fairly, we have found it important to dislocate these prejudices in advance. In that respect, we do approach the discussion of Marx and Marxism from the perspective that some views, while held by students for understandable reasons, are wrong.[4]

Our hope is that what follows here, organized in pairs of related but distinct narratives, will encourage more instructors to find ways for occupying their classrooms with embodied, radical potential, critique, and imagination—the forces of conservatism and liberal capitalism have succeeded in doing the exact opposite for decades, every time the oppression, exploitation, and hypocrisy of the status quo has been ignored in their classrooms.[5] Each narrative sub-section represents commentary on the respective strategies we have used in confronting these shared experiences. We have found that, while manifold techniques are useful, the most effective strategies for teaching Marx in Miami include reflexive confrontations with the anti-Marxist ideological presupposition of our students.

## 2  Fidel Castro: Intellectual Heir of Karl Marx?

Perhaps the most serious obstacle to teaching Marx is getting students to take him seriously in the first place. Without some kind of impetus to do otherwise, most simply reject in advance the possibility that he might have something

---

4  Again, Engels (1978, 766) remarks, "Ideology is a process accomplished by the so-called thinker consciously ....but with a false consciousness."
5  A superb text for those interested in a lucid exposition of several of the arguments we will be exploring in this essay is Terry Eagleton's *Why Marx Was Right* (2011).

to offer them. Of course, there are some reasons for this. Firstly, there is often an inclination by undergraduates to resist reading seriously texts that might challenge their tidy vision of reality, whether those ideas originate with Marx, Plato, Nietzsche, or Thomas Paine. College students are recovering teenagers, and most teenagers have already convinced themselves that political disputes are only the result of old people who were probably born cranky curmudgeons. Secondly, despite their flirtations with rebelliousness, most undergraduates arrive in college as products of their local ideological apparatuses. Parents, religious affiliations, friends, and other influences often serve to reinforce the view that a special place in Hell is reserved for Marx and all of his apparently mindless followers who wake up in the morning and hate freedom. If the idea of "America" is depicted as an unqualified good, then Marx and Marxism are obviously the antithesis of that moral purity.[6] Why? Because the greatest enemy faced by the United States was supposedly the Soviet Union, a nation built in Marx's image and which would have undoubtedly received his nodding approval, just as the United States is presently the country that George Washington, James Madison, and Thomas Jefferson clearly wanted. In order to teach Marx, it has been helpful to displace students from this sort of ingrained error.[7] This challenge of exposing our students to a world of heterodox ideas is tremendously rewarding. As they are compelled to reflect on their ideological baggage in order to learn, we have to do the same in order to teach.

In Miami, however, there is the further, and very entrenched, difficulty of Cuba. While most students, even now, can vaguely identify the Soviet Union as an adversary, they often do so in the most impersonal terms. I have yet to meet a student whose parents spent time in a gulag. The Russian students I have had bear only a vague memory of life under "communism." In Miami, the animus toward Marxism is often rooted in far more personal experiences. Practically all of my students hailed from families who fled what they described

---

[6] The idea that capitalism and America are synonymous is certainly not peculiar to Miami. I have found that a very effective remedy to this misconception is to ask my students the following questions:
   a. Which part of the Declaration of Independence or Constitution forbids socialism? Of course, the answer is that no such provision exists.
   b. If we cannot find a prohibition against socialism, then surely some part of our nation's fundamental documents must endorse capitalism. If socialism is "un-American," and capitalism is so essential to American life, it must be there. Which part of those documents gives countenance to capitalism? The look on their faces as they realize that there is no constitutional basis for capitalism is quite refreshing.

[7] The same is true for many other historical thinkers, such as the authors of *The Federalist Papers* or other figures from the American founding, whose views are frequently distorted to serve as proxies in contemporary controversies.

to us as the genuine misery of Fidel Castro's poorly named "revolution." Many directly observed the censorship and repression, or had family members who experienced it firsthand. Some had family who were political prisoners. And Fidel Castro, infamously, declared some kind of allegiance to the Soviet sphere of influence, and communism, despite admitting to have read no more than a fraction from the first volume of *Das Kapital* (Cameron 1964). Because of the history they normally receive, the idea of impartially discussing Marxism is generally a non-starter for most students, but Cuban-American students, quite understandably, have a heightened degree of obstinacy against this subject.

While those resistances are understandable, the problem is that they are clearly misplaced. Castro is not the fault of Karl Marx. Stalin's murderous purges are completely unsupported by anything Marx or Engels wrote. The pedagogical challenge, then, is to dislocate prejudice from the text while conveying respect for the very real experiences many of the Cuban émigrés have suffered.

*Bryant Sculos*: I say the word Marx and I notice several students immediately look nauseated or worse, angry. I expect this. I offer them a challenge from the outset. If you find specific textual evidence for the horrible atrocities committed by Stalin, Mao, Che Guevara or Fidel Castro in the writings of Marx, show them to me, we will discuss them and you will receive ten points on your final grade. Some students seem intimidated by the challenge, but others have seemed quite eager to attempt to prove me wrong, confident they will be able to meet the challenge. I have offered that challenge many times, and I haven't had a single student able to provide text-based arguments for such a connection. Weirdly, Marx never actually advocates the mass killing or imprisoning of political opponents. He never suggests that industrialization should proceed under authoritarian guidelines. In fact for Marx, industrial capitalism is a necessary stage in our human progress towards socialism and communism. Agrarian societies are not prepared for socialism according to Marx (1998, 44).[8] I tell them, in the next class we will discuss the concept of post-scarcity,

---

8  This interpretation, along with many of the others offered in this chapter, while generally accurate, are often necessary simplifications that elide some of the complexities and incongruities across Marx's (and Engels') various texts—simplifications necessary and appropriate for undergraduate courses that are often students' first serious academic experiences with Marx and Marxism. It is also worth noting that some of the events and contributions in the classroom discussions that serve as the bases for these narratives are not included for the sake of clarity. These narratives also involve the merging of multiple class sections across multiple semesters.

but until then let us look at why you all think that Cuba—their principal "counter-example" to the viability, seriousness, or democratic core of Marxism—is a Marxist state.[9]

"Is it because Castro told you that is where he got his ideas? Is it because that is what he told your parents? And maybe he did get some ideas from Marx, and maybe he initially meant well towards those ideas." I present them the positive accomplishments of the Castro regime compared to the Batista regime and its predecessors: increased literacy, decreased poverty, increase in the quality and availability of basic health care, and increased agricultural production (Glennie 2011). We look at the dark side as well. That is not enough to placate them. They seemingly hate me at this moment. I expect this. What I tell them next is what earns me a bit of their trust again: "What we will be doing over the next several classes will not prevent you from criticizing the ills and atrocities of the Castro regime. I promise. You can end up agreeing with everything Marx says, and you will actually be in a better position to criticize that regime. After all, there was a reason Marx said towards the end of his life, 'I do not know what I am, but I am not a Marxist.' He saw people were already perverting his arguments and theories."

"Now then why do we accept Castro's claim that his policies and practices represent the ideals of Marx? Many of your parents and friends have told you their own horror stories of the Castro regime (or similarly "socialist" regimes) or you yourself experienced them; you "know" how terrible Castro is, so why is it that you all seem to accept his platitude that he and his regime are simply applying Marx's theories? Let us think about what I believe to be an apt analogy." I write on the white board:

KU KLUX KLAN : _____ :: ISIS : _____ :: CUBA/USSR : _____

I call on students to fill in the blanks one at a time. Most pick up on the point I am trying to make with this analogy rather quickly, even if many disagree with the validity of the comparisons at first.

KU KLUX KLAN : CHRISTIANITY:: ISIS : ISLAM:: CUBA/USSR : MARXISM[10]

---

9   On the problem of the entire idea of a "Marxist state" see Narrative #2.
10  This analogy is adapted from the one I have heard religious scholar and public intellectual Reza Aslan make on many occasions. His analogy only includes the KKK and ISIS, but I am deeply indebted to his pedagogical attempts on Fox News and CNN. Luckily, my students handed my altered challenge better than the anchors Prof. Aslan has had to deal with (especially most recently over the publication of his 2013 book *Zealot*).

I ask them, "Do most Christians accept that the Klan has the correct interpretation of Christianity?" A student blurts out, "I didn't know they were even Christian..."

I tell him, "That is because of how warped and ignored their interpretation is by any respectable Christian." Another student calls out, "But ISIS does actually represent Islam."

I reply sharply, "Are you Muslim? Or more relevantly, are you a scholar of the Koran or the Hadith?" He asks what the Hadith is. I reply, "This is precisely why we need to be a bit more humble and skeptical about how much or how little we actually know about the things we hear on the news, especially if for some terrible reason your chosen channel happens to be named after an orange canine." It takes them a moment or two, then I get the laugh I was hoping for. The laughter dies down, and I bring us back to the analogy. "But honestly, do most Muslims agree with ISIS's interpretation of Islam?" A few students assert that they do. "Look at all the support they have! Of course, maybe it's not all Muslims, but it sure seems like most."

"Why does it seem that way?" I push back. No response. I ask the whole class now, "Which country is home to the largest percentage of Muslims worldwide?" They begin guessing, Pakistan, India, Saudi Arabia. Then someone finally gets it: Indonesia. "Yes, it is actually Indonesia, and there is barely statistically measurable support for ISIS in Indonesia. Additionally though, statistics globally including the Middle East, show that most Muslims oppose ISIS. So just as with the KKK, we should not accept ISIS's interpretation of Islam." I call on a student, "So what you're saying is that Castro and Stalin and people like them have perverted Marxism and we believe them?"

"That is exactly what I am saying to you."[11]

*Sean Walsh*: My strategy has been a sort of dialectical exorcism: let's begin with what we all "know." I begin the first class on Marx, almost always pertaining to "On the Jewish Question," by asking the students to list any so-called "Marxist states" that have ever existed. The first round of responses are immediate: the Soviet Union, China, Cuba. With some prodding, the list usually grows to include former Eastern Bloc nations: Yugoslavia, Czechoslovakia, Albania, East Germany, Hungary. If I ask emphasize the term "ever," students with some knowledge of history might suggest Spain during the Civil War era. At this

---

11   Another analogy I have occasionally used is: "If I prance about your home wearing a red suit, place a present for you underneath a tree near your house while you sleep, and I attach antlers to my cat, would you believe me if I told you I was Santa Claus? No? Why? Because you know the myth of Santa Claus includes so much more than these superficial characteristics. Why is then that so many people, without ever actually reading Marx, accept the claims of dictators that they embody Marx's (or even Lenin's) theories?"

point, I will normally jab the students by pointing out how Eurocentric the list appears. This leads to a flood of African, Asian, and South American nations: Mozambique, Eritrea, Angola, Nicaragua, Vietnam, Cambodia, Laos. Some will hesitantly offer Venezuela under the regime of Hugo Chavez, or Evo Morales' Bolivia. Frankly, I will include whatever they want, as long as the list does not include something like Thatcher's England or de Gaulle's France.

Depending on how frenetic my handwriting appears, the chalkboard is generally consumed by the list. It is at this point that, starting with the Soviet Union, I cross out every nation listed and explain what every serious reader of Marx knows: there has never been a genuine "Marxist state." Further, I admit to the students that I have asked them to do the impossible because there can be *no such thing* as a Marxist state. Starting with the latter point, my normal approach is to explain first the impossibility of a Marxist state by offering preliminary comments on how Marxism, in total opposition to what they have heard, is incompatible with the state. The point is never to take my word for it, but to read what Marx actually had to say on the subject. As we delve further, and read *The Communist Manifesto*, they see for themselves how Marx and Engels insist the state exists for no other purpose than managing the common affairs of the ruling class (Marx and Engels 1985, 82). They see for themselves how, once class antagonisms are resolved through revolution, the state has no further use, and withers into nothing (105).

I have found, for a fair reading of Marx, it becomes useful to demonstrate that not only were the nations listed "not Marxist," but they also represent merely another kind of capitalism. As I explain to my students, it is perfectly fair to examine Marx' ideas and disagree with them. It is patently unfair, however, to point to the failings of various political entities that had only the most nominal, superficial connection to his work as evidence of his errors.

Since students tend to begin from the prejudice that capitalism is good, and communism is not, I pose a direct question: what is capitalism, or what is the central feature of capitalism? Invariably, the answer points to free markets and minimal government interference. In other words, the students express the commonly held view that capitalism is identical with some kind of freedom. This myth is easily dispensed with a tour of political systems that were both deeply authoritarian and capitalist: Chile, Argentina, the fascist regimes of Germany and Italy, and American war economies top the list of counterexamples. At this point, I introduce what Marx considered the secret of capitalist production, surplus value. Virtually all of my students have been middle and lower middle class. Most of them work. Despite the complexity of the three volumes of *Capital*, they are usually quick in grasping the concept, as it is readily observable in their own experiences. They understand the value of what they produce and how they are expected to work in excess of their own compensation in order to generate even more value for someone else. And this is when we return to the list of crossed-out "Marxist states." After discussing the meaning of surplus value, it becomes a rather simple matter to explain that in *every* single state on the list—Russia, China, Cuba, East Germany, Vietnam, Cambodia, all of them—one will find the establishment of surplus value. In other words, they come to understand that, whatever banners it flew, and however hard it pretended to be otherwise, neither the Soviet Union, China, nor even Cuba was anything other than an authoritarian form of capitalism in which surplus value was generated for the benefits of those who owned the means of production, most often the elites of the ruling party.

Some students remain skeptical. Some remain incredulous. All of us have a difficult time looking past what we have been taught by parents, pastors, and other local influences.[12] Whether it succeeds, or not, this is a start to a more honest conversation and I have found this prefatory dialogue useful. Why? Because students from Cuba perceived firsthand how their families lived in squalor, while Castro and his associates enjoyed living in relative opulence. The concept of surplus value, whereby the labor of many is exploited for the benefit of a few, makes sense to them, and, while some remain intransigent, *most* of the students start asking why they have been taught what are now apparently distortions, if not outright lies, about Karl Marx and his ideas.

## 3  The Twisted Trees of Human Nature

While the students can now recognize that the excesses and crimes of the Soviet Union or Cuba no longer count as evidence against Marxism, other prejudices persist. Part of our snarky inner monologue has been to conclude that whatever failings are said to go on in America's high schools, they must be excelling in courses on human nature, because, in general, undergraduates, regardless of their major, often arrive utterly confident that they can speak unerringly on the subject. More seriously, the "fact" of human nature is almost exclusively used as an attempt to foreclose the discussions. However, we refuse to abandon this ground to prejudice. We understand why students appeal to this argument, but our reading of Marx and like-minded thinkers has lead us to believe withholding conceptions of human nature is central to our students'

---

12   Some students also refuse to accept the superiority of Darwin's theories to the fictions of scripture. Some students refuse to accept math (I was one of those). No pedagogical strategy is perfect, but these have helped us greatly.

developing a sense of self-critical consciousness in terms of questioning the existing political and economic system, as well as to them taking alternative theories like Marxism seriously.

In his *Social Contract*, Jean-Jacques Rousseau (1993a, 240) claimed that democracy was a government fit only for a race of gods, and not for human beings. In our experience undergraduate students tend to agree with this principle, at least when it is made clear that Marx and Engels (1985, 104) are among the few political thinkers, ever, to advocate explicitly on behalf of democracy. Raising this point in class yields some very interesting discussions, as students learn that the authors of the Constitution of the United States were aghast by the idea of democracy, whereas Marx was motivated by the promise of political equality. To the degree that they oppose Marxism, and support a republican form of government designed to minimize the passions and participation of the masses, students are called into considering their own potentially tepid commitment to anything like real democracy. Indeed, many are surprised to learn that Marx (1978, 30) speaks so fervently about the idea of genuine "universal human emancipation," freedom from a system that they often recognize in advance of their encounter with his ideas as being grossly unjust, exploitative, racist, and misogynist.

But prejudice and resistance still lingers on. Even if, at this point, the students have come to discard the absurd lies that Marx wants to enslave them all and make them share underwear, they maintain the view that his ideas are unworkable because human beings are of a nature that is inimical to cooperation, collectivity, and harmony.[13] It is perhaps a view drawn from Immanuel Kant's liberalism, which bemoaned, "Nothing straight can be constructed from such warped wood as that which man is made of" (Kant 1991, 46). At this point, the pendulum has swung to the other extreme. Unburdened from having to answer for the Soviet Union and Cuba, the problem is no longer that Marx' ideas represent unmitigated evil. Rather, now the problem is that his ideas are *too good*, and human nature is essentially too wicked for those ideas to work. Of course, this refutation is hardly unique to Marxism. The respective ideas of Plato, Hobbes, or pretty much anything that fails to immediately resemble the status quo is subject to scorn, since obviously the present system works so well (unless, you happen to be poor, non-white, female, an animal, a tree, etc.).

*Sean Walsh*: I have found that, in Miami, the indictment against human nature can be particularly acute. Students are likely to suggest that human

---

13  As Marx and Engels (1985, 99) explicitly state, "Communism deprives no man of the power to appropriate the products of society; all that it does is to deprive him of the power subjugate the labor of others by means of such appropriation."

beings are necessarily selfish and competitive and only cooperate when there is advantage. To their credit, this view is derived and reinforced by scenes from their environment. The geography and culture of Miami seem only to encourage self-absorption, consumerism, and narcissism. Locked, for the moment, by the Everglades National Park (a sprawling zone of, for now, protected wetlands) on one side, and the Atlantic Ocean on the other, Miami is a highly condensed, overcrowded megalopolis. Perhaps owing to the authoritarian nature of Castro's regime, the prevailing attitude in Miami-Dade County seems to be grotesquely individualist. For example, driving an automobile in Miami is a decidedly hazardous undertaking. This is not merely anecdotal. Miami is among the most dangerous places to drive, "First in automotive fatalities, first in pedestrian strikes, first in the obscenity-laced tirades of their fellow drivers" (Palmer 2014). There is no such thing as courtesy for one's fellow human being, and using a turn signal is generally seen as a sign of weakness. Consumption is necessarily conspicuous. In this place, the point of all consumption is conspicuous. It seems unlikely that most of the people purchasing vehicles from BMW, Mercedes Benz, and Jaguar can afford them, but the object remains to appear as though you can. It is not only a culture of "me," but "have you seen me (as I was running you off the road)?" There is often little concern for community or neighborhood.[14] Noise abounds at all hours, noise from car stereos, televisions sets, and very loud mouths.

As for crime, by some estimates, Miami ranked as the seventeenth "most dangerous city in the country" in 2011, putting it in company with perennially infamous cities such as Detroit, Baltimore, Oakland, and Cleveland (*Huffington Post* 2014). When I ask my students how many of them live in a home with an alarm, some hands go up, depending on how many can afford such luxury. When I ask them how many live in a home with bars on the windows, many more hands go up. When I ask them how many live in a home with a gun, almost all of their hands are raised. Indeed, as my students in Miami generally attest, there is a great deal of evidence to support Kant's indictment against human nature.

Rousseau (1993b, 57) offered one of the first rebuttals to this fell accusation, when he claimed that theorists indicting man in his natural state had confounded "the savage man with the men we have daily before our eyes." The same basic response holds true for Marx, following from his theory of historical materialism.[15] The manner in which production takes place at a given historical

---

14 Students have frequently regaled me with stories of awful neighbors whose transgressions ranged from throwing dead rats into their backyard to having gunfights with the Miami-Dade County Sheriff's Department.
15 Lukács (1968, 1) describes historical materialism as the basis of Marxism, and the defining factor of a Marxist. While Marx never used the term "historical materialism," though

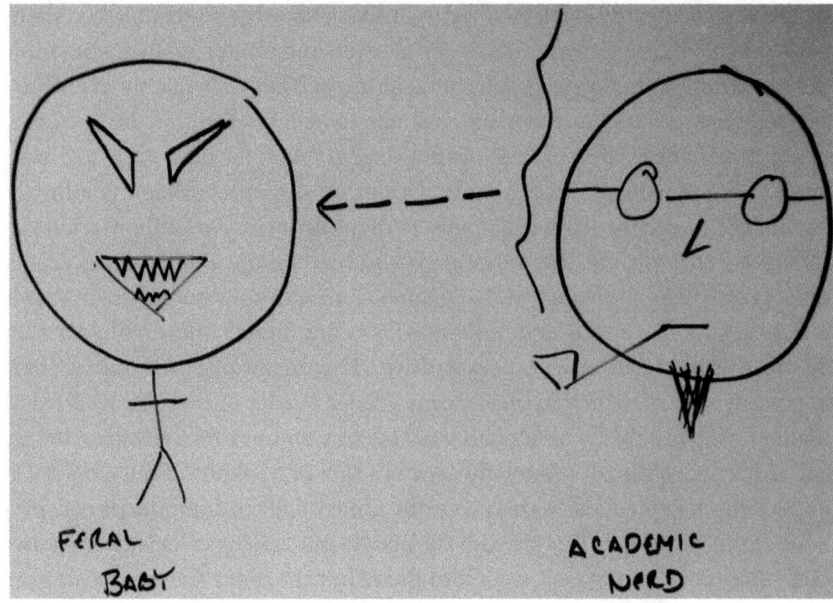

FIGURE 3.1  "Feral Baby" (by Dr. Sean Noah Walsh)

moment is what supplies the character of ideas, politics, religion, art, and philosophy (Marx 1970, 20–21). Indeed, human being itself is largely configured by the historical particularity of production.[16] The basic concept of historical materialism is fairly straightforward and most undergraduates grasp it quickly. But the human beings in front of them are the only kind they have ever known, and grasping the *extent* to which production influences what passes as human nature can be more challenging. Indeed, for Marx, we do not even really know what authentic human being looks like because our subjectivity has been so thoroughly perverted by the mechanisms of capitalism. In order to illustrate this point, I have employed a heuristic device, which I call "Feral Baby."[17]

The drawing (Figure 3.1) begins with the figure on the left, the eponymous feral baby. As its name suggests, Feral Baby was left in the woods far from civilization before any kind of socialization or education could take place. The child has no language, no concept of human society or any of its trappings. Raised

---

Engels (1978, 760) describes their joint effort to establish a "materialist conception of history."

16  As Marx (1988, 107) writes, "The transcendence of private property is therefore the complete emancipation of all human senses and attributes."

17  As readers can see by the expert drawing, only instructors with really advanced art skills should even attempt this.

by woodland creatures, probably squirrels or wild boars, it has no concept of itself as a human being and spends its day chasing birds and gathering acorns (which students with knowledge of survival skills have told me are inedible). On the right is "Academic Nerd," a pretentious pipe smoking member of the intelligentsia who pats himself on the back for writing research that does nothing to change the world, and makes inappropriately sarcastic jokes about conservative politicians to his undergraduate courses.[18]

I pose the question to the class, "If Academic Nerd is an anthropologist, sociologist, political scientist, or some similar profession, what would he want from observing Feral Baby? What reason would he have to observe Feral Baby?" Answers are usually quick to arrive at the idea that "Feral Baby" represents human nature, uncontaminated by civilization and its contents. Feral Baby represents human nature in its purest form, and could provide evidence for Academic Nerd as to whether or not human beings are essentially greedy, self-interested, and violent, which is how we often see them in capitalism. I then ask the class what problems are inextricably associated with this kind of practice, or asked differently, "Why will Academic Nerd be unable to access this truth of human nature from Feral Baby?" Sometimes they arrive at the answer themselves, other times require a bit of prodding, but, in any case, the problem is not with the truth of Feral Baby, but the truth of Academic Nerd. In fact, it is Academic Nerd who is quite thoroughly enmeshed in the capitalist mode of production. Academic Nerd is already a product of capitalism, already contaminated by its superstructure, its norms, ideas, educational apparatus, and concepts. In effect, Academic Nerd is unable to assess Feral Baby in a manner unobstructed by capitalism; he will necessarily impose concepts onto Feral Baby (such as "feral" and "baby") that are generated within a historically given superstructure. "Feral Baby" does not recognize the difference between civilized and feral; those are Academic Nerd's concepts, drawn from this historical mode of production, and he takes them with him wherever he goes. It does not matter if Academic Nerd is on his way to the bank, or, like the Marxist anthropologist Claude Levi-Strauss, he is on his way to study the Nambikwara; he takes capitalism with him. The lesson for our students is that while the nature of human beings in capitalism is there for them to observe, they have no vantage point from which to correctly assess human nature outside of, or beyond, the mode of production that has constituted their perspectives. There is no Archimedean view to be had. The trans-historical truth of human nature is inaccessible to us.

---

18   Most of my students verbally acknowledge the resemblance between "Academic Nerd" and me.

According to the Marxist view, if human beings appear rotten to the core, it is because the capitalist system we inhabit violently encourages pernicious behaviors. The idea, going back to at least John Locke (1980, 21), that the rich are the industrious and the poor, unreasonable and lazy, is clearly shown to be backward. In fact, the poor have to work much harder for their survival, whereas the objective of achieving riches is quite clear: it provides the advantage of not having to work nearly as hard, if at all. In that sense, the "Feral Baby" exercise helps dislocate prejudices against human nature and demonstrate how the capitalist system encourages laziness by making it the end goal.

*Bryant Sculos:* No matter how often I explain to my students that Marx does not offer a conception of human nature in the conventional sense of that phrase— however oversimplified I might think this interpretation of Marx is— it seems they have a fundamental difficulty wrapping their heads around it. I explain why Marx makes this argument and how it fits into his overall theory. Consciousness, our psychologies and resulting behaviors, our beliefs and our desires, are all shaped by our historical social conditions in which we are raised and live (Marx 1998, 42). There is usually an astute student who will push deeper and ask: "Well isn't species-being like a kind of human nature, that people regardless of their social conditions, are at their best and freest when they are laboring as they choose?"

"Well yes, it is like a concept of human nature, but it differs from conventional uses of the phrase 'human nature' in that Marx (1988, 69) argues quite lucidly that how we labor or how we would choose to labor is also determined or at least shaped by our existing social conditions. The broad idea of freely-chosen labor may be trans-historical, but how it would manifest itself in reality is deeply particular."[19] This is typically where the thoughtfulness ends though, sadly.

The next set of questions invariably revolves around the same theme: "But aren't competitiveness and self-interest and greed natural, biological aspects of human beings as animals?" or more accurately those "questions" are typically posed as statements. "These characteristics *are* part of human nature and you and Marx are both naïve fools for thinking otherwise" (or so their tone often suggests). As much as I may have the urge to walk out of class and drink, I don't. I take a deep breath and reply with a question or set of questions that encourages the student(s) to consider the (potentially ideological) basis for such

---

19  Now perhaps this question is based on how I teach the idea of species-being based on Erich Fromm's very accurate elucidation of what he takes to be Marx's socio-historical conception of human nature as the manifestation of species-being in a particular mode of production (Fromm 1961; 1962).

a claim. "Are all people equally competitive?" "Is there any consistently verified DNA markers or other biological evidence which points to comprehensive genetic determinism regarding these varying levels of competitiveness across time?" "Are you examining this question from a neutral, asocial point of view?" We go around on these questions for a little while as they come closer and closer to understanding the historical and social essence of their preconceptions.

However, regardless of these questions and that my students' minds tend to be more receptive at this point, they are often largely unconvinced of the potential accuracy or feasibility of the alternative, Marxian perspective. In order to more fully unlearn the assumptions that prevent them from fully appreciating the value of Marx's position, I now ask, "How many people think that texting and driving improves their safety and well-being on the road?"[20] One student raises their hand, as a joke. Next, "How many people text and drive?" Almost every hand goes up. I then simply ask them to consider the social roots of that pervasive norm that so obviously and knowingly endangers their safety and even their lives. We discuss it. I transition, "Now think about the news on Black Friday over the past few years. People are getting trampled *to death* at Wal-Marts. People are literally murdering each other for a discounted, slightly larger TV than the one they probably have at home. Think about that, it isn't even for something they need to live, and it isn't something they probably wouldn't otherwise be able to experience some version of."

To drive the point home, I ask them: "How many people have heard of these people who jump onto subway tracks to save complete strangers? How many of you have ever done a single thing that didn't benefit you? Even small things. How many of you have done these things at some sort of risk to yourself?" They share their stories. They feel more optimistic. The atmosphere of the room is changing before me, slowly and cautiously I press on: "Is it at least plausible that our current socioeconomic system, capitalism, promotes certain beliefs and behaviors at the expense of others? That we are capable of both great creativity, compassion, and selflessness as well as narcissism, hedonism, and thoughtlessness, but that our system promotes the latter practices more than the former?" I get a lot of nods here. With class typically about to end at this point, I tell them to think about this over the next two days until our following class meeting, and to try to come up with other examples, either for or against this view so we can discuss them then. It is not the point that they admit to accepting Marx's view on human nature or any of these alternative concepts so much as is the pedagogical victory in getting them to seriously question their

---

20   This is an especially pertinent question in Miami.

belief in the trans-historical naturalness of some of the most pernicious normative and behavioral aspects of capitalist society.

About as often as students suggest that the basic psycho-social manifestations of capitalism are natural, universal traits of human beings, I hear students bring up the question of incentive and laziness when we discuss socialism, communism or possibilities of a post-capitalist political economy. Though Marx (1985, 99) himself says very little on the topic, contrary to prevailing opinion, what he does say makes it possible for me to answer this student inquiry fairly easily. "So if everyone receives what they need, and contributes what they can, what prevents people from free riding or taking advantage of those who work hard?" I tell them, "First, remember, Marx argues that people naturally want to labor and be productive, creative members of society, but it is the existing social conditions and relations of production that either prevent them from laboring how they would otherwise choose, or turns the work they are compelled to do to survive (e.g., stocking shelves or pulling a lever for eight hours at a time) into pure toil. Marx (100) argues that you would want to work if you could work how you wanted."

Still they push pack, "What would make someone want to contribute if they didn't need to? Wouldn't they take a few too many days off? Wouldn't overall societal innovation decrease? People need incentive to put in those extra hours to invent things." I agree with them; "People do need incentive, but why does that incentive need to be profit or consumer goods?" I offer them the example of the inventor of the Polio vaccine. "He gave it away to the world. His motivation to innovate was purely to contribute to the betterment of the world. Sure maybe his ego wanted the privilege that comes with solving such a difficult problem. Marx would have no problem with this." I call on the next student: "Okay I generally agree with you," He says, "but...." I interrupt him, "You mean Marx? You agree with *Marx* on this...I want to hear you say it out loud." [Everyone laughs]. I ask him to continue. "So I agree with Marx, but how do we get people to want to do the really terrible jobs like cleaning the sewers?" I make sure he knows how thoughtful and important this superb question is, and it is a challenge to which the left must respond. It is indeed one of the enduring challenges of the Marxist and socialist tradition: how can people be convinced that there is a viable democratic, egalitarian alternative?

Though I typically engage in a more Socratic style, I lecture at length now: "Well Marx doesn't give us an explicit answer to that question, but he does offer two very important arguments that can help us come up with a solution using his ideas. First, both socialism and communism require post-scarcity, which means we have developed enough technologically to provide for every person on earth in all their basic necessities and likely beyond that to include some luxuries. This means that maybe we'll have already developed a technology to clean sewers or pick up trash for us. Anyone here LOVE vacuuming?" I ask. A couple students raise their hands. "Well most of us don't, so guess what? Now we have Roombas. Why is it so difficult to imagine that we could invent a sewer version of a Roomba? The second aspect of Marx's work that is important to remind ourselves of is that his notion of post-capitalism is not utopian, that is it is not supposed to be imagined as a perfect society where there are no problems or unhappy people or disagreements. If you think this is the case, I will give extra credit to anyone who finds textual support in Marx's writing for such an interpretation.[21] So maybe you'll get to labor how you freely choose for six hours of the day, but for two hours you'll have to pick-up garbage. We can all hope that as problems come up, the more creative people will be there and be motivated to help us deal with them. There are people who love robotics and computer science here right? I'm looking at you to invent those poop-eating robots." Speaking of poop, where I teach, many of my students are older or at least work, many full-time, alongside being parents. In one instance I asked one of my more outspoken critics in a class whom I knew had two children, "When your daughter was a baby did you change her diapers?" He of course says yes. I ask him why.

He tells me, "Because I love her, and it is my job to make sure she is healthy and happy and taken care of." "So not for profit or self-interest then? For love? How ridiculous. Where is the profit in that?"[22]

## 4    "It" Looks Good on Paper

Dispensing with the myth of phony Marxist "states," and distortions of human nature clears the way for students to read Marx on his own terms, just as one ought to read any political philosopher. Many begin to appreciate that

---

21    *This* challenge is conveyed more clearly as facetious—as opposed to the genuine one discussed earlier.
22    I spoke to this student after class quite often, and on this occasion I thanked him for his thoughtful participation and contribution because I thought many of his peers got something very important from it. Closing down the avenues of dialogue for anyone but the most heinous racists or sexists (and even then pointing out the regressive nature of their views can be productive for others who hold the politically correct versions of them) is often the worst thing we can do. When discussing Marx especially, allowing students of the most fundamentally misguided views space to present their supposedly well-reasoned arguments and simply questioning them (or even allowing their peers to question them) can be exceptionally fruitful.

capitalism might not be the unmitigated good they had been otherwise led to believe, and that perhaps some of Marx's criticisms remain warranted. Potentially, the denizens of capitalism are largely alienated in a system where they have no control over their own labor, and nothing left to sell but their bodies. Exploitation is not the exceptional condition of some sweatshop in a remote developing nation. Rather, exploitation is the norm, no matter how luxurious the vestments in which it is garbed.

Still, there is usually one prejudice that normally remains. This one usually arrives in the form that, despite his insistence that he was putting socialism on a scientific basis, Marx was naïve, idealist, and ultimately utopian. "It looks good on paper," they say, "but it would never work in the real world." This objection, which may overlap in some ways, is different than the idea that human nature precludes the possibility of communism. Rather, the presumption here is that the mechanics of reality itself simply do not permit a mutually beneficial society based on collectivity and cooperation, or, as Marx (1938, 10) states, "from each according to his ability, to each according to his needs." Put more crudely, our undergraduate students are often convinced of the idea that someone always has to get screwed. Even more to the point, someone has to get screwed, and better you than me. This unfortunate fact, they contend, is not merely an idiosyncrasy of capitalism, but all possible politics.

In Miami, a city with enormous disparities in wealth, where the gaudy opulence and ostentatiousness of South Beach is mere minutes from the abject poverty and crime of Liberty City, the supposedly immutable rule of kill or be killed is on vivid display. The Miami area is home to fantastically wealthy individuals, banks, and major corporations. Yet, in sprawling slums like Overtown and Opa Locka, others "live on as little as $11 a day" (Olorunnipa 2014). According to a report by the United States Census Bureau, Miami-Dade County had the second highest level of income inequality in the country (Bee 2012).[23] In an environment so patently unfair, reeking as it does of staggering poverty, it becomes understandable why so many students see the wholly artificial, and remediable, problem of inequality as inevitable. For them, all societies must be this way to one degree or another, and a Marxist society, well intentioned as it may be, is naïve in defying this basic principle of reality. It simply would not work.

*Sean Walsh:* My approach for addressing this prejudice has been twofold. First, I pose a question, asking, "You have told me that 'it' would not work. What is this 'it' to which you are referring?" The response is usually an incredulous, "Marxist society (duh)." "Fine," I will state, "but what is that? What is this 'it'?

---

[23] Only the greater New York area was higher.

How does 'it' work? How are things arranged? How do decisions get made? How does production occur? What kind of mechanism is there for order?" Now, after a few minutes the students realize they do not know, and the reason for that, I explain, is because Marx *never tells us*. He provides abstract principles for the communist society that arises after the revolution. It is clearly democratic, but the concrete details concerning what that means and how that will work are conspicuously absent. It is mutually beneficial insofar as "the free development of each is the free development of all", but how that actually transpires is nebulous (Marx and Engels 1985, 105). In fact, Marx does not explain how a communist society would actually work. He could not do so for two reasons. First, as a product of the capitalist mode of production and, as Lenin (1987, 74) said, a member of the bourgeoisie, he was in no position to imagine the specifics of a genuinely communist society. To do so would merely draw from the imagination provided by the capitalist mode of production. Secondly, given his commitment to democracy, it simply was not up to him to decide for all of us what that society should look like. It remains up to those who will inherit that world. It is, therefore, impossible to say "it looks good on paper, but would never work," because it is *not on paper*, so we cannot possibly assess whether or not it would work. There is no "it."[24] In effect, what I want to convey to the students is that Marx does not really write about communism. The overwhelming majority of his work is actually about capitalism, which is probably why Fredric Jameson refers to Marxism as "the science of capitalism" (Jameson 1996).

Secondly, the idea that "it" would not work also hinges on the concept of what works. While some are indifferent, many of the Miami students already recognize the inhumanity of conditions in their city. Judging by the rather obvious state of inequality, I ask, "Does capitalism work, if, by work, we mean providing for human needs? We are told that hard work ought to be rewarded. Is a single mother working three jobs at minimum wage not working? Is she, in all likelihood, not working harder than the CEO of a major corporation, yet earning only an infinitesimally small fraction of his earnings?" Oftentimes, our students realize that the moral foundations they arrived with are incompatible with the exploitative and unjust nature of capitalism, and better fit, if not the absent specifics, the egalitarian principles of Marxism.

---

24  Readers of Marx may note his commentary from "Critique of the Gotha Program," in which he provides certain details of a post-revolutionary society. While his views here are sometimes mistaken for concrete details of communism, they belong only to a transitional phase. As Marx says, an intermediary phase would appear between capitalist society and "a higher phase of communism" (Marx 1938, 10).

*Bryant Sculos:* After I take my students through what little Marx actually says about communism, I bring the discussion back to what Marx should be much more well-known for, namely his exposition and critique of capitalism. I ask my students, "Though we have just looked at how Marx doesn't actually say very much beyond guiding principles for communism: non-exploitation, democratically organized labor, collective ownership of the means of production, and an egalitarianism based on need and ability, if we are intent on applying the logic of 'It looks good on paper, but' consistently we should look at capitalism in the very same way."

There is nothing wrong with the logic of criticizing a theory for being problematic when practiced, so long as there is actually a theory there to point to and the applications that were supposedly attempted actually mirror that theory. Capitalism is a much better example than Marxism in this case.[25]

I ask them, "What are the principles of capitalism?" Profit. Supply and demand. Market-determined prices. Wage labor. Freedom (or free enterprise). These are the ideas my students come up with, though I am quick to point out that Marx's (1991, 297) definition would only include wage labor and profit as they relate to surplus-value and commodification of labor.[26] "Now, if you were to read Ludwig von Mises, F.A. Hayek, Milton Friedman, or even Steve Forbes, some of the foremost capitalist thinkers, you would find many if not all of these things mentioned. Western governments over the past 150 years have been attempting to implement these principles into policy in various ways. "So are people free in this country?" I ask.

One student responds, "No, but that is because the government over-taxes and over-regulates our lives—specifically when it comes to financial stuff." Gold star for the future Fox News correspondent.

I immediately point out where we are: a public-university, deeply subsidized by taxes. They often complain about tuition, and rightfully so, but if we look at private universities, their tuition is significantly higher on average. I go back to the concept of free enterprise. "Let's look at free enterprise. What is the first rule of investment that you may learn in an introductory course (and something my grandparents have taught from a way too young age)? 'You need money to make money.' So then free enterprise can be very expensive, or impossible if you are poor. How is it free? How are we all free if we all aren't free to even participate in one of the basic aspects of the system according to these

---

25 Though there are certainly left critics like Noam Chomsky who have long-suggested that true capitalism has never really existed either.
26 Specifically, Marx states, "All that matters in any sphere of production is to produce surplus-value, to appropriate a definite quantity of unpaid labor in labor's product."

thinkers? So then someone else, tell me how we are free? This ideal of capitalism, freedom. Where do we see it?"

A different student steps up, "We are mostly free, yes. We can choose the career we want. We can choose not to work if we don't want. No one is forcing you to shop or invest or work." While this point is superficially true, I respond, "Is that really all we mean by freedom though? It is certainly not what Marx meant. Don't tell me all the people who work three full-time jobs would actively choose that life. Look at me, I love my job teaching, and as hard as I do work, I also had the benefit of a great public school education, which got me a near-full scholarship to a fairly prestigious private university, which then got me a paid position in the PhD program here. At the same time as I had all that opportunity and good luck, I still can't play in the NBA. Not only am I 5'5" and slower than a dried-out snail, but I was also never taught how to play. Can I just go up to the Miami Heat and say 'Okay I don't really know what this sport is but I am positive I will be terrible at it, I'm on the Heat now'? So I can choose to not work or work an unspecified job that no one is under any obligation to provide for me *even if I am qualified*, and so there's a good chance I'll be sporadically unemployed or work jobs there is a likely chance I'll hate? If that's freedom, I'll take the opposite thanks." We all laugh.

"No of course not. I am very restricted in terms of how I am allowed to labor, and now imagine a world where most people have far less opportunity and luck than I did. Say, the world we currently live in perhaps. This is all completely consistent with the principles of capitalism, but are we comfortable calling this freedom? Look at how many people hate their jobs. Even if you are one of the lucky few that doesn't hate their job, is it your dream job? Would you do it if you won the lottery? If you wouldn't keep doing your job if you didn't need the paycheck, how can you say that you are free? You work to make money to survive and live a moderately enjoyable life, or provide a better one for your kids."

The broader point I am trying to make to these students is to be fair in their criticisms (that is, to not make up things and say "Oh yeah, Marx said this"), but to also be weary of shallow critique (to not think Marxism looks great on paper and then not look and see if perhaps the same argument can be used against the system they agree with). There are theories which are pro-capitalism that look good on paper and suck in practice and there are theories which are pro-capitalism which when we really look at them suck both on paper and in practice. Marx never really put his ideas on paper regarding communism. What he details about capitalism though is pretty horrible, and when we look around we can see much of what he theorized about capitalism looking pretty crappy in practice as well.

## 5 Conclusion

Although addressing these prejudices can be frustrating, we have found the results rewarding. The discussions and dialogue that follow, more closely pertain to the texts and the criticisms tend to be better informed. We judge the success of these strategies, not by converting students, or having uniform agreement in the classroom, but by having given them something else to think about as they start reading Marx. While we have no wish to offer empirical evidence to support their value, readers can judge for themselves if these strategies, or derivations adapted for specific environments and student populations, merit application in their own classrooms. We have seen them open the minds of students in class who refuse even to make left-turns in traffic. More importantly we think, they become more critical of the ideological nature of capitalism and more sanguine regarding the possibilities of new twenty-first century instantiations of post-capitalist democratic politics without falling into the traps of the failed state capitalism represented in countries like Cuba, China, and the USSR. Our praxis is about dislocating the extant indoctrination with critique, not an alternative doctrine, at least not necessarily. Against the increase in online instruction that is part of the corporatization of the United States University system in recent years, we believe a physical classroom is a crucial space to occupy in order to use the practices discussed here. Being able to deploy various counterexamples in the moment, before a student has a chance to have their counterrevolutionary ideology further entrenched by the various distractions and ideological internet media sources available to an online student which can serve to undermine pedagogical praxis. Pedagogical praxis, like the kind detailed in this essay, is about the critical examination of the prevailing indoctrinating apparatus of neoliberal capitalism. It is about dislocating this doctrinal hegemony, which seems at every turn trying to dismantle praxeological space by moving more classes online (at often greater cost to the student) or making the instructors' position more precarious by overloading classes, converting permanent positions to temporary, or tenured to non-tenured. However, capitalism cannot escape its own contradictions, or at least it has yet to do so, and thus this praxeological opportunity—and demand—remains.

### Acknowledgements

The authors wish to gratefully acknowledge Joaquin Pedroso and Rudy Leal-McCormack for their efforts and commentary on early versions of this essay. We would also like to thank the anonymous reviewers at *Class, Race and*

*Corporate Power*, where an earlier version of this chapter originally appeared, for their insights and highly constructive suggestions. Finally, we are grateful to our students who tolerate our corny jokes and our well-intentioned if very imperfect pedagogical experiments. They have challenged us to improve our teaching, and ourselves, every semester.

## Bibliography

Bee, Adam (2012) "Household Income Inequality Within U.S. Counties: 2006–2010." United States Census Bureau. February, 2012. http://www.census.gov/prod/2012pubs/acsbr10-18.pdf

Cameron, James (1964) "Cuba's Fumbling Marxism: An Eyewitness Account." In *The Atlantic*. http://www.theatlantic.com/magazine/archive/1964/09/cubas-fumbling-marxism-an-eyewitness-account/305929/

Eagleton, Terry (2011) *Why Marx Was Right*. New Haven: Yale University Press.

Engels, Friedrich (1978) "Letters on Historical Materialism." In *The Marx-Engels Reader*. Ed. Robert C. Tucker. New York: W.W. Norton & Company.

Fromm, Erich (2004) *Marx's Concept of Man*. London: Bloomsbury.

Fromm, Erich (1962) *Beyond the Chains of Illusion: My Encounter with Marx and Freud*. New York: Simon & Schuster

Glennie, Jonathan (2011) "Cuba: A development model that proved the doubters wrong" in *The Guardian*. http://www.theguardian.com/global-development/poverty-matters/2011/aug/05/cuban-development-model

Huffington Post (2012) "Miami Ranked 17th in 'Most Dangerous Cities in America' List.'" In *Huffington Post*. http://www.huffingtonpost.com/2012/11/05/miami-ranked-as-17th-dangerous-city_n_2076782.html

Jameson, Fredric (1996) "Five Theses on Actually Existing Marxism." In *Monthly Review*. Vol. 47:11.

Kant, Immanuel (1991) "Idea for a Universal History with a Cosmopolitan Purpose." In *Kant: Political Writings*. Ed. Hans Reiss. Cambridge: Cambridge University Press.

Lenin, V.I. (1987) "What Is to Be Done?" In *Essential Works of Lenin*. Ed. Henry M. Christman. New York: Dover Publications.

Locke, John (1980) *Second Treatise of Government*. Ed. C.B. Macpherson. Indianapolis: Hackett Publishing Company.

Lukacs, Georg (1972) *History and Class Consciousness*. Trans. Rodney Livingstone. Cambridge, Massachusetts: The MIT Press.

Marx, Karl (1938) *Critique of the Gotha Programme*. Ed. C.P. Dutt. New York: International Publishers.

Marx, Karl (1970) *A Contribution to the Critique of Political Economy*. Ed. Maurice Dobb. New York: International Publishers.

Marx, Karl (1978) "On the Jewish Question." In *The Marx-Engels Reader*. Ed. Robert C. Tucker. W.W. Norton & Company.

Marx, Karl (1988) *Economic and Philosophic Manuscripts of 1844*. Trans. Martin Milligan. Buffalo, New York: Prometheus Books.

Marx, Karl (1991) *Capital, Volume 3*. Trans. David Fernbach. London: Penguin Books.

Marx, Karl (1998) *The German Ideology*. Amherst: Prometheus Books.

Marx, Karl and Friedrich Engels (1985) *The Communist Manifesto*. London: Penguin Books.

Olorunnipa, Toluse (2014) "Miami's Poor Live on $11 a Day as Boom Widens Wealth Gap." In *Bloomberg Business*. May 3, 2014. http://www.bloomberg.com/news/articles/2014-05-02/miami-s-poor-live-on-11-a-day-as-boom-widens-wealth-gap.

Palmer, Brian (2014) "Which City Has the Worst Drivers?" In *Slate*. August 27, 2014. http://www.slate.com/articles/health_and_science/science/2013/07/which_city_has_the_worst_drivers_boston_baltimore_washington_d_c_miami.single.html.

Rousseau, Jean-Jacques (1993a) "The Social Contract." In *The Social Contract and Discourses*. Trans. G.D.H. Cole. London: Everyman.

Rousseau, Jean-Jacques (1993b) "Discourse on the Origin of Inequality." In *The Social Contract and Discourses*. Trans. G.D.H. Cole. London: Everyman.

CHAPTER 4

# Marxferatu: Introducing Marx through the Vampire Metaphor

*Jess Morrissette*

Our modern understanding of the vampire draws extensively on the work of Bram Stoker. Through Stoker's 1897 novel *Dracula* we know the vampire's habits, the vampire's abilities, and the vampire's weaknesses. Stoker, however, was far from the first author to write about vampires.[1] In fact, if we look back a few decades prior *Dracula*'s publication, we discover another author with an intense interest in vampires. This earlier author's work would go on to be translated into dozens of languages and shape the lives of well over a billion people worldwide. The author is, of course, Karl Marx.[2]

Despite the undeniable significance of Marxist thought across a wide range of academic disciplines—including political science, economics, film studies, geography, history, literary criticism, philosophy, sociology, and beyond—teaching Marx to an undergraduate audience poses certain pedagogical challenges. Obviously, students cannot fully appreciate the intricacies of "The Manifesto of the Communist Party" during a 15-minute skimming of the text prior to class. The language is dense, the arguments are sophisticated, and the early industrial era during which Marx and his collaborator Friedrich Engels wrote seems like ancient history to today's college students. Moreover, in an increasingly polarized American political climate, a growing number of students enter the classroom prepared to actively resist any attempts at "Marxist indoctrination" by their "agenda-pushing" professors. Therefore, the challenge is making Marx relevant, accessible, and applicable to twenty-first century undergraduates. In this capacity the vampire metaphor is particularly effective.

In this article, I demonstrate the utility of the vampire metaphor as a tool for teaching Marx in a manner that is both pertinent and readily comprehensible to today's undergraduate students. Whereas Stoker wrote about a supernatural

---

1 Earlier prominent works of vampire fiction include Goethe's *The Bride of Corinth* (1797), Lord Byron's *The Giaour* (1813), John William Polidori's *The Vampyre* (1819), James Malcom Rymer's *Varney the Vampire* (1847), and Joseph Sheridan Le Fanu's *Carmilla* (1872).
2 "Marxferatu" is a portmanteau that blends Marx's surname with *Nosferatu*, a synonym for vampire most famously used as the title of director F. W. Murnau's unauthorized 1922 film adaptation of *Dracula*.

vampire, this approach to teaching Marxism recasts capitalism as a form of *economic* vampirism. In this interpretation of Marxist theory, factory owners step into the role of the vampire, draining the surplus value of the worker's labor to further enrich themselves, in much the same way that Stoker's vampire sucks blood from victims to grow ever stronger. Seduced by the capitalist's spell—the comforting distractions of religion, politics, consumer culture—the worker suffers a "loss of self" and emerges as little more than a walking corpse.

Although the young women and men who step onto college campuses today may not have spent considerable time pondering the inherent contradictions of capitalism or the broader implications of class struggle, they are remarkably well-versed in vampire lore.[3] After all, the current generation of college students propelled Stephenie Meyer's *Twilight* saga to sell more than 100 million copies worldwide and helped make television's *True Blood* the most-watched series on HBO since *The Sopranos*. In turn, the ubiquity of vampires in contemporary popular culture makes the vampire metaphor a particularly valuable pedagogical tool to introduce undergraduate students to key concepts in Marxist philosophy and political economy.

This article begins by exploring in greater detail the challenges faced in teaching Marx to an undergraduate audience, followed by a brief discussion of Marx's use of the vampire metaphor in his own work. Then the article extends the vampire metaphor to demonstrate its potential as a teaching tool to introduce three essential concepts in the Marxist critique of capitalism: class conflict, alienation, and false consciousness.

## 1   The Challenges of Teaching about Marxism

In most academic disciplines, introducing undergraduate students to Marxism consists of more than simply describing Karl Marx as a historical figure and briefly summarizing his work. Isser (1981) explains the task at hand as follows:

---

3  Certainly, the "rules" and assumptions of vampire fiction vary considerably from one fictional work to the next. For instance, vampires who sparkle when exposed to sunlight, as depicted in the *Twilight* saga, are a significant departure from the vampire archetype popularized in Stoker's *Dracula*. For this article, however, I work from three defining traits—that is, characteristics that tend to appear consistently in nearly all fictional portrayals of vampires. First, vampires are distinct from, and prey on, humans. Second, vampires survive and draw strength by draining the life force, typically blood, from their human victims. Third, vampires possess the ability to enthrall their would-be victims, whether through supernatural means or sheer beauty and charisma. These core traits reappear consistently in historical and contemporary vampire fiction. Moreover, they create a starting point that is accessible to nearly any student or instructor acquainted with even the general concept of a vampire, whether or not they are aficionados of the genre.

The students need to develop intellectual insights into complex economic and social conflicts as well as a rigorous analysis of political theory. They must perceive the philosophical and ethical dimensions of these societies, such as the dilemma of liberty versus equality, or the disparity and difficulty of maintaining individuality in a collective society. (61)

This task is further complicated by the fact than many undergraduate students, at least in the United States, enter college with relatively little knowledge about Marxism. For instance, a study of first-semester freshmen conducted by Manton and English (2000) indicates that only 37.2% of respondents could correctly identify Karl Marx as the "father" of communism on a multiple-choice questionnaire.[4] Clarke and Mearman (2003) also note that students "will invariably have a whole host of preconditioned ideas, including perceptions of 'communist' or 'socialist' regimes, " all of which make teaching about Marxism "harder, although not impossible" (74).

Ollman (1978) argues that the absence of a vital socialist movement in the United States "makes most students approach Marxism too much in the spirit of another academic exercise, just as it confirms them in the belief—before study begins—that Marx's analysis cannot be correct" (15). He suggests that "how one approaches and organizes the subject matter, where one begins and concludes, the kind of examples used, and especially what one emphasizes have considerable influence on the degree of success" (16) in teaching students about Marxism. In turn, the vampire metaphor is an accessible approach that works around students' lack of knowledge on Marxism by capitalizing on their familiarity with the vampire mythos. Furthermore, this metaphor has the advantage of divorcing Marxist thought from an immediately "political" context, helping to assuage any preconceived notions or biases that students may bring to the classroom.

## 2  Marx's Use of the Vampire Metaphor

Although the characterization of communism as a "specter" haunting Europe is arguably the most prominent example of supernatural imagery in the Marxist canon, Neocleous (2003) argues that "the vampire metaphor plays a significant role in Marx's work, a role perhaps even more significant than the ghostly or spectral" (669). In *Das Kapital,* for instance, Marx (1867/2008) describes capital

---

[4] The same study indicates that only 26.6% of freshmen respondents could correctly identify Adam Smith as the "father" of capitalism, suggesting more generalized deficiencies in teaching economic history in American high schools.

as "dead labor, that, vampire-like, only lives by sucking living labor, and lives the more, the more labor it sucks" (149). He also suggests that the elongation of the working day "quenches only in a slight degree the vampire thirst for the living blood of labor" (159) and warns that the vampire "will not lose its hold...'so long as there is a muscle, nerve, a drop of blood to be exploited'" (181). Similar blood-sucking imagery also appears in *The Eighteenth Brumaire of Louis Napoleon* (1852), the *Grundrisse* (1858), the Inaugural Address to the International Working Men's Association (1864), and elsewhere in Marx's work (Neocleous 2003).

Why does Marx revisit the vampire metaphor and use blood-related imagery so often in his work? Perhaps Marx's references to vampirism merely serve as a literary device to enliven his prose. Alternatively, we could also situate it against the broader backdrop of nineteenth-century Europe's fascination with vampire fiction. However, Neocleous (2003) argues that the vampire metaphor is more than a simple rhetorical device or a reflection of popular literary trends; rather, it is central to Marx's understanding of capitalism:

> Marx uses it to illustrate one of the central dynamics of capitalist production—the distinction between living and dead labor, a distinction that picks up on a more general theme in his work: the desire to create a society founded on the *living* of full and creative lives rather than one founded on the *rule of the dead*.... The vampire as monster both *demonstrates* the capabilities of capital and acts as a *warning* about it. (684)

Just as vampirism was a potent metaphor in illustrating the relationship between bourgeoisie and proletariat in Marx's time, it remains effective for teaching the basic principles of Marxist thought today—perhaps to an even greater degree considering the resurgent "vampire craze" in contemporary popular culture.[5] The following section expands on the vampire metaphor and illustrates its value as a pedagogical tool.

## 3   Extending and Applying the Vampire Metaphor in the Classroom

As Barrows (2006) observes, "Count Dracula has proven the most persistently adaptable and resilient of popular icons, retaining his power to intrigue and

---

[5] Notably, the vampire's cultural context has shifted somewhat since the era of Marx and Stoker. Whereas vampires were still a source of genuine fear for many eighteenth-century readers (and, therefore, a powerful allusion for Marx to draw on), contemporary depictions of vampires increasingly portray the vampire in a sympathetic light, the victim of his or her own curse—or even glamorize the bourgeois wealth and power of the vampire lifestyle.

frighten audiences across generational and cultural divides" (69). Moreover, Newitz (2006) characterizes monster stories, including tales of the undead, as "one of the dominant allegorical narratives used to explore economic life in the United States" (5). With that in mind, how can we extend Count Dracula—and the vampire metaphor as a whole—to introduce undergraduates to Marx's critique of capitalism? In this section, I explore three central concepts in Marxist thought: class conflict, alienation, and false consciousness. In each case, I first introduce the traditional Marxist understanding of the concept and then draw parallels with works of vampire literature, film, and television to demonstrate the value of the vampire metaphor as an instructional approach.

## 4  Class Conflict: The Living and the Undead

As Marx and Engels write in "The Manifesto of the Communist Party"(1848), "The history of hitherto existing society is the history of class struggles. Freeman and slave, patrician and plebian, lord and serf, guild-master and journeyman" (473–74). Certainly, the bifurcation of society into oppressor and oppressed is a hallmark of Marxist thought. Marx (1844/1978) argued that "the whole of society must fall apart into the two classes—the property-*owners* and the propertyless *workers*" (70), locked into an exploitative relationship that inevitably breeds conflict.

To illustrate this fundamental division of society into bourgeoisie and proletariat in the classroom, I compare the distinction between vampire and human that defines so much of the vampire canon. "In the figure of Count Dracula," Hatlen (1988) argues, "Stoker created an image of 'otherness'" (129)—not just physically, but also culturally and socially. Vampire fiction typically draws a clear line of separation between the living and the undead, creating a social demarcation between vampire and victim. Bill Compton, the vampire lead in HBO's *True Blood* series, gives voice to this division when he matter-of-factly declares to his human paramour, "I am not human, Sookie. I am vampire" ("Burning House of Love," 1.7). Moreover, as Bill explains to Sookie in an earlier episode, "We don't have human values like you" ("Strange Love," 1.1). In fact, *True Blood*, the *Twilight* series, and other contemporary works of vampire fiction increasingly depict entire clan-based vampire societies with their own laws and social norms that exist outside mainstream human society.

As discussed earlier, patterns of exploitation and inevitable conflict define the relationship between Marx's "dead labor" (capital) and "living labor" (the working class). Motivated solely by profit, factory owners emerge as a form of *economic* vampires, improving their bottom line through longer hours, lower wages, and poorer working conditions. Capitalists are, in effect, draining away the value of their workers' labor to enrich themselves—just as supernatural vampires drain their victims' life force to grow stronger.

The parallels with vampire fiction are evident. As Shaviro (2002) notes, "The vampire grows, not through any productive activity of its own, but by expropriating a surplus generated by the living" (282). Sims (2010) concurs: "For vampires, the cost of staying alive, or at least staying not quite dead, is the price of lives other than their own—as if, when they have exhausted their own allotted wealth, they can steal someone else's to keep the creditor at bay" (6). According to Forry (2006), "Vampires are the ultimate affirmation of individualism, escaping from human moral obligation, caring only for themselves, and free from regret or remorse for their actions" (237). Finally, Moretti (1999) draws the following comparison between the vampire and the capitalist:

> His curse compels him to make ever more victims, just as the capitalist is compelled to accumulate. His nature forces him to struggle to be unlimited, to subjugate *the whole of society*. For this reason, one cannot 'coexist' with the vampire. One must either succumb to him or kill him. (46)

As Count Dracula states in the 2004 film *Van Helsing*, "I'm at war with the world and every living soul in it!" In a similar vein, Marx (1847a/1978) defines the stakes in the conflict between the bourgeoisie and proletariat as "combat or death: bloody struggle or extinction" (219). The vampire metaphor, in turn, has the potential to drive home the primacy of class conflict to students encountering Marxist thought for the first time.

## 5   Alienation: The Exsanguination of the Working Class

Questions about what it means to be human are central in vampire fiction, dating back to Stoker's *Dracula* and running through the present in works like *Buffy the Vampire Slayer* and *Twilight*. Perhaps unsurprisingly, this is also an important concern in Marx's work. As a staunch materialist, he centers his theory of human nature on the individual's labor and productive activity. For instance, Marx argues in "Wage Labour and Capital" (1847) that labor "is the worker's own life-activity, the manifestation of his own life" (204). Singer (2000) elaborates that "labor in the sense of free productive activity is the essence of human life. Whatever is produced in this way—a statue, a house, or a piece of cloth—is therefore the essence of human life made into a physical object" (35–36). According to Marx, our ability to create freely and enjoy the products of that labor defines us as human beings and gives meaning to our lives.

Marx argues, however, that the relationship between workers and the value of their labor fundamentally changes under capitalist modes of production. When a worker sells the surplus value of his labor to a factory owner in exchange for wages paid, Marx calls it "a sacrifice of his life" (1847b/1978, 204). This process alienates humans from their own nature, and it is the factory owner who ultimately accumulates profit from the worker's labor. "Estranged from the material embodiment of their labor," Latham (2002) observes, "workers find themselves integrated into the factory system as cogs in the productive apparatus their own energies have spawned" (3). The worker is reduced to little more than the next stop on the assembly line, a monotonous process that results in a "total loss of humanity" according to Marx (1844/1978, 64). "As a result, therefore," Marx continues, "man...no longer feels himself to be freely active in any but his animal functions—eating, drinking, procreating...and in his human functions he no longer feels himself to be anything but an animal" (74). In turn, alienation from the product of his labor "enforces on the laborer abstinence from all life's enjoyments" (Marx 1867/2008, 333). Drained of his human spark, a worker's life loses all meaning. At the risk of mixing monster movie metaphors, the "loss of self" (Marx 1844/1978, 74) that results from capitalist production transforms the worker into little more than a zombie—a slave to the capitalist.

Whereas Marx's theory of alienation is a sophisticated argument, the vampire metaphor once again proves itself quite useful as a way to make the concept accessible to an undergraduate audience. In this context, compare the Marxist concept of alienation with the loss of humanity suffered by victims of the vampire's bite. Look no further than Lucy Westenra, the first character to suffer the Count's fangs in Stoker's *Dracula*, to find the archetypal victim of the vampire. Visiting her at night, Count Dracula slowly drains Lucy's blood and leaves her anemic and bedridden. Once vivacious, Lucy becomes pale, listless, and visibly weakened. "She was hardly able to turn her head," the character of Dr. Seward writes in his journal, "and the little nourishment which she could take seemed to do her no good" (Stoker 1897/1973, 143). The same character later notes, "Presently she woke, and I gave her food, as Van Helsing has prescribed. She took but a little, and that languidly. There did not seem to be with her now the unconscious struggle for life and strength that had hitherto marked her illness" (Stoker 1897, 149). Just as Marx's view of alienation suggests that capitalism drains the worker of his humanity and separates him from all life's enjoyments, so too does the vampire's bite drain Lucy of her will to live and eventually transform her into the walking dead.[6]

---

6 Marx's theory of alienation further argues that workers are themselves reduced to a commodity as a result of capitalist modes of production. We might compare this with the

## 6  False Consciousness: Under the Vampire's Spell

When we discuss the Marxist perspective on the exploitation and alienation of the working class, students often pose a familiar question: why don't the workers just rise up? Following through with the vampire motif, we compare the failure of the working class to mobilize against the bourgeoisie with the victims who passively surrender to Dracula's attacks. The vampire has seduced his victims and placed them under his spell. In much the same way, Marx argues that capitalism casts its own spell over the working class.

Marx attributes the failure of the working class to rise up against its oppressors to a lack of class consciousness—that is, a collective unawareness concerning social and economic standing among the workers. In fact, engendering a stronger sense of class consciousness among European workers is the *raison d'être* behind Marx and Engel's "Manifesto of the Communist Party." However, the workers are distracted from the realities of economic exploitation (the "base" in Marxist terminology) by politics, ideology, culture, religion, and the commodities that capitalism produces (all parts of society's "superstructure"). For example, Marx's oft-quoted dictum that religion is "the opiate of the people" (1843, 54) alludes to vague promises of future rewards in the afterlife in exchange for enduring earthly hardships in the present. Similarly, Marx (1867/2008) argues that the social value ascribed to the wages paid and the goods produced under capitalism creates "commodity fetishism" that further diverts the worker's attention from the harsh realities of exploitation. Political ideologies are yet another distraction; as Marx and Engels (1846) note, "the ideas of the ruling class are in every epoch the ruling ideas." These social, cultural, and political aspects of the bourgeoisie-dominated superstructure create a false consciousness that distracts workers from the economic base and, ultimately, their own best interests. The social order produced by capitalism is designed to immobilize the worker long enough for the factory owner to effectively drain him dry.

Similarly, the title character in *Blade* (1998) describes the base and superstructure that defines the film's setting when he declares, "You better wake up. The world you live in is just a sugar-coated topping. There is another world beneath it—the real world." Seduction is arguably the most potent talent in the vampire's repertoire, dating back at least as far as Count Dracula's

---

depiction of vampires treating humans as private property in *True Blood*. Bill repeatedly refers to Sookie as his possession, other vampires speak of keeping humans as pets, and vampire law explicitly forbids one vampire from feeding on another vampire's human.

"hypnotic" eyes and the "fascination" they evoke in Lucy. For instance, Hood (1988) refers to Dracula's powers of enticement, "in which he inflames the irrational desires of his world-be converts for those corrupt but intoxicating powers and pleasures to which he has access" (216). While *Buffy the Vampire Slayer*'s Spike dismisses Dracula's hypnotic powers as "nothing but showy Gypsy stuff," the Count nevertheless succeeds in placing the formidable Buffy under his thrall, however briefly ("Buffy vs. Dracula," 5.1). Meanwhile, in the *True Blood* universe, the vampiric ability to mesmerize and mentally control human beings is known as "glamouring." After all, as *True Blood*'s Bill observes, "humans are shockingly susceptible to just about every form of thought manipulation" ("I Don't Wanna Know," 1.10).

Turning to the *Twilight* series, Edward Cullen does not rely on any preternatural vampiric powers to enthrall his prey. Rather, he does this through old-fashioned emotional and physical attraction. As Bella Swan, the target of Edward's affection, puts it, "I wasn't *interesting*. And he was. Interesting...and brilliant...and mysterious...and perfect...and beautiful...and possibly able to lift full-sized vans with one hand" (Meyer 2005, 79). Bella goes on to expound, "About three things I was absolutely positive. First, Edward was a vampire. Second, there was part of him—and I didn't know how potent that part might be—that thirsted for my blood. And third, I was unconditionally and irrevocably in love with him" (195). Meanwhile, Edward is clearly cognizant of his charm, declaring to Bella, "I'm the world's best predator, aren't I? Everything about me invites you in—my voice, my face, even my smell. As if I need any of that!" (79). In summary, the vampire—whether through psychic powers or sheer physical beauty—creates its own sense of false consciousness in humans to more easily feast on their blood. Once again, the parallels with Marx's critique of capitalism are evident.

As the father of communism, where does Karl Marx fit into the vampire narrative? We might equate Marx with Stoker's Professor Abraham Van Helsing—a savvy intellectual endeavoring to warn those around him that a vampire is on the loose. After all, as Van Helsing cautions in *Dracula* (1931), "The strength of the vampire is that people will not believe in him." When Marx and Engels urge workers of the world to unite in *The Communist Manifesto*, they are not simply urging the proletariat to join a labor union. Instead, they are calling on the working class to stop acting like Lucy, the Count's passive victim in *Dracula*, and start acting like Buffy the Vampire Slayer. With their very humanity on the line, Marx and Engels urge workers to wake up from the vampire's spell and drive a stake through the heart of capitalism, laying it to rest once and for all.

## 7 Conclusion

McLellan (1999) describes the history of interpreting Marx in Western societies as "a history of the attempts to come to terms with, and even incorporate, the successively dominant intellectual trends in these societies" (955). In turn, I argue that using the vampire metaphor to teach Marx is a constructive exercise in reconciling the Marxist critique of capitalism with dominant trends in contemporary popular culture. This analysis demonstrates that it is possible to draw meaningful parallels between Marx's work and familiar tropes in vampire fiction, illustrating key Marxist concepts without diluting their intellectual significance. Moreover, this approach to teaching Marxist thought offers several pedagogical advantages.

First, and perhaps most importantly, the "barriers to entry" are low. Neither the instructor nor his or her students must know the intricacies of the entire vampire genre to benefit from the metaphor's application. Rather, a basic knowledge that vampires are supernatural creatures that somehow enthrall and suck the blood from their human victims—a threshold of understanding that many American students will have met and exceeded after their first few experiences trick-or-treating during childhood—is a sufficient starting point to draw the necessary parallels with Marxist concepts like class conflict, alienation, and false consciousness. A second advantage of the vampire metaphor is its scalability. Depending on the particular course and the instructor's learning objectives, this approach to introducing Marxist thought could constitute a single lesson plan, or, if the instructor chooses to explore it in greater detail, span over the course of several class periods. In fact, I have used the vampire metaphor as a cornerstone in building an entire undergraduate course titled Politics of the Undead, in which we examine topics ranging from political economy to social contract theory to gender and sexuality through the lens of fictional vampires, zombies, and mummies. Finally, as the preceding analysis suggests, the pedagogical approach lends itself readily to incorporating multimedia into the class with vampire-related film and television clips.

One must remain mindful of the fact that the vampire metaphor potentially risks reducing the complexities of Marxist thought to the oversimplified notion that capitalism "creates monsters who want to kill you" (Newitz 2006, 3). To that end, it is an equally valuable classroom exercise to examine the ways in which the vampire metaphor is an *imperfect* representation of Marx's ideas. The portrayal of the capitalist as a predator intent on draining away the life essence of the worker, for instance, fails to adequately capture Marx's structural understanding of class relations, replacing it with a decidedly individualistic depiction of exploitation.[7] In addition, while the vampire metaphor provides helpful insights into class conflict, alienation, and false consciousness, it is more difficult to find proximate thematic connections to other key Marxist concepts, including historical materialism, Marx's theory of revolution, and the dictatorship of the proletariat. In other words, the vampire metaphor is not intended as a *substitute* for the in-depth scholarly study of the many facets of Marxist thought. It is merely an *entry point*—the beginning of an intellectual discussion intended to make the subject matter more immediately engaging to an undergraduate audience.

In conclusion, by taking something that is both very real and vitally important—the impact of economic forces on modern society—and recasting it in terms of fictional blood-sucking creatures, we arrive at a teaching practice that helps make Marx relevant to a generation of students well-versed in the finer points of vampirology. Furthermore, the vampire metaphor works across the wide range of disciplines in which Marx is studied, from political science to literary criticism. Therefore it is a valuable instructional approach that makes Marx accessible and comprehensible to twenty-first century students, so many of whom have grown up immersed in both classical and contemporary vampire fiction.

## Bibliography

Barrows, Adam (2006) "Heidegger the Vampire Slayer: The Undead and Fundamental Ontology." In *The Undead and Philosophy: Chicken Soup for the Soulless*, ed. Richard Greene and K. Silem Mohammad, 69–79. Chicago: Open Court Press.
*Blade* (1998) Directed by Stephen Norrington. New Line Home Video, DVD.
*Buffy the Vampire Slayer: The Chosen Collection* (2005) Twentieth Century Fox Home Entertainment, DVD.
Clarke, Peter and Mearman, Andrew (2003) "Why Marxist Economics Should Be Taught but Probably Won't Be!" *Capital & Class* (79): 55–80.
*Dracula* (1931/1999) Directed by Tod Browning. Universal Studios, DVD.

---

7 Even in this instance, Marx's tendency to waver back and forth in his work between characterizations of the bourgeoisie as either willfully predatory or simply a product of larger structural forces arguably parallels depictions of vampires who enthusiastically embrace their malevolent instincts and other "nobler" vampires who treat their condition as an inescapable curse. For example, *True Blood*'s Bill Compton represents the latter archetype, whereas his frequent rival, Eric Northman, represents the former—at least during early seasons of the series.

Forry, Joan G (2006) "'Powerful, Beautiful, and Without Regret': Femininity, Masculinity, and the Vampire Aesthetic." In *The Undead and Philosophy: Chicken Soup for the Soulless*, ed. Richard Greene and K. Silem Mohammad, 237–247. Chicago: Open Court Press.

Hatlen, Burton (1988) "The Return of the Repressed/Oppressed in Bram Stoker's *Dracula*." In *Dracula: The Vampire and the Critics*, ed. Margaret L. Carter, 109–16. Ann Arbor: University of Michigan Institute Research Press.

Hood, Gwenyth (1988) "Sauron and Dracula." In *Dracula: The Vampire and the Critics*, ed. Margaret L. Carter, 215–230. Ann Arbor: University of Michigan Institute Research Press.

Isser, Natalie (1981) "Teaching about Communism." *Improving College and University Teaching* 29 (2): 60–63.

Latham, Robert (2002) *Consuming Youth: Vampires, Cyborgs, and the Culture of Consumption*. Chicago: University of Chicago Press.

Manton, Edgar, and Donald English (2000) "The Ability of College Freshman to Identify Adam Smith and Karl Marx." *College Student Journal* 34 (3): 468–71.

Marx, Karl (1843/1978) "Contribution to the Critique of Hegel's *Philosophy of the Right*: Introduction." In *The Marx-Engels Reader* (2nd ed.), ed. Robert C. Tucker, 53–65. New York: W. W. Norton.

Marx, Karl (1844/1978) "Economic and Philosophic Manuscripts of 1844." In *The Marx-Engels Reader* (2nd ed.), ed. Robert C. Tucker, 66–125. New York: W. W. Norton.

Marx, Karl (1847a/1978) "The Coming Upheaval." In R. Tucker (Ed.), *The Marx-Engels Reader* (2nd ed.), ed. Robert C. Tucker, 218–19. New York: W. W. Norton.

Marx, Karl (1847b/1978) "Wage Labour and Capital." In *The Marx-Engels Reader* (2nd ed.), ed. Robert C. Tucker, 203–17. New York: W. W. Norton.

Marx, Karl (1867/2008) *Capital: An Abridged Edition*, ed. David McLellan. New York: Oxford University Press.

Marx, Karl, and Engels, Friedrich (1846) *The German Ideology*. Retrieved from http://www.marxists.org/archive/marx/works/1845/german-ideology/index.htm

Marx, Karl and Engels, Friedrich (1848/1978) "Manifesto of the Communist Party." In *The Marx-Engels Reader* (2nd ed.), ed. Robert C. Tucker, 473–500. New York: W. W. Norton.

McLellan, David (1999) "Then and Now: Marx and Marxism." *Political Studies* 47 (5): 955–66.

Meyer, Stephenie (2005) *Twilight*. New York: Little, Brown and Company.

Moretti, Franco (1999) "*Dracula* and Capitalism." In *Dracula: Contemporary Critical Essays*, ed. Glennis Byron, 43–54. New York: St. Martin's Press.

Neocleous, Mark (2003) "The Political Economy of the Dead: Marx's Vampires." *History of Political Thought* 24 (4): 668–84.

Newitz, Annalee (2006) *Pretend We're Dead: Capitalist Monsters in American Pop Culture*. Durham, NC: Duke University Press.

Ollman, Bertell (1978) "On Teaching Marxism." *The Radical Teacher* (9): 15–21.

Shaviro, Steven (2002) "Capitalist Monsters." *Historical Materialism* 10 (4): 281–290.

Sims, Michael (2010) "Introduction: The Cost of Living." In *Dracula's Guest: A Connoisseur's Collection of Victorian Vampire Stories*, ed. Michael Sims, 1–20. New York: Walker Publishing Company.

Singer, Peter (2000) *Marx: A Very Short Introduction*. Oxford: Oxford University Press.

Stoker, Bram (1897/1973) *Dracula*. New York: Doubleday.

*True Blood: The Complete First Season* (2009) HBO Home Video, DVD.

*Van Helsing* (2004) Directed by Stephen Sommers. Universal Studios, DVD.

CHAPTER 5

# Neoliberal Feminist Monsters: Where to Find Them and How to Slay Them

*Maylin M. Hernandez*

> *Theory is not inherently healing, liberatory, or revolutionary. It fulfills this function only when we ask that it do so and direct our theorizing towards this end.*
>
> —bell hooks, Teaching to Transgress: Education as the Practice of Freedom (1994, 61)

⁂

I was once sitting in a graduate seminar when the professor began a discussion on the role of women in the classroom. This discussion was prompted by an event that had occurred the week before at the university, which a small portion of the class attended. During this event, the women from the classroom were positioned on the periphery seating whereas the male student attendees were placed at the main discussion table.[1] During this class meeting, the professor called attention to the fact that the women did not engage in the same behavior as the men because they did not ask for a seat at the table as well. This led the professor to "coach" these women on their need to engage more in the classroom in a similar style to the men. The result of this discussion was not that men were oppressing women structurally, but that in some way, the women were repressing themselves from obtaining the same benefits and praises as the men who were more vocal and more likely to ask for better seats. Discussions like this are likely happening at universities across the country; women are frequently given advice on behaviors they should engage in, how they should

---

1 It was learned later that the same professor had sent out a request to all the students in the course to take periphery seats if they were not highly invested in the talk due to limited seating—in response all students from this course that attended, male and female, agreed to sit in the periphery. The male students found themselves at the table after asking during the event to be moved to the table.

participate more (almost always in comparison to the men in their classes), and even warned about the difficulties they will face in an academic environment due to their gender. These discussions, while usually well-intentioned to respond to the common internalization of patriarchal norms that encourage women to act in certain, usually subordinate, ways, in fact, produce a new problem; a problem that posits that for women to overcome their external and internal oppressions they must behave in ways that garner them the same opportunities and responses that men receive. Thus, "feminine" behaviors are discouraged and individualistic, "masculine," behaviors are encouraged as successful to all students. This begins to (re)produce a form of oppression on women via the well-meaning, but systematic, praise of masculine qualities at the expense of feminine ones. An oppression that is observed before the current neoliberal period[2] but manifests itself in a new way in the current moment—particularly in the popularity and the rise of neoliberal feminism. As such, I argue that a revised socialist-feminism, gained from important insights from foundational texts in the discourse, offers us a way of teaching within neoliberal society while avoiding the same reproduction of capitalistic forms of femininity. Part of this revision focuses on the disruption of traditional gender norms and behaviors, and places value and emphasis on encouraging collective and nurturing characteristics in the classroom.

The oppression of women has been written about widely in both socialist-feminist and critical pedagogical literatures, although usually in relation to women's role in the family and within the division of labor in capitalism. While women's experiences in education have been a topic of some discussion, few have attempted to theorize how a wide variety of engagement in the classroom benefits a radical socialist-feminist agenda and critique of capitalism, with bell hooks' *Teaching to Transgress* (1994) as one of a few notable exceptions. Thus, this chapter revisits the scholarship done by earlier socialist-feminists and critical pedagogical scholars and aims to reorient them towards the specific ways that contemporary capitalism and mainstream feminism have co-opted and undermined their teachings and insights in the twenty-first century classroom, in addition to the ways in which movements towards the eradication of patriarchy (and overcoming the specific oppressions of women and sexual minorities) that occur outside of the university have been lost while teaching students. This leads to a situation in which the university promotes aspects of neoliberalism and neoliberal feminism. Neoliberal feminism is used to sell wars, shoes, apartments, and careers, as it is molded to fit into every aspect of our lives. But perhaps a detour is first needed to situate this work in the larger neoliberal and

---

2   See for example, in Freudian psychoanalysis on the origins of female sexuality, penis-envy, and castration, which is discussed in more detail later.

neoliberal feminist literature. Due to the myriad evocations of neoliberalism throughout academia (often without explicitly using the term "neoliberal"), it becomes crucial to ground this text in prior scholarship. Wendy Brown offers a succinct definition of the shift neoliberalism has taken from liberalism,

> Neo-liberalism is not simply a set of economic policies; it is not only about facilitating free trade, maximizing corporate profits, and challenging welfarism. Rather, neo-liberalism carries a social analysis which, when deployed as a form of governmentality, reaches from the soul of the citizen-subject to education policy to practices of empire. Neo-liberal rationality, while foregrounding the market, is not only or even primarily focused on the economy; rather it involves *extending and disseminating market values to all institutions and social action*, even as the market itself remains a distinctive player. (2003, 40)

Neoliberal feminism, by extension, represents a feminist politics that is in sync with the neoliberal agenda described above; "Neoliberal feminism, in other words, offers no critique—immanent or otherwise—of neoliberalism," nor capitalism more broadly (Rottenberg 2013, 2). It is a feminism that reproduces the neoliberal order and one that encourages women to participate in creating a functioning work-life balance and shifts problems resulting from gender inequality to one that holds the individual and their work ethic responsible for shortcomings (Rottenberg 2013, 3).

Neoliberal feminism, with its consumeristic dimension(s), applied pedagogically, promotes the individuation of students through (false) empowerment narratives. To address this issue more broadly, we must discuss the pressing need to take a socialist-feminist approach to teaching in order to be both intersectionally inclusive of various sex, race, gender, and class identities and to provide an academic space that continues to challenge capitalist conventions regarding feminism. Overall, the aim is not to provide a definitive answer as to what a successful socialist-feminist pedagogy would look like, but rather to address why it is crucial to orient teaching towards a critical assessment of the co-optation of the emancipatory impetus of feminism by capitalistic structures and norms happening in education—and why this is such a destructive trend—while simultaneously challenging these norms as they appear in the classroom. An emphasis will be placed here on the development of a socialist-feminism that not only seeks to change how women interact with the world, but also one that shifts away the overwhelming pressure for women to conform to "masculine" behaviors to succeed. An ideal approach will try to do so in at least two ways; by encouraging traits in women that are historically shunned or discouraged and by seeking to change the environment in which men and women interact with one another. The only way that this can be achieved, I believe, is by promoting a socialist-feminist approach to the classroom that resists the encouragement of capitalistic modes of attributing positive and negative values towards masculine and feminine gender traits,[3] respectively, and instead creates and radically promotes an environment in which value is not ascribed to these traits. Doing so, I hope, will lead to what bell hooks celebrates in teaching as the creation of a new scholarly environment that can urge "all of us to open our minds and hearts so that we can know beyond the boundaries of what is acceptable, so that we can think and rethink, so that we can create new visions, I celebrate teaching that enables transgressions—a movement against and beyond boundaries. It is a movement which makes education the practice of freedom" (1994, 12). Articulating this as a movement also draws attention to the fact that there will be constant struggles and failures in trying to ultimately get to the most effective kind of socialist-feminist pedagogy that this chapter aims to outline. The various authors mentioned here have all succeeded in pushing socialist-feminism and critical pedagogy forward, and yet all have elements that they miss, things they do not take into account, and points that are not pushed far enough where they cease to reproduce the problems they are trying to eradicate. This chapter strives to tread through these texts to highlight where our past failings have occurred in the hopes of moving critical socialist-feminist pedagogy forward.

## 1    Socialist-Feminist and Critical Pedagogical Literature

Very little of the major contemporary socialist-feminist arguments take a direct look at the education system within capitalist societies.[4] Those that do tend to link the experiences and qualitative results of the education of women

---

3   It is important to note that I consider these traits to be a result of structural discursive social conditioning and not in any way related to a kind of deterministic essentialist binary.
4   By this I am referring to insights into education internally, regarding not just the general structure of primary, secondary, and higher education but the classroom in particular. Generally, major authors who include discussions of education (like Michele Barrett who will be discussed in length later) focus typically on the statistical results of female education—that women are less represented in certain fields, or that women congregate in traditionally feminine professions or courses, like cooking or sewing. While these investigations are important they don't delve deep enough into the face-to-face interactions that occur within the classroom—either between professors and students or among students themselves.

in order to make direct connections to women's location in the division of labor. Put more simply, the focus of women's education in socialist-feminist literatures tends to focus on what comes after her schooling, not what is instilled, encouraged, and discouraged during it. At the foundation of socialist-feminism is Friedrich Engels' *On the Origin of the Family, Private Property, and the State* (1884) due to the significance it plays in texts that connect women's oppression in education to their roles as workers in the home and, later, to disadvantages they face in the broader division of labor. Although Engels' piece does not address the education of women within society, it poses a few questions that led to its place as a foundational piece in the on-going investigation into the construction of masculine and feminine subjects. First, it brings to light the socially constructed nature of gender hierarchies and privileged sexualities.[5] Second, Engels acknowledges the struggles and oppression of women as the primary repression experienced by a class in modern history (Marx 1978, 739). Third is his construction of the repression of women as becoming necessary within a capitalist society (among the bourgeoisie) in order to reproduce the species and, essentially, the forces and relations of production.[6] Finally, perhaps one of the aspects of this piece that is most taken up by Marxist-feminists deals with Engels' assertion that introducing women into the workforce is the prerequisite for their emancipation from male domination.[7]

With all that said, as Michele Barrett points out, feminists have found a multitude of problems with the latter part of Engels' work by

> arguing against the view that the family as the site of women's oppression is merely a relic of the pre-capitalist era. They have argued to the contrary that the oppression of women and the sexual division of labour are entrenched in capitalist relations of production and must be analyzed in

---

5   What Engels calls societies consists of "all savages and all barbarians of the lower and middle stages and partly even of the upper stage" (Marx, 735). These pre-capitalist societies placed the woman in a highly respected social position, in comparison to the slave-serf hybrid social and sexual relation that women find themselves in in capitalist societies.

6   From the preface to the first edition: "According to the materialistic conception, the determining factor in history is, in the last resort, the production and reproduction of immediate life. But this itself is of a twofold character. On the one hand, the production of the means of subsistence, of food, clothing and shelter and the tools requisite thereof; on the other, the production of human beings themselves, the propagation of the species."

7   Specifically, he writes, "It will then become evident that the first premise for the emancipation of women is the reintroduction of the entire female sex into public industry; and that this again demands that the quality possessed by the individual family of being the economy unit of society be abolished" (744). This presents a striking connection to the aims of neoliberalism detailed earlier.

that light. Marxist feminists have argued that Marxism must take account of women's domestic labour, their poorly paid and insecure position as wage-labourers, and the familial ideology which contributes to their oppression. (1978, 29–30)

In addition to this, Engels' view that proletarian women are not oppressed in marriage (in the way he describes female oppression among the bourgeois class) because they have no access to property and production (and this likely serves as the basis for his claim that without these relations women's oppression would end) does not take into account the prevalence of domestic abuse against women across classes, often due to the frustrations experienced from barely being able to reproduce oneself, let alone a family. Even with its historical inaccuracies on the specific daily experiences of a variety of proletarian family situations, *On the Origin of the Family, Private Property and the State* has allowed feminists to bring forth questions on the nature of women's oppression and the reproduction of capitalism. By providing a foundation for a materialist analysis of gender relations, Engels' piece sparked a shift towards an analysis "of the problem of women's 'collusion' in their oppression at the level of sexual politics requires an account of the operations of ideology and the structuring of gendered personality, temperament and subjectivity" (Barrett 2014, 47). Although what Barrett outlines as being the trajectory of feminist scholars after this piece (a trajectory placing a strong emphasis on women's relation to the division of labor and the social reproduction of capital) acknowledges the creation of a "sexual script," it does not account for the ways outside the domestic sphere in which it is still reproduced today.

The reactions from both Marxist-feminists, and feminists more broadly, towards Engels' *On the Origins of the Family* highlights a key dimension of the difficulty of merging Marxian and feminist analyses in general. By including the prevalence of patriarchy in capitalist society, Engels reveals on-going problems with the theoretical use of "patriarchy." Many socialist-feminists offer their own insights into the productive or unproductive uses of "patriarchy" as an object of analysis. Barrett, as a representative of the group that believes "patriarchy" as a category is problematic, notes how Marxist-feminists struggle to utilize it in a way that is not completely oppositional to other feminisms. These attempts however, result, for her,

> in posing patriarchy as either completely independent of capitalism, or as the dominant system of power relations, it completely fails to provide an analysis of women's oppression in a society characterized by capitalist relations of production.... In the absence of a body of coherent analysis

of women's oppression under capitalism, we have to work towards this through insights gained from political work. (2014, 38)

The other side of this debate argues that patriarchy necessarily must have various and, at times, conflictual definitions within various theories because of its long historical usage. Speaking directly to the arguments posed by Barrett, Sylvia Walby, in *Theorizing Patriarchy*, argues that patriarchy remains a useful theoretical concept because of its rich and varying history. Charting its use since Weber, Walby presents a conception of patriarchy that acknowledges its multi-uses while still being useful for a socialist-feminist critique. Walby understands patriarchy to be a system that not only exists alongside capitalism[8] but as one that consists of "social structures and practices in which men dominate, oppress and exploit women" (1991, 20).[9] Among these social structures, Walby identifies education, which I find begs for the critical theoretical look at the implications of a capitalist patriarchy within the university with which this chapter is concerned. In this way, I find that both feminism and Marxism are mutually dependent when developing an adequate critique of capitalist and neoliberal modes of being. Barbara Ehrenreich (2018) makes this exceptionally clear when discussing how she views the space that socialist-feminism has been trying to carve out for itself. She claims that, "it is a space free from the constrictions of a truncated kind of feminism and a truncated version of Marxism—in which we can develop the kind of politics that addresses the political/economic/cultural totality of monopoly capitalist society. We could only go so far with the available kinds of feminism, the conventional kind of Marxism, and then we had to break out to something that is not so restrictive and incomplete in its view of the world." A successful socialist-feminist approach to the classroom needs to combine the politics that surround students (even as they exceed gender-based problems) with a critical insight into how these issues are produced and replicated.

## 2      The Classroom—Creating Liberatory Spaces with Students

As this chapter seeks to chart its way within socialist-feminist pedagogical dialogues towards a unique critique of capitalism, there exist many trends

---

8   She also notes racism here as well.
9   Walby identifies six non-abstract structures of patriarchy: "the patriarchal mode of production, patriarchal relations in paid work, patriarchal relations in the state, male violence, patriarchal relations in sexuality, and patriarchal relations in cultural institutions," the one being most relevant for this project being the latter (20). It is also crucial to state that Walby explicitly rejects biological determinism as the cause of these structures.

stemming from discussions around Marxist-feminist pedagogy and critical pedagogy writ large. This section will outline just a few to introduce the kinds of discussion had within these discourses and the shortcomings found within them from not recognizing the reproduction of masculine characteristics, as the basis for success in society, at the expense of feminine ones. While it is important to salvage the value of historically "feminine" traits, the goal of a socialist-feminist pedagogy is to approach compassionate and collective-oriented traits rather than simply reversing the masculine-feminine divide. Doing so requires a critical look at the way we teach, and learn, in the classroom.

To begin this, an important aspect to touch on is the revolutionary potential of critical pedagogy. To this end, Peter McLaren's chapter "Critical Pedagogy as Revolutionary Practice" in *Marxism and Education* (2011), provides key insight into the approach I find most appealing towards re-emphasizing the importance of maintaining, or establishing, a socialist-feminist pedagogical approach to the classroom. McLaren sets up the ultimate goal of critical pedagogical approaches being one which,

> ...deals with the becomingness of human beings, which is tautologically the defining feature of education, but it does so with a particular political project in mind—anticapitalist, anti-imperialist, anti-racist, antisexist, and prodemocratic and emancipatory struggle....Here critical pedagogy serves to make the familiar strange and the strange familiar (refiguring how we see the relationship between the self and the social so that we can see both as manufactured, as the social construction of multiple dimensions, and, at times, as the obverse of each other, and the suppressed underside of each other).
> JONES 2011, 216

Thus, the socialist-feminist pedagogy that I find worth pursuing and advocating for is one that strives to "make the familiar strange and the strange familiar"— an intention that I find most neglected in the critical and feminist approaches to education in the literature generally. Part of this push towards making the familiar strange is the need for an investigation of the ways in which patriarchically determined feminine characteristics are continually shunned as being oppressively associated with women and the response is typically a complete rejection of these traits. What I want to propose with the subsequent critiques of Marxist- and socialist-feminist writers discussed in this chapter is that a rejection of characteristics simply because they are labelled feminine promotes a non-radical orientation towards the classroom and effectively causes masculine characteristics to be seen as ideal for both genders instead of a social-behavioral pluralism between gender expressions that radically challenge notions of ideal and unideal expressions, including those who have multiple or unstable identities (and draws attention to the reality within capitalism that male traits in particular are seen—and actually are—more profitable, for both workers and their bosses).

As another part of the same edited volume on the intersections between Marxism and education, Sara Carpenter and Shahrzad Mojab detail the Marxist-feminist approach they utilize when teaching at the university level. In this article, "Adult Education and the 'Matter' of Consciousness in Marxist-Feminism," the two detail an important psychological dimension of the problems posed within capitalism that encourages individuals to move away from a natural cooperative mode of community. They write,

> For Marx and Engels, human life would not exist without humans living and working in "cooperative" social relations in order to produce and reproduce their lives. These "cooperative" relations were not necessarily peaceful, but rather cooperative in the sense that humans live and reproduce socially, their existence is evidence of this connection. However, one of the central characteristics of life within a capitalist mode of production is that we do not experience our lives as "social" or "cooperative." Rather, we work under the conception that we are individual, independent, and self-sufficient.
> 
> JONES 2011, 120–1

Unfortunately, Carpenter and Mojab do not take this shift from the cooperative to the individualistic far enough in terms of engagement with and between students in the classroom. While it is certainly the case that capitalism promotes an individuality that typically manifests itself as competition, both in and outside the classroom, there is never attention drawn to the ways in which these individual and self-sufficient tendencies arise and are inadvertently reproduced in daily life. Instead, the two authors focus on the importance of getting their students to question some forms of knowledge through epistemological questions like "how do we know what we know?"

While epistemological critique aids in the development of a critical outlook towards other kinds of socially accepted behavior, the utilization of this kind of question in the classroom never fully seems to come together within a Marxist-feminist, or even feminist, scope. By spending considerable time in their piece stressing the importance of asking students "how do we know what we know," the authors neglect to provide insight into how this approach aids in a Marxist-feminist pedagogy that challenges the perpetuation of an individualistic, independent, and self-sufficient society. Thus, the major shortcoming of this pedagogical work is that it seems incomplete in its attempt to merge critical, Marxist, and feminist thought together. But more than this, the authors seem to suggest that because Marxism aims to take down capitalism, and feminism to take down patriarchy, the two are naturally inclined to work together because "capitalism without patriarchy or patriarchy without capitalism is impossible, and together they constitute a social whole" (136). While this is certainly true to some extent, it is also misleading, because patriarchy can easily be said to have existed in feudal societies, as distinct labor divisions between the genders were existent there as well.[10]

That is not to say that capitalism and patriarchy do not, together, have a different and more sinister relational existence now, but it is to say that without a feminist perspective, Marxism is also subject to the same gender problems that a variety of modes of production (capitalist, feudal, etc.) have had and this becomes necessary to recognize to the further importance of a Marxist/socialist-feminist perspective to teaching that explicitly acknowledges the gaps between these two schools of thought and works towards the bridging of both in a way that reduces the reproduction of any patriarchal and capitalist modes of existence.

The importance of this is best stated by bell hooks in her book *Teaching to Transgress: Education as the Practice of Freedom* (1994) that we must remember "the classroom remains the most radical space of possibility in the academy" (12). hooks' work is very near what I hope a renewed socialist-feminist pedagogy will look like in the future. When describing her early education in an all-black school during segregation, hooks recalls the effort her primary school teachers put into learning about where students came from, what their home lives were like, what things they excelled at, and what things they struggled with in order to orient their teaching towards the success of black students in society writ large. There was a clear effort to create a community within the classroom that allowed students to explore their interests and critique the society they lived in and what they are been previously taught. This is an effort that hooks notes was not repeated when segregation ended or during much of her post-secondary education. Instead, she notes that her schooling shifted from a collaborative effort to one of memorization and the ability to regurgitate the knowledge of the professor. This is still the fundamental issue of our educational system, in that, whether as individuals we strive to challenge it, our students have already spent the vast majority of their lives being told to repeat information to receive high marks, to compete with others for the favor of their teachers and professors, and not to challenge the authority at the front of the classroom. As hooks astutely notes, "the vast majority of students learn through conservative, traditional

---

10  As was identified by Engels in "On the Origin of the Family, Private Property and the State" in addition to feminist critiques of the work, mentioned above.

educational practices and concern themselves only with the presence of the professor, any radical pedagogy must insist that everyone's presence is acknowledged" (1994, 8). This is ultimately one of the most difficult challenges in teaching because, even in smaller groups, students are hesitant and reluctant to communicate with each other, or at least with others they are not already familiar with, and this is one that we have yet to have fully overcome.[11] This issue also demonstrates where even bell hooks' views on teaching fall short; while a focus on *all* students in the classroom is key, the way students interact with one another, and not just the way that teachers help students develop their own curiosity for learning, is deeply important for moving beyond the reproduction of universal "masculine" behaviors over subordinate "feminine" ones, and not encouraging a complete dismissal of productive, collective, and nurturing traits often associated as "feminine."

## 3   Going on a Neoliberal-Feminist Hunt

And so, while they are still limited, socialist-feminist texts have in some ways discussed the issues surrounding particular teaching structures in a capitalist system, and particularly the negative consequences the ideologies that schools promote for the success of women in general. Michele Barrett spends a considerable amount of time in *Women's Oppression Today* (2014) detailing the research done in regard to the British education system on girls, but she also draws attention to what she finds to be a major problem of traditional Marxist-feminist cooperation when dealing with the education system[12] when she writes,

> Hence the *substance* of Althusser's argument would need to be modified in profound ways for it to be of use to feminists. Nor am I convinced that

---

[11]   I, myself, find trouble with this often when trying to encourage students to answer questions to the entire class and not only to me. I frequently remind them that I am not the only person in the room, and I am certainly not the only person who could benefit from their answers. This is an everyday challenge that I struggle with in trying to teach and also trying to encourage students to see each other as equals, as others they can bounce ideas off of, and not just another anonymous body in a classroom.

[12]   Here, Barrett will evoke problems surrounding the use and works of Louis Althusser, the French Marxist philosopher, most famous for his work on ISAs and RSAs in *Ideology and Ideological State Apparatuses* (found in *Lenin and Philosophy and other essays*, 1971). It is in relation to this work and the debate among Marxist-feminists on whether "an Althusserian approach to the reproduction of capitalism can provide an analysis of the reproduction of gender division in capitalism" (Barrett 2014, 138).

the *method* which seeks to understand education and training processes in terms of the reproduction of relations of dominance and subordinacy can be transposed on to the question of gender. To do this would be to argue that just as the capitalist class is reproduced in a relationship of total dominance over the working class, so men are reproduced as totally dominant over women. Without denying the general pattern of male dominance, we can still see particular drawbacks in this argument. It would be difficult to argue, for instance, that the qualifications and skills imparted to a girl at a major independent school would in any sense 'equip' her for a place in the division of labour that was subordinate to that of a woorking [sic] class boy who left school at the minimum age with no formal qualifications. (139)

The problem with this statement is its focus on gender oppression being materialized only in one's physical appearance and thus an Althusserian structuralist analysis of education would not be a fruitful endeavor. Although Barrett is absolutely correct that a woman with the kind of education and training described would likely not work in a professional environment where she would be subordinate to a man with the education and experience of the one described above, she is still likely to be subordinate to other men with lesser educations than her in the same field, or, more common now, she will be subordinate to other women who reproduce the very masculine characteristics that are applauded and encouraged throughout ones education and which continues in the workplace.[13]

We see this latter situation in our everyday lives and even more commonly in our popular culture. For example, in *The Proposal*, Ryan Reynolds, playing a publisher executive assistant, is subordinate to Sandra Bullock, the executive. However, Sandra Bullock is in the position she is in, not because she is a *woman,* but *because* she carries herself in a masculine way—she embodies the cold-heartedness of a typical male CEO *in order to* be successful—an embodiment that causes her to be hated by her subordinates (likely because of the female playing the male role). Additionally, this same embodiment causes her to hate herself, a key element to the plot which becomes more fully developed

---

13   To take up the modern terminology of "mansplaining"(Solnit 2014), I would suggest that this behavior emerges from women understanding that patronizing modes of discourse are valued when expressed in male bodies (similar to Mitchell's application of penis-envy described later) and thus they reproduce the same behavior—sometimes in unique ways, and sometimes by "switching back-and-forth" between stereotypically feminine and masculine behaviors. See, also: https://www.gsb.stanford.edu/insights/researchers-how-women-can-succeed-workplace.

when the two characters are forced into a matrimony ploy together and as we slowly see Bullock's character achieve happiness when she loosens the reins on her success and career and allows the space for Reynolds to play a more dominating role in the relationship. This film thus illuminates a major problem with Barrett's analysis of the benefits of a higher education for women—notably because these women, in order to be successful in the ways Barrett predicts, must replicate and embody a very particular set of traits that are often seen and well-received when they are found in a male body. The second problem arises when we watch Bullock's character development occur because she ceases to "fake" her masculine characteristics and relearns her feminine ones to be successful in all aspects of her life (love and work, but likely less so in her career than she was before). A reproduction of the patriarchal status quo results as the couple resembles the nuclear heteronormative couple. Although Barrett may not ultimately claim that women are happier in the final situation depicted in the film, ultimately, we find that the only path towards career success is a masculine one, and other paths are distinctly feminine—and detrimental to personal success. Yet Barrett's book never strives to address the assumption that masculinity in a capitalist society is ideal for the individual happiness and internal success of any individual as all genders would likely face similar stressors that Bullock finds herself confronted with throughout the plot of the film.

Barrett's path-breaking work does provide important insights into the nature of the education of women and girls in the British system by bringing in various studies and referencing the research done by other feminist scholars on the behaviors encouraged and discouraged in the classroom. One such study that she cites is by Elena Belotti who observed that in elementary schools "the assumption that girls should perform domestic services for boys is acted out in the classroom at a very early age in the various tasks of clearing up and so on that little girls are enjoined to perform" (Barrett 2014, 140). While this still remains nothing new in a large portion of elementary classroom settings, girls, and later women, who want to overcome the behaviors of domesticity that this encouragement provides will look towards what the boys do, how they act, and what leads to their having privileges that prevent them from having to necessarily partake in the cleanup process that the girls all participate in in the classroom.

This attempt to mimic what those in better positions do has been frequently observed in psychoanalytical writings as early as 1925 in Freud's "An Autobiographical Study" in which, as Juliet Mitchell characterizes it, the female becomes angry at her lack of a penis and strives for a masculinity in which she cannot obtain (Mitchell 1975, 219). Due to an inability to fully achieve this masculinity (by presumably being unable to obtain a penis), the female becomes "envious as though 'by nature'; she demands privileges and exemptions ('pedestal treatment') to compensate her for her supposed biological inadequacy" (87). Both reactions reproduce a feminine subject that either strives to be as masculine as possible to imitate the success of men, or demands privileges that amount to an equality with men within the same system—and thus continues to reproduce a neoliberal feminist perspective that does not challenge the privilege attributed to masculinity in the first place.

These observations will ultimately lead to a revaluing in girls' minds of the characteristics associated with their male peers as being desirable and those that led them to be enjoined to perform the cleaning ritual noted above as undesirable. Barrett also presents a study which finds results that would, I believe, easily lead to this same negative revaluing of their femininity when she recounts that; "male teachers tended to marginalize or simply ignore the female students" which lead to a depreciation of their self-esteem but also serves to teach girls that the behaviors that will get them acknowledged by their teachers or professors in a positive way are those similar to what allows male students to receive the attention they do (Barrett 2014, 141). Thus, feminine characteristics are what are viewed as the problem, and the solution rests in a reorientation of personal traits that value masculinist ones—instead of a structural reevaluating into what reproduces the feminine-masculine divide and why the divide itself is not challenged—and who profits off both the endurance of masculine dominance or the marketization of suitable "female" traits—suitable here defined as those that do not directly conflict with capitalism.

For those females that do not wish to reidentify themselves with the idealized traits of their male peers, these women and girls often end up being encouraged throughout their entire education to be more conformist in school than what is encouraged with male students (141). And as such, we see situations arise where "adolescent girls were implicitly and even explicitly 'coached' by their teachers into appropriately feminine behaviour" that lead to them learning specific definitions about adult masculinity and femininity due to the long period children spend in the schooling system (141). As the anecdote that opened this piece indicates, "coaching" no longer performs the same explicit household/workplace-female/male divide that was commonly expressed in education during earlier periods. Instead, it can now manifest itself in new ways that seem helpful and liberating (like trying to encourage female students to engage in class discussion more) but ultimately lead to a censorship and control on the feminine personality. A censorship that results in the internalization of masculine behavior in the classroom and the perpetual devaluing of historically and socially defined "feminine" characteristics. Challenging the feminine-woman and masculine-male divide is crucial, but not at the expense of discouraging everyone (regardless of gender) from wanting to have or express historically feminine characteristics because of an existing divide of the feminine as undesirable and the masculine as desirable. This too often results in female, or female-identifying, students given advice and neglects to discuss these same issues with the male, and male-identifying, students in the room. The discussion that is usually conducted in these situations functions more to alienate the women, especially if they disagree in any respect, and does little to promote that everyone is "present" in the room (to harken back to bell hooks' statement mentioned earlier). Very little is done in the classroom in the majority of these situations (including the anecdote cited above) to confront the way men behave in the classroom—including, but not limited to, the use of a condescending and presumptuous tone and the frequent interrupting of others, particularly female students. [14]

We often see the way in which women-identifying individuals have to alter their behavior or perform additional tasks to make the transition from traditionally female fields to traditionally male ones. One such example frequently occurs in journalism, where female writers who are employed by women's fashion/beauty magazines face difficulties if they try to crossover to more "serious" writing at places like *The New York Times*, *Harper's*, or any number of other similarly high-profile outlets. The few instances in which women are able to make the jump, they often speak ambivalently about their past work and try to distance themselves from preconceived notions of their skills. Other times, women must symbolically relinquish their femininity and embrace masculinity while soothing the egos of men that may be intimidated by their success.[15] As Karen Jesella writes in her piece "Paper Dollhouse: why can't style writers get any respect?" that some of the few notable examples of women who have

---

[14] The criticisms on female behavior in the classroom in this regard mirror the social issue we have with blaming rape victims for their assaults. These women are often told the things that they did wrong (dressing provocatively or consuming alcohol or drugs) and what they should do to avoid unwanted attention (which is never avoided regardless if one were to take this advice) and the men are often excused as "boys being boys" and are hardly taught not to rape and not to assume that any other person's body or affection is due to them. The difficulty of challenging these prevalent societal norms also goes back to bell hooks' reminder that our students were brought up and taught under conservative (and I would add patriarchal) educational systems that will continuously be challenges to any attempts to promote self-critique on these behaviors and capitalism itself.

[15] Again, here success refers to what is deemed profitable to capitalism; not the skill or influence the work itself may have. Success is also another capitalist category that drives individuals towards solitary, and often, conniving competitive behavior—a socialist-feminist perspective on success may focus more on collective achievement.

made the shift from style magazines to more complex reporting—she references Jamaica Kincaid, Kennedy Fraser, and Lillian Ross—did so by "disowning the womanly world of fashion and beauty, they renounce their femininity. By allying with older, male *New Yorker* writers, (Ross was [William] Shawn's longtime lover;[16] Kincaid married Shawn's son; Fraser married another writer at the magazine), they get it back again—and they get literary power, too. If they emasculate the men by being writers, they remasculinize them by becoming their lovers" (2006, 44).[17]

When describing the university experience of women, Barrett acknowledges the persistent inequity among female students, in what we may now refer to as STEM fields, to male students when writing, "the girl who does decide to proceed to university in, say, an engineering subject, will find herself in a department dominated by men and an ethos of masculinity" (Barrett 2014, 143–4). Now, despite a broader inaccuracy that STEM fields are the only fields in which there is a clear gender unevenness (research suggests that this is common in many fields and departments), Barrett misses a key critique in her observation. Departments across the university system are dominated by an ethos of masculinity that does not always show itself as such today. An ethos of masculinity still exists in most facets of women's lives because of the way in which their own liberation seems to be encouraged by their ability to "play the boys' game better" and perform better in an educational setting than their male peers in the only ways they are likely to get recognition—by the enacting and embodying of masculine characteristics. Returning briefly to the STEM fields for a moment, Isabelle Stengers and Vinciane Despret acknowledge that,

> For a scientist, to claim that it is "as a woman" that she signals the singularity of her practice is certainly a way to contribute to the feminist struggle, but at the price of giving ammunition to those who were precisely waiting for it in order to avoid questions which demand hesitation, lucidity,

---

16  William Shawn was the editor of the *New Yorker* at the time.
17  While this is a very particular example, and Jesella is very clear to highlight that there is no indication that these women "slept their way to the top," it highlights the troubling field that women professionals have to navigate in order to continue down their desired career paths. These women had to simultaneously denounce their femininity (because it caused them to be read as too frivolous and, thus, their writing was not serious enough for highly regarded outlets) but also to reclaim it while in these new positions in order to not shift workplace gender balances more than their presence already does. This is a key aspect that a socialist-feminist pedagogy needs to address in the classroom and solutions should be discussed that strive to not discourage feminine qualities in typically masculine environments.

and attention to problems of pertinence. The woman who is a bother will no longer be a colleague but a distraction who intends to "politicize science," to make it a cause that is "unscientific." (2011, 39)

Thus, not only are woman pressured to conform to masculine traits during the education process, we find that they are also encouraged to conform to a "gender-neutrality" that ignores their positionality as women at the expense of not being able to perform their research.[18] When women do connect their gender with their politics in the pursuit of new scientific knowledge they are often shunned in a similar way. As Keely Savoie details from an American Association for the Advancement of Science (AAAS) seminar on The Evolutionary Aspects of Gender and Sexuality, Dr. Joan Roughgarden remarks that

> research that eschews those archaic and sexist assumptions about gender and sexuality is routinely marginalized, ghettoized, swept under the rug, ignored, avoided, and ridiculed. Passive and active sexism in scientific research, she says, have resulted in a skewed and incomplete picture of the world that only a feminist overhaul of existing and future research can correct. (2004, 37)

To a claim like that I have just made, Barrett offers a rebuttal of sorts, by arguing that "the necessary process of revaluing the characteristics attributed to 'femininity' (such as 'sensitivity') may lead to an unreflective assertion of these as pre-given characteristics of women" (2014, 150). These responses are highly problematic because they do tend to lead towards a social recapitulation towards "gender-neutral" (read, masculine) traits that challenge the "naturalness" of any feminine characteristics, but not those identified as masculine.

For my purposes here, the goal is not to claim that socially-construed ideals of naturalness are more valuable, but rather, that the emphasis on revaluing socially-constructed feminine characteristics *instead* of valuing these same feminine traits within a broader set of human characteristics (ones that can be possessed by both males and females) is problematic under a socialist-feminist pedagogical approach. The goal is not to perfect our categorization of biologically-determined characteristics, but instead, to view both perceived and constructed gendered traits in more scrutiny to avoid the common pitfall

---

18   Stengers and Despret depict this through the story-telling of Adrienne Zihlman whose research was discredited, rejected, and her orientation proclaimed to "pollute" science because of her identification of her research with her status as woman (2011, 39-41).

of attempting a neutrality that ultimately favors capitalist-approved masculine traits.

## 4  Co-optation: The Final Struggle Against Neoliberal-Feminism

As the previous section points out, the specific kind of socialist-feminist pedagogical project that I find necessary for a productive and radical affront on the co-optation of the university by neoliberal-feminism is difficult to achieve and, oftentimes, attempts to do so run into the same problems they aim to confront. In fact, recent discussions that intend to focus on the ways masculine traits are encouraged in the classroom, while feminine ones are discouraged, also reproduce this same neoliberal-feminism in unintended ways. The popularity of discussing texts like Anne-Marie Slaughter's *Why Woman Still Can't Have It All* and Sheryl Sandberg's *Lean In*, that encourage, and teach, women to "act" like men to succeed in the workplace has been done in one of these attempts to call out the problems of neoliberal feminism's attempts at co-optation of feminist movements. One popular critique is found within Nicole Aschoff's *The New Prophets of Capital* (2015) in which Aschoff calls attention to the danger of faddish feminists arising, like Sheryl Sandberg and Hillary Clinton.[19] For her, these "feminists" essentially offer only a re-telling of the same Betty Friedan 1970s "mistaken choice" paradigm. In this paradigm it is argued that women are conditioned to make poor choices, that they have to choose a "comfy" life as a stay-at-home mom instead of getting down and dirty with the corporate boys, or that they are destined for lower-earning cubicle jobs instead of making it as top CEOs in the companies they can now *choose* to work at. The problem with neoliberal feminism is that it continues to reproduce the notion of a "mistaken choice." However, contrary to some of the beliefs of a Sheryl Sandberg or Hillary Clinton, women are not mistakenly choosing to gain less or to be less ambitious, just as they are not actively choosing not to sit at the table, lean in, or raise their hands until they are called on. These characteristics, and other similar ones evoked to help "shatter the glass ceiling" these neoliberal feminists propose, is one that ultimately finds its success in a women's ability to more successfully mimic men within capitalism, not one that engages in dismantling and challenging a system that encourages individuals to be aggressive, assertive, and often-times cruel on their way to the top (even while most remain closer to the bottom). The problem of advocating and promoting any

---

19   Hillary Clinton's role in faddish feminism will be discussed in more detail later. See also: *False Choices: Faux Feminism and Hillary Rodham Clinton* (Verso, 2016).

pedagogical approach other than a socialist-feminist one is that it will always necessarily reproduce the valuing of a distinctly masculine behavior. And thus reaffirms that these women are only as successful as they were because they have acted like the men, and as is often the case, because of still-present gender biases, they did it better.[20] This is not to say there are not career-paths where stereotypically "feminine" traits are sellable, but rather that these career-paths nearly without exception are nowhere near the highest paying careers—and we also should be questioning the entire capitalistic basis of the notion of success resting on how much one can sell oneself for (though the irony of the world's oldest profession, and its criticisms being historically feminine should not be lost on us). Even within nursing, a profession dominated by women, the highest paid specialization, anesthesiology, is the one with a higher percentage of men than women (Luthra 2015).

Aschoff's phrase for neoliberal feminism throughout her book—"trickle-down feminism"—is an apt term for the kind of feminism produced from a capitalist/neoliberalist ideology. This neoliberal feminism promotes only the successes of very specific women, like Sandberg and Clinton, and uses them as an exemplar of the achievements of all women if they work hard enough and make the right (read: male) decisions. By encouraging the successes of a few key women, neoliberal feminism is successful in maintaining the capitalist mode of production by encouraging all women to look to these icons to help make their everyday working conditions improve instead of urging for their own collective bargaining—or fighting for an egalitarian, non-sexist post-capitalist alternative. As Nina Power points out in *One Dimensional Woman,* there is a false belief that "all women want is another woman" (2009, 8). By encouraging a small group of women to "lean in" the ultimate effect of the larger population of women for whom corporate jobs just are not possible is to "hold on."

Aschoff, however, still falls victim, in a way, to reproducing the value of masculine characteristics at the expense of feminine ones when she begins to praise Sandberg, writing,

> Sandberg is right that women hold themselves back as a result of patriarchal norms that push them to be caring and nice. Women do need

---

20   Although much can be said about the pressure women face to out-perform their male counterparts in order to be viewed as competent or successful, we see countless examples of women's performances being rated less than their male colleagues, or women being held to higher standards. A few cases have recently garnered attention, especially surrounding the #MeToo movement, including Michelle William's $625,000 pay for reshooting scenes for "All the Money in the World" in comparison to her co-star Mark Wahlberg's $5 million despite both having roughly equal screen time (http://www.nydailynews.com/entertainment/mark-wahlberg-paid-4m-michelle-williams-money-article-1.3766399).

to stop worrying about being perfect mothers/wives/daughters. Women do need to take the lead and enter positions of power. This part of her story needs to be shared and internalized. But Sandberg's version of leaning in reinforces the fundamentally exploitative social relations that characterize our society and strengthen a system that permanently divides women at the top from women at the bottom. (2015, 40)

Although her critique on the meanness of certain woman who have taken these power positions, like Marissa Mayer,[21] or less directly, Jen Holleran,[22] are important to note, Aschoff's suggestion that any part of Sandberg's advice, particularly one suggesting that women being "caring and nice" is merely a product of patriarchal norms encourages women to be the opposite as a way to challenge these norms. What we should be encouraging is not more "manly women" or more women who are self-interested and mean; but, encouraging traits like caring and kindness in both men and women *more*. What do we reproduce when we encourage women to "take the lead" and resist being held back by these barbaric traits like kindness? Do we not reproduce women who further reproduce the same capitalistic mentality of a dog-eat-dog world?[23] What is the result of masses of women "taking the lead" in this way? And why does most feminist advice center on getting women to change their behaviors, or resist the traits that are historically and socially encouraged in them? What is so bad about being kind? Is it just that kindness is exploited in a capitalist system? Then why promote negative social behaviors instead of drawing attention to the problems that affect men and women in capitalism? Instead of encouraging daughters, sisters, female students, and female friends to push against patriarchal norms of kindness, let's encourage our sons, brothers, and male students and friends to push against these same patriarchal norms and be more compassionate and kind.[24]

---

21    The former president and CEO of Yahoo! She announced her resignation in June 2017.
22    In 2010, Holleran was recommended by Sandberg to Mark Zuckerberg to head his foundation The Start Up: Education in order to try and improve the standardized performance of Newark Public Schools. Holleran was a mother of twins whose husband had not been taking a big role in their rearing when the position was offered to her. However, because she "leaned" in, her husband helped out, her marriage equalized, and she successfully undermined hundreds of Newark schoolteachers (most of whom were women too) who were fired for lower testing scores (Aschoff 2015, 36-7).
23    On the concept of the capitalistic mentality, see Sculos 2017a; 2017b
24    In the same spirit and logic that we would want to rally against these patriarchal norms among both genders in retaliation against the patriarchal norms that accepts blaming a rape victim for their attire or whether or not they consumed alcohol.

## 5 How a Socialist-Feminist Pedagogy Slays the Beast

These questions should strive to orient us towards a socialist-feminist pedagogy that privileges the cultivation of a teaching environment in which capitalist and neoliberalist ideologies are challenged and fundamentally obstructed. This chapter advocates for the collective work towards developing particular pedagogical strategies aimed towards empowering female, male, or non-gender-conforming students in the classroom without relying on patriarchal characteristics of "masculine" and "feminine" and attributing values on ideal and non-ideal modes of classroom engagement. Capitalism and neoliberalism are constantly acquiring new territory on their ceaseless quest for the co-optation of all radical and resistant modes of being and thinking—the university should be among one of the most rigorously protected against this systemic attack.[25]

In order to begin the process of this work, we need to recapitulate the dangers of continuing with a neoliberal-feminist orientation towards the education of men, women, and non-conforming individuals in the university. By encouraging women, or those who express themselves in stereotypically feminine ways, to act in ways that are socially valued in men—such as certain kinds of interrupting behavior in the classroom, mansplaining, aggressiveness, occupying large areas of space (as in manspreading), or leaning in—(and denying them success when they refuse to conform), we reproduce values of exploitation and domination against "the original proletariat" and thus bastardize any claimed variation of a socialist or Marxist agenda. However, it is crucial not to propose that the solution against gender-specific values is the encouragement of a "gender-neutral" script of accepted behavior, because these scripts ultimately serve to bolster the dominance of masculine characteristics. Instead, a socialist-feminist pedagogical approach to the classroom that nears the approach this chapter aims to approximate is one that encourages multiple ways of engaging in learning that resist the reproduction of tropes of behavior based on either classically patriarchal or capitalistic norms. This approach should strive not to reproduce, neither in whole nor part, modes of behavior that promote individualism as these are traits valued and encouraged in a capitalist/neoliberal society. Rather, an active promotion of stereotypically feminine traits that are dismissed in capitalistic modes of learning because they are unprofitable—like genuine kindness and sensitivity—should be encouraged

---

25  For further discussion on resistance and neoliberalism in higher education, see *Counterrevolution and Repression in the Politics of Education: At the Midnight of Dissent*, Sean Noah Walsh, 2014, Lexington: Plymouth, UK and *Neoliberalism's War on Higher Education*, Henry A. Giroux, 2014, Chicago, IL: Haymarket Books.

behavior regardless of a perceived biological connection between these traits as female, but of communal and productive human characteristics. This is not to exclude beneficial masculine traits, or even traits that may not fall neatly in this historically socially-reproduced binary but the focus on just (more often repressed) stereotypical feminine traits serves as an example of the necessity and radical potential generated by encouraging and reproducing traits that do not serve to further or benefit the everyday operations and co-optation characteristic of capitalist modes of (re)production.

## Bibliography

Aschoff, N.M. (2015) *The New Prophets of Capital*. Verso.

Barrett, M. (2014) *Women's Oppression Today: the Marxist/Feminist Encounter*. London: Verso.

Brown, W. (2003) "Neo-liberalism and the End of Liberal Democracy." *Theory & Event*, 7(1). DOI:10.1353/tae.2003.0020

Ehrenreich, B. (2018) "What is Socialist Feminism?" *Jacobin*. https://jacobinmag.com/2018/07/socialist-feminism-barbara-ehrenreich.

hooks, b. (1994) *Teaching to Transgress: Education as the Practice of Freedom*. New York: Routledge.

Jesella, K. (2006) "Paper Dollhouse: Why Can't Style Writers Get Any Respect?" *Bitch Media*, Issue no. 32, 40–5.

Jones, P.E. (2011) *Marxism and Education: Renewing the Dialogue, Pedagogy, and Culture*. Basingstoke: Palgrave Macmillan.

Luthra, S. (2015) "Pay, But Not Equity, Improves For Female Anesthesiologists." *NPR.org*. https://www.npr.org/sections/health-shots/2015/09/18/441198354/pay-but-not-equity-improves-for-female-anesthesiologists.

Marx, K., & Engels, F. (1978) *The Marx-Engels Reader* (R.C. Tucker, Ed.). New York: W. W. Norton.

Mitchell, J. (1975) *Psychoanalysis and Feminism: Freud, Reich, Laing and Women*. London: Vintage Books.

Power, N. (2009) *One-Dimensional Woman*. Hants: O Books.

Rottenberg, C. (2013) "The Rise of Neoliberal Feminism." *Cultural Studies*, 28(3), 1–20. DOI:10.1080/09502386.2013.857361.

Savoie, K. (2004) "Unnatural Selection: Questioning Science's Gender Bias." *Bitch Media*, Issue no. 24, 37–41, 90–1.

Sculos, B.W. (2017a) "The Capitalistic Mentality and the Politics of Radical Reform: A (Mostly) Friendly Reply to Michael J. Thompson." *New Politics*. Vol. XVI No. 2, Whole Number 62.

Sculos, B.W. (2017b) "Demystifying the Capitalistic Mentality: Reconciling Adorno and Fromm on the Psycho-Social Reproduction of Capitalism." *Constellations*, 25(2), 272–286.

Stengers, I., & Despret, V. (2011) *Women Who Make a Fuss: The Unfaithful Daughters of Virginia Woolf* (A. Knutson, Trans.). Minneapolis, MN: Univocal.

Walby, S. (1991) *Theorizing Patriarchy*. Oxford u.a.: Blackwell.

# PART 2

*Rethinking Critical Theory & Critical Pedagogy*

∴

CHAPTER 6

# The "Great Refusal" Redux: Antidote to Mindless Syncopation

*Mary Caputi*

Teaching Marx in the twenty-first century is a hard sell. The pervasive neoliberal ideology that dominates globalized markets and an omnipresent media culture renders the Marxist theory of "scientific revolution" implausible to most students, for the anticipated transition from capitalism to communism appears nowhere in sight. Indeed, the perceived magnitude of Marx and Engels' misdiagnosis of the historical situation often causes students to dismiss their theory wholesale, labeling it as quaint, quixotic, and hopelessly utopian. What might have sounded convincing in the late nineteenth century bears no connection to the interdependent, commercialized, high-tech world that students now inhabit such that Marxist theory gets catalogued alongside Platonic Forms and the Stoics' "universal city." Nevertheless, this sweeping rejection of Marxist orthodoxy often becomes attenuated when the syllabus moves to the more nuanced and adaptable revisionism of later thinkers. Once students realize that many tenets of Marx's thinking have been seriously and thoughtfully reworked to fit a contemporary historical framework, his ideas undergo favorable reappraisal and he escapes the epithet "obsolete."

Herbert Marcuse represents a revisionist thinker to whom students often relate meaningfully. As is well known, Marcuse was an iconic figure of the student revolts of the 1960s, and his writings lent theoretical ballast to that decade's progressive politics and anti-establishment sensibility (Marcuse 1964, 1969, 1974; Andrew T. Lamas, A.T., Todd Wolfson, T., Funke, P. 2017). At that time, students identified deeply with his revisionist thinking as it translated orthodoxy into a critique of *their own* society; they saw the relevance of his writings to politics, aesthetics, and sexuality as these applied to the more disturbing aspects of the twentieth century. Hence in his writing, Marcuse praises what he terms the "Great Refusal" of the sixties' generation that demanded a collective rethinking of America's capitalist and imperialist agenda; he applauds that generation's insistence that mainstream corporate culture be transformed along more humane, egalitarian lines and that it fundamentally rethink its metric for human success (Marcuse 1971).

Importantly, Marcuse underscores the Great Refusal's ability to distinguish "progress" from manipulation and indoctrination into the mainstream. He endorses the rebelliousness of sixties youth who, resisting conformity, refuse the domesticating power of advanced industrial societies and instead cultivate other values: e.g., the spirituality found in nature, the need to nurture community and discourage competition, a life focused on things other than money-making and career advancement. Refusing cooptation by corporate culture and creature comforts, disaffected sixties youth interpreted these as little more than tools of ideological persuasion and subsequently nurtured an iconoclastic counterculture. In *An Essay on Liberation,* Marcuse praises their discernment and moral tenacity:

> they recognize the mark of social repression, even in the most sublime manifestations of traditional culture, even in the most spectacular manifestations of technical progress. They have again raised a specter (and this time a specter which haunts not only the bourgeoisie but all exploitative bureaucracies): the specter of a revolution which subordinates the development of productive forces and higher standards of living to the requirements of creating solidarity for the human species....
> MARCUSE 1971, 8

Today, of course, things are different, with students facing a much altered, more economically and politically polarized society from that of the 1960s. Today's students face different challenges and do not claim the luxury of a robust economy and expansive middle class, both of which ensured that even agitating radicals would enjoy a comfortable lifestyle. Nevertheless, the lessons contained in Marcuse's writings still hold the potential to raise awareness regarding the "cognitive devastation" that so often accompanies our unknowing indoctrination into a system that in reality does not serve our interests (Kangussu, Kovacevic, Lamas 2017). Here, I examine Marcuse's ability to reach twenty-first century students thanks to his emphasis on the critical faculty whose near liquidation jeopardizes our relationship to mainstream culture. While a bona fide counterculture does not appear to be materializing, I illustrate that his concept of the "Great Refusal" remains pertinent today, and that teaching Marcuse alongside Marx still exerts an enlightening power, thereby keeping alive the demanding, rebellious spirit of cultural disaffection that we witness in recent social movements.

## 1 Work, "Stuff," and Naturalized False Needs

In *One-Dimensional Man,* Marcuse famously argues that the affluence and comfort of advanced industrialized societies serve to obfuscate the undesirable and indeed inhumane qualities that such societies foster. As avid consumers of the many goods and services offered, great swathes of our time and energy are devoted to purchasing and paying for the creature comforts that we naturalize and thus come to expect. Like other members of the Frankfurt School, Marcuse laments the degree to which we find our worth in our possessions and measure the value of our lives in terms of material accumulation. Human beings assume a "one-dimensional" intellect when we lose critical distance on what the society offers, but simply accept its culture of affluence as confirmation of its innate goodness and success. The seduction of creature comforts provokes the hasty conclusion that the modern world is surely "advanced," and that ample consumer goods designate social success. Blinded to the more sinister dimensions of "progress," we cannot discern the extent to which material gain has thwarted our perception. Marcuse writes:

> The efficiency of the system blunts the individuals' recognition that it contains no facts which do not communicate the repressive power of the whole. If the individuals find themselves in the things which shape their lives, they do so, not by giving, but by accepting the law of things—not the law of physics but the law of their society.
> MARCUSE 1964, 11

Writing in 1964, Marcuse observed that growth and accumulation were the unquestioned integral components of capitalist culture. The duty to work hard in order to accumulate things and accrue sizeable debt became naturalized rather than open to question. Thought, imagination, material resources, the organization of one's time: indeed all our energies are oriented around work such that the act of laboring and the remuneration it yields alone determine our worth. Whereas technological rationality could easily *release* us from long working hours and thus enrich the quality of our lives, the opposite trend has occurred. The pernicious, restless Faustian ideology that accompanies advanced industrial societies makes us want more, "need" more, and identify all the more deeply with what we own. Sadly, "the apparatus imposes its economic and political requirements for...expansion on labor time and free time, on the material and intellectual culture" in ways that diminish our lives (Marcuse 1964, 2–3). The self-realization within reach is thus thwarted by the naturalization of market values and the seductive, entangling ideology of consumption (Brown 2015).

Recent authors expound on Marcuse's observations, bringing his mid-twentieth century critique of the system even more up-to-date. In *The Problem with Work*, for instance, Kathi Weeks writes of the "irrationality of our commitment to work" resulting from its being "the most stubbornly naturalized and apparently self-evident elements of modern...capitalist societies" (Weeks 2011, 43). Weeks analyzes the manner in which the Protestant work ethic ingrains itself in our psyches, inducing us to engage in a "constant and methodical productive effort" lest—in keeping with that ideology—we become idle and hence depraved. In Western capitalist societies, the compulsion to prove industrious bores into our thoughts and emotions with such authority that we remain "haunted by the legacy of the Puritan ethic," eager to compete in the marketplace where our value is easily gauged by the indicative signs of income, the accumulation of consumer goods, investment strategies, and financial planning (Weeks 2011, 39).

Yet if the moralizing austerity of the Protestant work ethic is what originally impelled us to work, the emergent ideology has subsequently shed any allegiance to the self-sacrificing, self-effacing dimension of that ethos that saves its money for a rainy day. Today we work to shop, to accumulate "stuff" under the aegis of an expanding consumerism that often takes the place of religion. Moreover, the culture of credit has made it easy to adhere to that religion's tenets. We are awash in things to buy, credit card bills to pay, and a technologically driven ethos in which expensive gadgetry becomes ever more quickly obsolete. It is hardly hyperbole to state that, for many, the mall now functions as a church or temple, their counters and storefronts operating as an altar, and the commodity-on-display as the revered entity that promises fulfillment: communion. According to comedian George Carlin, we succumb to this ideology to such an extent that life becomes nothing more than the accumulation of "stuff;" our homes are "a pile of stuff with a cover on it...a place to keep your stuff while you go out and get more stuff" (https://www.youtube.com/watch?v=MvgN5gCuLac).

Western societies are so saturated with commodity culture that we risk being inured to the saturation. In 2015, Red Crow marketing estimated that most Americans see between 4,000–10,000 advertisements per day, overwhelming our minds with commercial interests and so colonizing the imagination as to make disposable merchandise appear as essential as air, water, and food (http://www.redcrowmarketing.com/2015/09/10/many-ads-see-.oneday/). We all know how cleverly entertaining advertisements can be, and their preponderance in our lives naturalizes their claims about what we need and can afford. An attained level of creature comfort—often beyond our means yet presented as easily within reach—thus assumes an insidiously pharmacotic dimension as the very things that enrich our lives can easily enslave us to more debt, more stress, more hours spent laboring in order to pay the bills and accumulate "stuff" (Derrida 1981). Each new acquisition claims our time and energy, often exhaustively, yet the "new" commodity exudes such promise that to be without is to risk invisibility by our peers.

Indeed, because the pharmacotic attributes of these acquisitions prove so compelling, we lose the ability to imagine life without them wherein their benefits are not championed as essential to survival. The acquisition of more goods and services resonates deeply with the American Dream such that "the more factor"—our national signature—mandates and assumes continued growth, continued expansion, the satisfaction of desires on an ever-increasing scale. In "The More Factor," Laurence Shames argues that America's optimistic "habit of more" lies deeply embedded in our expansionist history of growth, opulence, and self-recreation. "The habit of more seemed to suggest that there was no such things as getting wiped out in America," Shames explains. "A fortune lost in Texas might be recouped in Colorado...There was always a second chance...in this land where growth was destiny and where expansion and purpose were the same thing" (Shames 2011, 91). Accumulation indeed constitutes a core American value and operates as our most respected metric of success. True, a movement to declutter has arisen as a reaction against this rampant consumerism (Kondo 2014). Yet any trip to the mall reveals that shopping, cell phone use, texting, messaging, and accumulating "stuff" remain a widespread passion.

Indeed, it has been estimated that many of us check our cell phones no fewer than 150 times a day thanks to the manufacturing companies artfully conceived strategies at "sucking you in" and "taking your time" (Wise, K. "Your Cellphone Is Trying To Control Your Life," *PBS Newshour*, January 30, 2017). The buzz, the ding, the vibration are deftly conceived to command our attention and that of our pocketbooks. Some even express concern that technology alters how we relate to one another. Sherry Turkle, for instance, has carefully examined the impact of social media on human interaction, sadly concluding that as a society we now engage less in face-to-face conversation, preferring the distance and control that technological mediation affords (Turkle 2012, 2015, 2016). At the extreme, persons highly dependent on screens and keypads have lost the ability to read facial expressions and thus to interpret human emotions; subsequently, they no longer experience empathy. According to Turkle, such a "flight from face-to-face conversation" loses some of the crucial ingredients of human exchange "where human meanings are understood, where empathy is engaged" (Turkle 2016, 29). Because face-to-face conversation leaves us vulnerable, open to "unpredictable and self-revealing" encounters in which "intimacy flourishes and empathy thrives," we prefer the safe distance of technology. The latter offers control and increased manipulation of human exchange, giving expression to "the robotic moment" capable of erasing the vulnerable uncertainties of real relationship (Turkle 2016, 33).

Yet the accommodating user-friendliness of sophisticated gadgetry that offers companionship as well as efficiency proves difficult to resist. Won over by the reigning ideology, we often cannot distinguish between Marcuse's "true" and "false" needs, but instead allow an insidious, disguised form of totalitarianism to inhere. Programmed to honor and pursue what is in fact unnecessary, we mistake an authoritarian system for "freedom" and succumb to the neoliberal claim that market ideology promotes "individuality." Marcuse writes:

> The organism is thus being preconditioned for the spontaneous acceptance of what is offered. Inasmuch as the greater liberty involves a contraction rather than extension and development of instinctual needs, it works *for* rather than *against* the status quo of general repression ...The latter appears to be a vital factor in the making of the authoritarian personality of our time.
> MARCUSE 1964, 74

Thus, while we conceive of the free market as the hallmark of American civil liberties, Marcuse invites us to perceive it as the obverse, and to read "totalitarian" where we typically see "freedom." He thereby underscores the insidious nature of authoritarian rule that deftly disguises itself as progressive: "For 'totalitarian' is not only a terroristic political coordination of society, but also a non-terroristic economic-technical coordination which operates through the manipulation of needs by vested interests" (Marcuse 1964, 3). To be sure, the cleverness of modern inventions lies not only in their persuasive sales pitch and claim on our pocketbooks, but also in their ability to insinuate themselves so profoundly into our lives as to become an extension of our bodies, our minds, and the way we perform the simplest tasks. The culture of Facebook, for instance, eradicates the distinctions between privacy and the public sphere, since, so often, private matters constitute the subject matter of Facebook conversations. "There is no space that is not invaded and taken over by social demands" write Imaculada Kangussu, Filip Kovacevic, and Andrew T. Lama, for "[t]he individual is forced to identify with society even in the utmost recesses of his or her soul" (Kangussu, Kovacevic, Lama 2017, 135).

While many advancements in science and technology unquestionably produce a more comfortable and efficient life for those who can afford them, Marcuse invokes a cautioning tone when the former simply reduces to the latter. Social media is now the lifeline for many, and its seductive, pharmacotic attributes oscillate between sustaining umbilical chord and toxic addiction. Sometimes "more" equates with less; other times it spells disaster. When what is truly good—social justice, democratic principles, beauty, peace—is vexingly confused with what is simply "new," "progressive," or "advanced," society has lost the ability to imagine its own reconfiguration in accordance with its deepest values. If we fail to query the 150 cell phone checks in the name of staying informed, we have erased the critical faculty capable of imagining a society less mediated by technological rationality. The never-ending text message, the ubiquitous hash tag, the YouTube video gone viral; in the worst-case scenario, we cannot distinguish Baudrillard's hyperreal from reality itself: if it's gadgetry, it's good (Baudrillard 1994). We play into our false needs since "the technological controls appear to be the very embodiment of Reason for the benefit of all social groups and interests—to such an extent that all contradiction seems irrational and counteraction impossible" (Marcuse 1964, 9).

Not entirely impossible, however. Acknowledging the atrophied state of the critical faculty presents a teachable moment for educators, a pedagogical opening that can raise awareness about the different cognitive functions at work (or not) in our technologically sophisticated, commercially overrun society. Because students' lives are mired in technology, bombarded by commercialism, and deeply enmeshed in the material goals of the American Dream, there exists plenty of material for educators to work with when introducing Marcuse's critique. The thralldom of the hyperreal itself ensures that class time devoted to the pharmacotic power of consumerist society invariably gets students' attention. Their very love of social media guarantees that the "rational character of its irrationality" when offered as a lesson plan will pique their curiosity (Marcuse 1964, 9). Hence the ingrained contradictions that Marcuse laments can function as a springboard for pedagogical strategies.

## 2 Syncopating with the Hyperreal

Students are well aware of how subliminal advertising, clever marketing strategies, and the power of commercial hype proves persuasive, inducing us to acquire material goods and incur debts that we could just as easily live without. Subsequently, the pedagogical room for maneuver particular to this generation centers not around commercial values per se; rather it is information technology, the manner in which "progress" is packaged in the form of social media that occupies a special place in today's ideological landscape. Herein lies the power to reach and to teach, since technology's pharmacotic allure proves integral to students' way of relating to the world. iPhones, iPads, computers, and other electronic devices provide information, do research, help with homework, give driving directions, and respond to our questions. They talk to us, give advice, promise friendship, cater to individualized tastes, and help us stay "in touch." They claim to enrich our lives immeasurably and widen our sphere of influence, thereby allowing access to sources of happiness that we could otherwise never tap. Their friendly voices even admonish us when we lose our temper, for Siri has been known to say, "I'll pretend I didn't hear that."

There can be no doubt that modern technology embodies some of the ideals of an enlightened world as promised in seventeenth- and eighteenth-century philosophy. In "Beyond One-Dimensionality," Andrew Feenberg convincingly argues that Marcuse himself saw value in *technē*, the technological base of society that can improve our lives by "rejoining imagination and reason in the creation of a new technological base" (Feenberg 2107, 233). It is therefore not a forgone conclusion that the advancements will turn back on themselves in Frankenstein fashion, controlling the intellect that conceived it, terrorizing the world that it was designed to improve. When "theoretical" purpose is in fact joined to "practical" means, much good can come of technological advancement. "The cognitive achievements made possible by the destruction of the traditional concept of essence are undeniable," Feenberg writes, "but so is the danger of spiritual and material extermination represented by a technology unrestrained by any limits" (Feenberg, 2017, 233).

Yet such unrestraint is the norm, and it goes by the name of "progress." It is interpreted as singularly rational by virtue of all that it makes possible, but where is the *qualitative* analysis of its articulation? Indeed, we can be sure that the oppositional imagination has atrophied when we stop questioning the value of our "enlightened" world and confuse the means with the end, the answer with the question. Why is it desirable to have so many "friends" on Facebook? Why is it important to be in constant "touch" with people through texting? Has shopping online truly enriched our lives? Checking our cellphones 150 times a day suggests that a conclusion has been accepted as indisputable rather than offered as a question. We have confused a *fact* with a *value*, pursuing a false need whose instant feedback obscures the destructive dimension of frenzied thinking. Beset by "cognitive devastation" thanks to the beautiful siren song of modern day gadgetry, we may even lack the ability to realize that critique has been extinguished, for contravening arguments are too often labeled "biased" (Kangussu, Kovacevic, Lamas 2017, 135). "This is the basis of Marcuse's critique of what he calls 'technological rationality,'" Feenberg writes, "a form of rationality that grasps its objects on purely functional terms without presupposing any goal except its own application and extension" (Kangussu, Kovacevic, Lamas 2017, 232).

Like his colleagues Max Horkheimer and Theodor Adorno, Marcuse thus laments our inability to distinguish enlightenment from myth, for the "curse of irresistible progress is irresistible regression" (Horkheimer, Adorno 2002, 28). And had he witnessed the texting ritual, the incessant tweeting, the voluminous Facebook "friendships" that claim so much of our students' energies, he would surely have spotted a teachable moment upon entering the classroom. Sadly, I now rarely ask my undergraduates to quiet down in order to begin class, since students are not speaking with one another. Only infrequently does the former chatter that animated the classroom prevail, and the absence of conversation makes me wonder whether they know each other at all. In solemn silence, every head is bent over a cellphone screen while students' fingers hurriedly work the keyboard with amazing dexterity. A hushed seriousness prevails. The fact that this inheres in my undergraduate but not graduate classes indicates that the deep attachment to technology which threatens to supplant friendship and conversation is generational. The boisterousness that typically reigns in my graduate seminar as I enter the classroom is therefore heartening, for the spirited cacophony suggests that they have been engaged in conversation for some time.

The disturbing silence among undergraduates nevertheless allows me to use texting, tweeting, Facebook posting, and selfie-taking as a pedagogical tool by introducing Marcuse's concept of "repressive desublimation," the notion that our freedom and agency have been colonized more than we know, that even when we believe ourselves free, we play into a script written for us. To suggest that Apple, Sprint, Verizon, and other carriers engage in a coopting mechanism that liquidates critical awareness raises the possibility that technological developments do not simply equate with human progress. Leaving aside the question of the carriers' intentions and the many benefits of communication technology as a whole, students are drawn into a conversation about whether a cellphone upgrade doesn't in fact set them *back*, rob them of experience, and dupe them. The latter lends credence to the Marxian premise that the commodity assumes an aggrandized, transcendental life form only to the degree that the worker/owner/operator is diminished and impoverished. Money "grows" and "earns interest" while we slave away; Siri talks to me while taking time away from my family, friends, and interests.

Herein lies a concrete example of the fetishized commodity, the simple item for sale whose emotional, social, and cultural weight has grown exponentially out of proportion to its real value. In *Capital*, Marx writes that whereas a commodity initially appears "trivial," just an item for purchase, in its fetishized, overvalued state it becomes "a very strange thing, abounding in metaphysical subtleties and theological niceties" (Marx 1990, 163). This suggestion that the cellphone has assumed undue importance in students' lives, allowing an inanimate object to command our attention and do our thinking for us, clarifies for them the tantalizingly fine line between empowered liberation and stealthy colonization. The line is indeed fine, pharmacotic to an extreme, and this ensures a battery of teachable moments that go to the heart of what students value. It causes them to consider whether their very desires have been manufactured in ways that benefit corporations rather than human need; perhaps their "individuality" is mass-produced. In *Eros and Civilization, A Philosophical Inquiry Into Freud,* Marcuse insists that "neither [a person's] desires nor [her]/his alteration of reality are henceforth [her]/his own: they are now 'organized' by... society. And this 'organization' represses and transubstantiates [her]/his original instinctual needs" (Marcuse 1974, 14–15). This control over our needs and manipulation of our instincts underscores the intellectual challenge for which Marxian analytic tools prove useful. For at the extreme, this lack of alternative interpretation signals an utterly moribund ability to engage in critique: everything is affirmative and self-referential, everything upholds what *is* rather than what might be.

Students' ears therefore perk up when they hear the claim that technologically granted "freedom" and "agency" may in fact represent cooptation. There is much to consider in asking whether being in touch is always desirable, beginning with the question of what it means to "be in touch." Asking students to consider whether the iPhone's texting feature has prefabricated and thus colonized how we communicate gets them talking, as do questions such as "When is more actually less?," "Why take so many selfies?" and "What is a Facebook 'friendship'?" Taking time to consider that perhaps our thinking has been appropriated for someone else's gain generates lively discussion, all the while affirming the pertinence of Marxian ideas to contemporary situations.

Certainly the ongoing belief in the American Dream and wishful thinking that it generates explains in part this devotion to screens, texts, hashtags, and the instant gratifications of a computerized world. After all, technological fluency insinuates a relationship with hugely successful innovators such as Steve Jobs, Bill Gates, and Mark Zuckerberg, thereby conferring a prosperous, up-and-coming image on those who purchase their products. Technology constructs an image that naturally appeals to many students given that it implies phenomenal success even in the absence of a college degree (Zuckerberg received an honorary degree after dropping out of Harvard). Cellphones connect us to corporate America; computers keep us attached, informed, plugged into news, to shopping options, celebrity gossip, Wall Street and Madison Avenue. Students' belief in the American Dream, often undaunted by a realistic assessment of whether they can achieve that level of success, is what Lauren Berlant terms their sense "self-interruption." Credulous vis-à-vis rags-to-riches stories thanks to the far-reaching hype of technology, they often view themselves as occupying a temporary in-between state, a hiatus of incompleteness that allows them to "ride the wave of the system...to syncopate with it...held in a relation of reciprocity" (Berlant 2011, 27).

The musical, rhythmic implications contained in the allusion to syncopation suggest a degree of pleasure and even delight in longing for an out-of-reach lifestyle, which students are programmed to desire. Syncopation invokes creativity, innovation, dancing, and fun, an activity that unfortunately sustains self-interruption rather than reflection and social consciousness. When the prevailing system causes us to continue to hope that quixotic, unrealizable aspirations may materialize, even when the opposing odds are overwhelming, we often dismiss this failure as an interim period, a hiatus that doesn't align with who we really are. We succumb to "the practices of self-interruption, self-suspension, and self-abeyance" that alone indicate how our current situation fails to represent who we wish we were: the success I'll become, the money I'll make, the famous person I'm evolving into (Berlant 2011, 27). Many forms of social media demand a happy face and, in linking us to Jobs, Gates, Zuckerberg, and others, the delights of syncopation divert our attention away from the suffering that the American Dream so often delivers, both at home and abroad, creating instead "a steady hum of livable crisis ordinariness" (Berlant 2011, 196). False needs become fun; the hyperreal diverts students' energies towards things that captivate and subdue. What pedagogical tools can help educators sharpen the remaining critical sensibility that this steady hum dulls?

## 3   The Great Refusal, Redux

Surely mindless syncopation does not exhaust our students' involvement with social media. In pharmacotic fashion, their immersion in technology also operates as a vector for political engagement that directly addresses Berlant's cruel optimism. Because technology facilitates communication within communities that it itself has helped establish, there exist more positive dimensions of its dialectical nature: namely, that it can inspire political activism by informing users about a larger social reality from which their busy lives might otherwise keep them. Here, the obverse of the hyperreal is at play, for technology is capable of awakening students to a harsh reality and often solicits their commitment to an important social cause. It provides them with the information necessary to not only raise their critical awareness about the social sphere, but transform this awareness into praxis: action in the streets, on the university campus, at the town hall meeting, at city hall.

Kangussu, Kovacevic, and Lamas correctly identify various instances of young persons' social engagement that have made an impact on society. They cite the Occupy Movement, World Social Forum, Tahir Square, and Black Lives Matter as examples of a changing ethos, and witness a "new sensibility" emerging among younger persons eager to expose injustice, hypocrisy, and exploitation and to see political change. To these examples I add the Million Woman March, Standing Rock, as well as the "Reclaiming Democracy Teach-Ins" held on my campus: lectures and open forum workshops organized around the themes of discrimination, fascism, mass media, and collective action. Contrary to the claim that young persons inhabit an aimless space of delusional self-interruption as they await a rags-to-riches watershed, these events underscore the passion, commitment, and intellectual curiosity that drives them to willingly engage and even to put themselves at risk for principles in which they believe. These events cannot be described as mere political theater or narcissistic posturing. Rather, they play out the other side of the pharmacotic dialectic, the beneficial side of technology's reach that is antagonistically linked to its coopting, repressive element. They dramatize what Christopher Fuchs deems "the antagonism of for-profit and not-for-profit (social) media, the antagonism of voluntarism and vulnerability of social-media-donation models, the antagonism of state-funded stability and control of alternative social media, the antagonism of for-profit organization and loss of autonomy...." (Fuchs 2017, 254). The younger generation participates in these events out of political conviction and social ideals (and yes, for the fun of it), and often experiences harassment, even arrest (http://www.huffingtonpost.com/2013/05/23/occupy-wall-street-arrests_n_3326640.html). At the teach-ins on my campus, for instance, students' questions and comments revealed a deep interest in the topics discussed, giving pause to the assertion that their intellects have been wholly ravaged by "cognitive devastation."

Kangussu, Kovacevic, and Lamas employ these examples as evidence of the hopeful dimension in Marcuse's thinking, a dimension that attenuates his more pessimistic observations by insisting that a forward-looking, imaginative energy still survives. The creative impulse ensures that a critique of society remains possible even in the face of a pervasive, damaging one-dimensionality marked by commodity fetishism, for the ability to conjure an alternative society remains intact so long as the imagination is at work. "Marcuse insists that imagination contains not only the backward-looking but also the forward-looking dimension," they explain, highlighting the power of the imagination to express refusal, to reject acquiescence in what is rather than in what could be (Kangussu, Kovacevic, Lamas 2017, 143).

Here, we must of course distinguish between the forms of transformative art that Marcuse identifies and the reality of social media, for surely the sublimating potential that he perceives in "a poem, play, novel, etc." differs radically from the highly commercial nature of, say, the internet (Marcuse 1978, 8). Marcuse found transformative power in art forms that tended to be far more esoteric than social media, catering to a rarified sensibility rather than to the immediate, self-gratifying impulses of the general public. Yet if we consider the precise aspects of art that allow sublimation rather than confirmation to take place, namely "a reshaping of language, perception, and understanding so that they reveal the essence of reality in its appearance," we see clearly how today's technology might allow for social transformation as well (Marcuse 1978, 8). Surely there is a great deal of creativity and imagination at work in all forms of social media, and given that these qualities are key to transformation, today's technology may just as easily participate in social *change* as in social conformity. Working the web will never equate to seeing a Brecht play, but it can engage the imagination just as thoroughly, albeit in a different genre.

The above-mentioned examples of social upheaval give witness to the imagination's survival amidst forces that would rather see its critical energies founder. Technology can thus prove an ally in political activism, and while some of its many attributes may weaken the intellect's attention span and encourage complacency with the status quo, the other side of its pharmacotic nature creates synergy among enthused, boisterous, often irreverent young activists. Forms of refusal are underway that make use of twenty-first century methods of community building.

In *The Aesthetic Dimension: Toward a Critique of Marxist Aesthetics*, Marcuse therefore expounds on the importance of imagination in sustaining critique. Originally published in 1977, this text confounds Berlant's disheartening claims by refusing the assertion that mindless syncopation constitutes the only response proffered by the younger generation. Because the imagination always retains the ability to propose alternatives to the existing order, aesthetic expression in any society functions as a repository for the values that are currently repressed. Today as in the mid-twentieth century, art in all its myriad forms—high, low, digital, performance, commercial—occupies a privileged position given that it nurtures a countercultural movement and thus provides an arena where the un-colonized, undomesticated instincts can express themselves freely. While art always belongs in part to the society that produced it, it simultaneously escapes the grasp of that society by allowing critique to be sublimated in an acceptable, non-threatening form. Marcuse writes:

> [T]he radical qualities of art, that is to say, its indictment of the established reality and its invocation of the beautiful image (*schöner Schein*) of liberation are grounded precisely in the dimensions where art *transcends* its social determination and emancipates itself from the given universe of discourse and behavior while preserving its overwhelming presence.
> MARCUSE 1978, 6

Admittedly, like Theodor Adorno who also promoted the emancipatory powers of aesthetics, Marcuse also acknowledges that any artwork contains a conservative pull given that it bears the society that produced it. Even the most radical exponents of the avant garde declare their indebtedness to the status quo despite themselves, for the means by which they are a produced, marketed, and distributed render them beholden to the powers that be. Even when its very purpose is indictment, art "stands under the law of the given" (Marcuse 1978, 11). And as Adorno's scathing criticism of the culture industry reveals, "the given" of society proves adept at colonizing our maverick impulses such that even our creative energies funnel back into the mainstream. It erases the difference between consumers and producers of culture, and orchestrates a mass-produced society that cleverly delivers conformity even among those who think themselves renegade. Adorno goes so far as to say that the culture industry operates "under the sign of terror," for its powers of persuasion are indeed convincing given the ridicule and opprobrium visited upon those who transgress its norms (Adorno 2001, 97).

Yet for Adorno and Marcuse alike, a hopeful dimension remains given that the aesthetic realm draws not on careful execution, meticulous conformity to rules, or adherence to set theorems, but in its use of the imagination whose very nature is generative. And while technology today surely does not exhibit the esoteric refinement of the oppositional art that interested Adorno and Marcuse, it nevertheless elicits an innovative resourcefulness and the desire to experience something new. The extensive reach of repressive desublimation is thus attenuated, for Marcuse himself acknowledges that the conservative pull of art (or Facebook, or tweeting, or anything that draws on the imagination) is thwarted by the alterity that it makes possible. Hence even the most mainstream aesthetic expression such as a hackneyed situation comedy or predictable Hollywood movie may nurture the oppositional imagination given that they draw out the inventive powers of the mind. Marcuse thus affirms that, "art...is committed to an emancipation of sensibility, imagination, and reason in all spheres of subjectivity and objectivity" (Marcuse 1978, 9).

At first blush it seems trivializing to state that the Great Refusal today reappears in the guise of texting, tweeting, Facebook posting, and selfies. To argue that Marcuse's insightful analysis of repressive desublimation is again given cultural purchase in the act of studying screens and posting inventive acronyms seems reductive: OMG, is this how revolutions are fought? Yet when the examples of the Occupy Movement, World Social Forum, Tahir Square, Black Lives Matter, the Million Woman March, and Reclaiming Democracy are proffered, social media suddenly assumes a serious dimension. Social media is the world our students inhabit and the language that they speak. Why not teach them Marcuse by making use of its many points of entry?

## Bibliography

Adorno, T. (2001) *The Culture Industry: Selected Essays on Mass Culture*. Bernstein J.M.(ed.), New York: Routledge.

Baudrillard, J. (1994) *Simulacra and Simulation*. Trans. S.F. Glaser, Ann Arbor, MI: University of Michigan Press.

Berlant, L. (2011) *Cruel Optimism*. Durham, NC: Duke University Press.

Brown, W. (2015) *Undoing the Demos: Neoliberalism's Stealth Revolution*, Brooklyn, NY: Zone Books.

Derrida, J. (1981) *Dissemination*. Trans. B. Johnson. Chicago: University of Chicago Press.

Feenberg, A. (2017) "Beyond One-Dimensionality." In Lamas, A., Wolfson, T. Funke, P.N. (eds.) *The Great Refusal: Herbert Marcuse and Contemporary Social Movements*. Philadelphia: Temple University Press, 229–240.

Fuchs, C. (2017) "Herbert Marcuse and the Dialectics of Social Media." In Lamas, A., Wolfson, T. Funke, P.N. (eds.) *The Great Refusal: Herbert Marcuse and Contemporary Social Movements*. Philadelphia: Temple University Press, 241–257.

Horkheimer, M., Adorno, T. (2002) *Dialectic of Enlightenment: Philosophical Fragments*. Trans. E. Jephcott. Stanford, CA: Stanford University Press.

http://www.huffingtonpost.com/2013/05/23/occupy-wall-street-arrests_n_3326640.html.

http://www.redcrowmarketing.com/2015/09/10/many-ads-see-one-day/.

https://www.youtube.com/watch?v=MvgN5gCuLac.

Kangussu, I., Kovacevic, F., Lamas, A. (2017) Mic Check! The New Sensibility Speaks. In Lamas, A., Wolfson, T. Funke, P.N. (eds.) *The Great Refusal: Herbert Marcuse and Contemporary Social Movements*. Philadelphia: Temple University Press, 132–156.

Kondo, M. (2014) *The Life-Changing Magic of Tidying Up: the Japanese Art of Decluttering and Organizing*. Berkeley, CA: Ten Speed Press.

Lamas, A.T., Wolfson, T. Peter N. Funke, P.N. (eds.) (2017) *The Great Refusal: Herbert Marcuse and Contemporary Social Movements*. Philadelphia: Temple University Press.

Marcuse, H. (1971) *An Essay on Liberation*. Boston, MA: Beacon.
Marcuse, H. (1974) *Eros and Civilization: A Philosophical Inquiry Into Freud*. Boston: Beacon.
Marcuse, H. (1964) *One-Dimensional Man*. Boston: Beacon Press.
Marcuse, H. (1999) *Reason and Revolution: Hegel and the Rise of Social Theory*. Amherst, NY: Humanity Books.
Marcuse, H. (1978) *The Aesthetic Dimension: Toward a Critique of Marxist Aesthetics*. Trans. E. Sherover, H. Marcuse. Boston: Beacon.
Marx, K. (1990) *Capital: A Critique of Political Economy*, Vol. 1. Trans. B. Fowkes, New York: Penguin.
Miles, M. (2012) *Herbert Marcuse: An Aesthetics of Liberation*. London: Pluto Press.
Shames, L. (2011) "The More Factor." In Maasik, S., Solomon, J. (eds) *Signs of Life in the USA, Readings on Popular Culture for Writers*. New York, NY: St. Martin's Press, 90–96.
Turkle, S. (2012) *Alone Together: Why We Expect More From Technology and Less From Each Other*. New York: Basic Books.
Turkle, S. (2016) "The Empathy Gap." *Psychotherapy Networker Magazine* (November 1): 29–54.
Turkle, S. (2016) *Reclaiming Conversation: The Power of Talk in a Digital Age*. Penguin Books.
Turkle, S. (2015) "Stop Googling. Let's Talk." *The New York Times* (September 26).
Weeks, K. (2011) *The Problem with Work: Feminism, Marxism, Antiwork Politics, and Postwork Imaginaries*. Durham and London: Duke University Press.
Wiggerhaus, R. (1994) *The Frankfurt School: Its History, Theories, and Political Significance*. Trans. M. Robertson. Cambridge, MA: the MIT Press.
Wise, K. (2017) "Your Cellphone Is Trying To Control Your Life." *PBS Newshour*, January 30, 2017.

CHAPTER 7

# Deep Critique: Critical Pedagogy, Marxism, and Feminist Standpoint Theory in the Corporate Classroom

*Allan Ardill*

## 1    Introduction

Inequality is a continuing feature of the capitalist world order despite booms and busts, and despite the waxing and waning of the welfare state. It has been this way since the industrial revolution and the shift from feudalism to capitalism. Over the same period of time science and technology have made enormous strides (not always good) and yet in social theory, public policy, and politics, the strides turned into circles. The paradox of legitimation following the postmodern turn, and the material and ideological pervasiveness of neoliberalism, gave rise to identity politics. Identity politics has been unable to grapple with growing inequality and the crises of world systems be they wars, the environment, or human crises. Without suggesting that ideas let alone university education can solve these tumultuous problems it remains the case that universities have some responsibility for the inability of social theory to grapple with these circumstances.

What does this suggest for those of us in the university system? It suggests a need to invigorate critical pedagogy despite the hostility of the corporate classroom. It suggests that through our research and teaching practice there is a need to explore ways of subverting the corporate university, pushing through the postmodern turn, re-centering Marxist critique, and problematizing the pluralism of identity politics to rebuild a culture appropriate to a more just world system. As someone who identifies with Feminist Standpoint Theory (FST) I engage with Marxism not just because of an historical connection between the two but because Marxism is essential to an understanding of class inequality and to what I teach – property law.

This chapter relates my approach to teaching compulsory property law courses with the aim of producing graduates with a propensity for deep critique by engaging with Marxism and Feminist Standpoint Theory. Deep critique is my attempt to practice what is described in the literature as critical pedagogy. While deep critique falls short of an extensive program of critical pedagogy, it shares the aims of critical pedagogies to produce students capable of critical self-reflection so that inequality and oppression can be confronted, perhaps overcome.

The chapter begins with an outline of inequality and the problems facing the world and the conditions giving rise to the corporate university before turning attention to critical pedagogy and its propensity to address conditions of inequality. It is argued that critical pedagogy needs to re-centre Marxist critique in order to grapple with the vacuousness of postmodern identity politics. To do this requires the "ruthless criticism" Marx (1843) described in a letter to Arnold Ruge, and fundamental to that practice is critical self-reflection of the Adorno and Freire kind. The chapter ends by linking these together with my experience of deep critique in the corporate university. It concludes that the greatest challenge to teaching in the corporate classroom is remaining authentic as a human being to a project of addressing inequality, and reconciling through both dialogue and action one's own privilege relative to others oppressed by that privilege.

## 2   Inequality and the Corporate Classroom

The OECD (2015) has cautioned against growing economic inequality as a drag on the global economy. Piketty's (2014, 571–77) comprehensive review of capital concludes that the biggest threat to western democracy is the extreme inequality that exists according to the historical formula that returns to capital grow faster than returns to labour and growth in outputs. Marxists have long recognised this as the extraction of surplus value (Singh 2017, 418–24). For those who live economic inequality, the daily deprivation and trauma that brings, means addressing inequality is all the more urgent.

Beyond the borders of the affluent west, the majority of the worlds people fare significantly worse off than those marginalised in the west. Meanwhile we teach a generation of students facing low wage growth and increasing casualization of their labour whether as students funding their way through university or later as graduates. Students face a global future where class mobility is more closely tied to exchange rates and inheritance than it is to individual merit. Students face challenges posed by an increasing concentration of wealth, privatisation of commons, global pollution and climate change. For Giroux (2013):

> Free market fundamentalists now wage a full-fledged attack on the social contract, the welfare state, any notion of the common good, and those public spheres not yet defined by commercial interests. Within neoliberal

ideology, the market becomes the template for organizing the rest of society. Everyone is now a customer or client, and every relationship is ultimately judged in bottom-line, cost-effective terms. Freedom is no longer about equality, social justice, or the public welfare, but about the trade in goods, financial capital, and commodities.

Students are "prepared" for these challenges by a privatised corporate education system that is increasingly tethered to neo-liberal capitalism whose emphasis is on reproducing existing conditions for profit while marketing student choice rather than questioning hegemony.

It is a system marketed to students on the promise they will become effective communicators, entrepreneurially individual, technically adept, capable of critical thinking and working in a team, and most often featured in marketing campaigns, "job-ready." The corporate university and the corporate school have dehumanised education:

> ... at the heart of this market driven regime is a form of instrumental rationality that quantifies all forms of meaning, privatizes social relations, dehistoricizes memory, and substitutes training for education while reducing the obligations of citizenship to the act of consuming. The production of knowledge in schools today is instrumental, wedded to objective outcomes, privatized, and is largely geared to produce consuming subjects. The organizational structures that make such knowledge possible enact serious costs on any viable notion of critical education and critical pedagogy. Teachers are deskilled, largely reduced to teaching for the test, business culture organizes the governance structures of schooling, knowledge is viewed as a commodity, and students are treated reductively as both consumers and workers.
> GIROUX 2013

The culture is one where students are not asked to understand and question this context but to take responsibility for it as individuals. In this highly competitive commodified education system with fewer prospects that academic performance will lead to full-time continuing graduate employment, it should be no surprise that students suffer increasing rates of anxiety and depression (Baron 2013, 276–79), and are increasingly sceptical of institutions other than the trusted logos and brands selling them an identity.

These conditions mean that students have become commodities themselves such that they are subject to the vagaries of global capital flows, market risks, and bear disproportionally the losses externalised by global capitalism. Locke's vision for property has meant wage-earners and sub-contractors bear the risks and excesses of capital without sharing proportionally in the benefits of trickle-down economics. From a pedagogical perspective our students are cultured into becoming self-absorbed utility maximisers well before they arrive at university. This is necessary if they are to navigate the conditions imposed upon them as individuals. They are made into solipsists where the only perceived truth is their individual atomised experience of the world, which is confirmed in silos of social media that echo this reality or their aspirations. As solipsists students are ill-equipped to grapple with their own circumstances, their education, their futures, let alone interrogate the conditions producing inequality and oppression.

The tragedy is that if students continue to be cultured in this way, who is going to address a world plagued by extremes of class inequality, abuses of human rights, poverty and hunger, war, colonial rule, and the prospect of environmental apocalypse? What should we be doing in the academy about this situation? What is our role in shaping the future? As Adorno (2005, 187) asked "What is to be done?"

It would be a mistake to presume that what happens in and around the classroom can be a panacea for these conditions or is solely responsible for making a better world. As Gerrard (2013, 186) reflected:

> I find myself increasingly unsure about the potential for education to alter long-standing social hierarchies of power. As much as education offers powerful possibilities for social action, systems of education have also played an unmistakable role in maintaining structures of inequality. Decades of work in the history and sociology of education clearly demonstrates that, in Basil Bernstein's words (1970, 344–47), "education cannot compensate for society," and that in many cases it compounds existing inequalities, exclusions, and disadvantages.

However that cannot be an excuse for acquiescence. Instead critical pedagogy affords two possibilities for a better world. The first possibility is the pre-emptive need identified by Adorno (2005, 191–204) to "prevent another Auschwitz", and the second possibility is the need for revolutionary cultural synthesis identified by Freire (1994, 157) to make a better world. In each case, "... it is therefore essential to have an increasingly critical knowledge of the current historical context, the view of the world held by the people, the principal contradiction of society, and the principal aspect of that contradiction" (Freire 1994, 157). In other words, preventing another Auschwitz or making a better world requires critical pedagogy.

For these reasons I am developing what I call "deep critique" which is my way of practising critical pedagogy as a means of preparing property law students to grapple with these conditions in the hope of a better future. Here I want to elaborate on the importance of Marx to critical pedagogy while differentiating it from the vocational critical thinking that has become fashionable in the corporate university. Long before the recent neo-liberal turn to vocational critical thinking (Davies 2016), Marxists, Feminists, and Critical Race activists were championing critical pedagogies.[1] The difference between vocational critical thinking and critical pedagogy goes to the heart of whether or not these sorts of questions can be addressed. Also, as argued below, critical pedagogy must reconnect its fragmented pedagogies through what Marx (1843) described as ruthless critical self-reflection, as opposed to liberal pluralism, if it is to have any effect beyond the fragmentation of identity politics. In saying this, there is no formula for teaching critical pedagogy other than a commitment to continuing the project commenced by Marx and taken forward by many others since.

## 3   Critical Pedagogy

Giroux scoffs at the idea there is an authentic form of critical pedagogy to be discovered in a mystical founder. He prefers the view that it is a movement based on praxis and for this reason it is a work in progress:

> … it is best to think of critical pedagogy as an ongoing project instead of a fixed set of references or prescriptive set of practices - put bluntly, it is not a method.
> GIROUX 2013

However, when Giroux said there is no correct methodology for critical pedagogy he did not mean that it is possible to do critical pedagogy by extricating its revolutionary intent. To do this is not to practice critical pedagogy but to teach critical thinking. Critical thinking is a necessary skill and indeed a component of critical pedagogy but it is not concerned with addressing oppression, rather equipping students with important life/workplace skills and innovation within the existing world order.

---

1   For example, in 1848 Marx and Engels (1998, 60) wrote: "And your education! Is not that also social, and determined by the social conditions under which you educate, by the intervention, direct or indirect, of society, by means of schools, etc.? The Communists have not invented the intervention of society in education; they do but seek to alter the character of that intervention, and to rescue education from the influence of the ruling class."

The possibility of a critical pedagogy begins with Marx's (1843) recognition that revolution requires material action as well as contesting ideas through ruthless criticism:

> If we have no business with the construction of the future or with organizing it for all time, there can still be no doubt about the task confronting us at present: the ruthless criticism of the existing order, ruthless in that it will shrink neither from its own discoveries, nor from conflict with the powers that be.

This is what Giroux meant. He was saying a critical pedagogy does not seek to remain faithful to a model if that model stifles the emancipation of the oppressed. It does not mean however, that Marxism is abandoned because it was imbued with enlightenment universalism (Traverso 1999, 21) or because it is incorrectly blamed for the Soviet experience, or more recently depicted by neoliberalism and postmodernism as another ideology. Similarly, to de-emphasise other so-called radical critiques of capitalism (e.g. critical legal studies, critical race theories, radical feminism, etc.) because they may appear controversial is to water down both the efficacy and essence of critical pedagogy (Appleby et al. 2013, 351). This argument is developed further below. For now, while it is important to avoid romanticizing Marxism, it remains absolutely integral to a better understanding "of the intersections between the existing schooling experiences of working-class communities and the potential for a radical or emancipatory orientation in working-class education" (Gerrard 2013, 191).

Critical pedagogy means learning from the past, listening to and working with the oppressed, and ruthlessly critiquing the existing world order. This is not possible if critique is reduced to critical thinking, or moments of individual political identity instead of understanding systems of power. To see gender inequality without recognising class and race inequality, or to see race inequality without gender and class inequality is to make the mistake of reductionism. It is akin to failing to see the forest for the trees. As Sengupta (2006, 635) has argued:

> Men do not oppress women because they are men; they do so because one of the forms in which oppression gets articulated happens to be patriarchy, which in turn has relationships with the ways in which forms of control over sexual or reproductive agency are tied to patterns of control over scarce resources. The factors that impel patriarchy are not unrelated to the factors that control other forms of agency in other resource and energy allocation and distribution scenarios in the material world; these can be and are inflected with tropes of ethnicity, race, caste, and the one that we most often forget to mention these days – class.

The common thread linking Marxism, Feminisms, critical race theories, and other critiques are the conditions that sustain and reproduce them. Emancipation is unachievable while fragmentation persists and in the absence of critical self-reflection. Freire recognised this because of his experience of life and his place in history. Freire developed his thinking through revolutionary praxis and by working with the poor and illiterate (McLaren 2000, 146) to produce several ground-breaking works, among them *Pedagogy of the Oppressed*. *Pedagogy of the Oppressed* analyzes the dialectical relationship between domination and oppression in the context of the historical development of capitalist education, against the backdrop of (un)successful revolutions (McLaren 2000, 146).

Freire (1994, 161), having observed the failures of revolutions maintained the vision of hope by learning from the past and combining it with critical reflection and dialogic action, or dialogic cultural synthesis. For Freire (1994, 30) the "central problem is this":

> How can the oppressed, as divided, unauthentic beings, participate in developing the pedagogy of their liberation? Only as they discover themselves to be "hosts" of the oppressor can they contribute to the midwifery of their liberating pedagogy. As long as they live in the duality in which *to be* is *to be like,* and *to be like* is *to be like the oppressor,* this contribution is impossible. The pedagogy of the oppressed is an instrument for their critical discovery that both they and their oppressors are manifestations of dehumanization.

Freire represents one of two discernible critical pedagogies, and was influenced by "Amilcar Cabral, a revolutionary leader who helped to liberate Guinea-Bissau from Portuguese domination in the 1960s" (McLaren 2000, 146). Freire like

> Cabral had understood that the political education of the peasantry had to be achieved first or else the revolution would be short-lived. Cabral always stressed that the political struggle was paramount over the military struggle, and that the guerrillas were to assume the role of the servants of the people.
> MCLAREN 2000, 146

From this experience it follows that authentic revolution is contingent upon cultural transformation in which leaders and teachers learn from the people, become integrated with the people, and do not impose their models:

> In their stead, there are actors who critically analyze reality (never separating this analysis from action) and intervene as Subjects in the historical process. Instead of following predetermined plans, leaders and people, mutually identified, together create the guidelines of their action. In this synthesis, leaders and people are somehow reborn in new knowledge and new action. Knowledge of the alienated culture leads to transforming action resulting in a culture which is being freed from alienation. The more sophisticated knowledge of the leaders is remade in the empirical knowledge of the people, while the latter is refined by the former.
>
> FREIRE 1994, 162

Clearly, this is very different from the history of countries like the former Soviet Union, China, and North Korea, which resulted in state dictatorships, and authoritarian capitalism in the case of China.

A second strand of critical pedagogy emerging from Marx's ruthless criticism and in response to history post-Marx was that developed by the Frankfurt School and in particular by Adorno. Adorno like Freire emphasised critical reflection albeit with a tendency to prevent barbarianism as opposed to a project of hope. For Adorno (2005, 203), "All political instruction finally should be centred upon the idea that Auschwitz should never happen again." This more pessimistic version of critical pedagogy was according to Gerrard (2013, 187) the result of lived experience:

> Following World War II, inspired by a deep skepticism toward the authority of scientific rationality and its universal tendencies, the notion of "emancipation" became radically refashioned. Led in large part by Theodore Adorno, Max Horkheimer, and others associated with the Frankfurt School, the "pessimistic turn" sought to abandon "action orientation" in the critique and challenge of capitalist power.

Crucially both strands of critical pedagogy emphasise critical self-reflection not as an instrument of self-indulgent neo-liberal individual psychology (Cho 2009, 90–91), rather as necessary to pedagogies of understanding how oppression is reproduced and how it can be confronted by connecting people through praxis. For example, Adorno's critical self-reflection "never stops at the level of the self" and instead "maps the self within the [at 77] conditions of society as a whole" so that the self is a "particular through which the whole is mediated" (Cho 2009, 76–77). The focus is on emancipation from dehumanisation in the case of Freire and on avoiding barbarianism in the case of Adorno.

Since Adorno and Freire, three interrelated factors have acted dialectically with critical pedagogy. The first of these was the postmodern turn and the emergence of new identity politics.

Another second factor was the increasing pervasiveness of neoliberalism and the corporate classroom giving rise to the appropriation of critical pedagogy as vocationally oriented critical thinking. The third was the call from Marxists to re-centre class. The call to re-centre class followed the impact of the first two factors which had effectively sidelined Marxism. Identity politics has proved impotent outside the west and in the face of growing inequality and the fallout of the GFC. As Best and Kellner (1998, 283) pointed out well before the 2008 Global Financial Crisis:

> The present conjuncture is highly ambiguous, positioning those in the overdeveloped Western and Northern areas between the era of modernity and a new epoch for which the term postmodernity has been coined, while people in other parts of the world are still living in premodern social and cultural forms, and on the whole the developing world exists in a contradictory matrix of premodern, modern, and postmodern forms.

Post-modernisms (mid- and late-twentieth-century women's, antiracist, queer, and post- (and de-) colonial movements) greatest success has been to problematize:

> ... the tenets of emancipatory authority in their experiences of exclusion and misrecognition in counter (as well as dominant) cultures. Wary of explanatory and exclusionary theories of social change that place authority solely in the hands of the working-class revolutionary subject, there is a "retreat from class-based, anti-capitalism struggles, and a move towards anti-system or more specifically, counter-cultural or identity-based struggles."
> GERRARD 2013, 188, quoting CHO 2008, 9

Class has regained interest because the burden of the GFC has been borne disproportionately by people with the least income and property rather than those who enjoyed pre-GFC profits. Calls to re-center class are not about revitalising Marxism but continuing the unfinished Marxist project of critiquing and understanding capitalism to be capable of creating a better future.

In other words, the postmodern new identity mantra "that class alone cannot name oppression", nor lead to emancipation of all forms of oppression (Gerrard 2013, 188) obscured the persistence of class inequality which accelerated due to the GFC and the neoliberal assault on the welfare state. At the same time sidelining class and over-emphasising "the philosophical dilemma that lies between the necessity and impossibility of 'emancipation'" (Gerrard 2013, 198), has buttressed the misplaced axiom that the capitalist world order is the best and only option. Yet capitalism is unlikely to be the end of history. So for Gerrard (2013, 198–99) this means embracing the "historicist and normative limits of social analyses and emancipatory discourses", and "the necessity to continue their production regardless":

> Thus, in the place of conceptual emptiness, universals such as "freedom," "equality," and "justice" can be defined, debated, and made constitutive through the act of emancipatory education. Indeed, the connection of class description to the potentiality of class action arguably opens the normative basis of class analyses to constant scrutiny. Or, in Freire's (*Pedagogy of the Oppressed* 1972, 61) words, "Once named, the world in its turn reappears to the namers as a problem and requires of them a new naming."

Central to this is the recognition that any vulnerability of Marxism to claims of 'preoccupation with enlightenment universals,' does not impair the need for Marxist critique. This would be to privilege early Marxism over the later more rigorous volumes of *Capital*. Later Marx is salient because class relations, "incorporate interweaving processes of culture, identity, and economy" and "they are, fundamentally, rooted in the work of capital" (Gerrard 2013, 200). At the heart of this formulation is the basic Marxist premise that social analyses must form the basis for the theorizing of injustice and inequality, and thus also for the understanding of their possible challenge (Gerrard 2013, 200).

Therefore, "as a marker for material relations of subjugation":

> By its very nature [class] is a historically embedded process, experienced and interpreted differently across temporal and cultural space, and ultimately interrelated with other forms of oppression and inequality.
> GERRARD 2013, 200

Class is not a static universal but to exclude it is fatal to critical pedagogy. In addition, it is through the instruments of class analysis that we are able to focus on material inequality as opposed to moments of oppression. That is to say:

> ... class analysis provides a means by which to understand the relations between cultural and material inequality and the broader processes of capital accumulation and expansion under neoliberal capitalism.
> GERRARD 2013, 193

By decentring class, critique turned to solipsism making the task of understanding and confronting oppression impossible. A project of critical pedagogy requires transcendence of the solipsism of identity politics, the hopelessness of what Žižek (2009, 157) referred to as "anti-communist Leftists," or those who might otherwise be disparaged as the career-driven postmodern intellectual Left.[2] In the words of Freire (1998, 40–41):

> To serve the dominant order is what many intellectuals of today who were progressive yesterday are doing when they reject all educational practices that unveil the dominant ideology while reducing education to a mere transference of contents that are considered "sufficient" to guarantee a happy life. ... [at 41] And they do this with the appearance of considering themselves up-to-date and able to transcend "old ideologies." They speak of the great need of professionalizing pedagogical programs even if they are empty of any possibility to understand society critically.

None of this means that a critical pedagogy sacrifices mastery of the technical abstraction necessary to disciplines. The two go together (Appleby et al. 2013, 351). As Freire (1998, 41) explains, "an educational practice is falsely progressive when it rejects the technical preparation of students so as to focus only on the political dimension of education" because "technical mastery is just as important for students as the political understanding is for a citizen." What critical pedagogy does is render disciplinary abstraction to a process of critique. It should do so in the sense that abstraction may harbour oppression as the appearance and price of a commodity obscures the nature of the exploitative productive relations that brought it to market.

Unfortunately the neo-liberal tendency in the corporate classroom is to prefer the technical and democratic aspects of Freire's pedagogy while extricating its revolutionary essence. For Giroux (2013) the focus on the technical as opposed to revolutionary essence of critical pedagogy means it "removes the classroom from larger social, political, and economic forces", so that the ultimate objective of education is to "to train students to compete successfully in a global economy". In other words, it is fashionable to cite Freire's (1994, 53) reference to "banking education" and his call to abandon traditional authority in teaching without an emphasis on neo-Marxism (Appleby et al. 2013, 346, 351).

---

2 Richard Shaull's Foreword to *Pedagogy of the Oppressed* makes a similar argument, "Fed up as I am with the abstractness and sterility of so much intellectual work in academic circles today, I am excited by a process of reflection which is set in a thoroughly historical context, which is carried on in the [at 14] midst of a struggle to create a new social order and thus represents a new unity of theory and praxis," in (Freire 1994, 13–14).

Active learning and democratising the didactic nature of education so that the teacher is a collaborator with students as opposed to their master coupled with pluralistic critical thinking is not going to change society. Necessary as active learning and critical thinking are to learning, by themselves they are not critical pedagogy. Democratising the classroom in the absence of understanding the historical construction of oppression and privilege means more of the same. Abandoning banking education and replacing it with active learning and critical thinking will not change oppression without teaching students about Marxism, neo-Marxism, radical feminisms, critical race and gender theories, amongst other "radical" pedagogies to historicise life and the construction of knowledge.

So rather than severing off and fragmenting oppression it is necessary to reconnect people through dialogic action aimed at cultural synthesis. This is not jargon. Freire (1994, 155–56) is very careful to explain the action:

> In order for the oppressed to unite, they must first cut the umbilical cord of magic and myth which binds them to the world of oppression; the unity which links them to each other must be of a different nature. To achieve this indispensable unity the revolutionary process must be, from the beginning, cultural action. The methods used to achieve the unity of the oppressed will depend on the latter's historical and existential experience within the social structure.

And to reiterate from earlier on:

> ... it is therefore essential to have an increasingly critical knowledge of the current historical context, the view of the world held by the people, the principal contradiction of society, and the principal aspect of that contradiction.
>
> FREIRE 1994, 157

A critical pedagogy is one that seeks to understand oppression and confront it through a "dialogical theory of action" where "Subjects meet in cooperation in order to transform the world" (Freire 1994, 148). For Freire (1994, 149) dialogue:

> ... must underlie any cooperation. In the theory of dialogical action, there is no place for conquering the people on behalf of the revolutionary cause, but only for gaining their adherence. Dialogue does not impose, does not manipulate, does not domesticate, does not "sloganize." This does not mean, however, that the theory of dialogical action leads

nowhere; no does it mean that the dialogical human does not have a clear idea of what she wants, or of the objectives to which she is committed.

This does not mean the teacher absconds as revolutionary leader, rather that the teacher does not impose "salvation" on the students "breaking the dialogical bond between them", and instead enables students to be co-authors in naming their oppressor and acting upon that knowledge (Freire 1994, 148). Critical pedagogy is therefore a movement aimed at preventing and replacing oppression by working with people to ruthlessly critique the world order through critical histories, critical self-reflection, and replacing solipsism with cultural synthesis. So what is deep critique, how does it fit with critical pedagogy?

## 4 Deep Critique in the Corporate Classroom

I am the course convenor of two compulsory property law courses out of the 24 courses necessary to qualify for a law degree at my university. I am required to teach the following topics for students to satisfy their admission requirements (known as the Priestley 11 "areas of knowledge" in Attachment 1 *Supreme Court (Admission) Rules 2004* (Qld)):

1. Meaning and purposes of the concept of property.
2. Possession, seisin and title.
3. Nature and type (i.e. fragmentation) of proprietary interests.
4. Creation and enforceability of proprietary interests.
5. Legal and equitable remedies.
6. Statutory schemes of registration.
7. Acquisition and disposal of proprietary interests.
8. Concurrent ownership.
9. Proprietary interests in land owned by another.
10. Mortgages.

OR

Topics of such breadth and depth as to satisfy the following guidelines. The topics should provide knowledge of the nature and type of various proprietary interests in chattels and land, and their creation and relative enforceability at law and in equity. Statutory schemes of registration for both general law land and Torrens land should be included. A variety of other topics might be included, e.g., fixtures, concurrent interests and more detailed treatment of such matters as sale of land, leases, mortgages, easements, restrictive covenants, etc.

In addition to this property doctrine I am also expected to layer it with the *Griffith Law School Strategic Plan*, *The Griffith Graduate*, and the *Australian Learning and Teaching Outcomes Project*. Prior to the neo-liberal cutbacks, the courses were once twice the credit point value with twice the contact hours and taught over 13 weeks. In the corporate classroom of today the two 12 week courses do not leave much time for critical pedagogy let alone a classic liberal education. For this reason only 3014LAW Property Law 1 involves critical pedagogy, while 3015LAW Property Law 2 is mostly doctrinal with some emphasis on critical thinking skills in the context of hypothetical problem solving. My student cohort is overwhelmingly middle-class.

What I call deep critique is not new or novel and like Gerrard (2013, 185) "I had come late to the party". Critical pedagogy was already "a well-established cohort of educational thinkers that had experienced numerous divisions and whose work had already been subjected to a range of critical analyses" (Gerrard 2013, 185). I did not know this until I started writing this chapter. What I have been practising as deep critique already had a name in "critical pedagogy," which was much more considered, practiced and sophisticated. Deep critique is my version of what Marx (1843) called "the ruthless criticism of the existing order," Adorno (2005, 193) called "critical self-reflection," Freire (1994) called "pedagogy of the oppressed," Giroux (2013) called "critical pedagogy," Gerrard (2013, 200) calls "emancipatory education," and others (McLaren 1998) have called "revolutionary pedagogy," and is much less than these critical pedagogies. It is much less because I do not practice deep critique beyond the confines of university life recognising that university and "private" life are completely intertwined.

To this extent I am both "an agent of reproduction" of the existing order and "a potential disrupter of social inequality and hierarchy" (Gerrard 2013, 200–201). I would like to think I spend marginally more employed time critiquing society than I do reproducing its inequality and oppression. However, I do not engage with the media to critique neo-liberalism, write blogs as a critic of the system, write letters to editors (Apple 2009, 94), or work with poor, oppressed communities (McLaren 2000, 46). Instead, deep critique is fundamental to my research and is practiced in one of the two compulsory law courses I convene.

I practise deep critique in the way I do research using Feminist Standpoint Theory (FST) which embraces class/group analysis to critically assess power by reading up the ladder of privilege (Ardill 2008). FST also informs my approach to teaching deep critique because it is a logical step to take to transcend the vacuousness of the postmodern fragmentation of critique. This is because although FST accepts the postmodern premise that political neutrality is an unachievable objective, it refuses to relinquish the possibility of understanding power and embraces critical voices. Apple (2009, 91) explains the connection between critical pedagogy and FST as both start critique from the standpoint of the most oppressed:

> The framework I have employed to understand this is grounded in what in cultural theory is called the act of repositioning. It in essence says that the best way to understand what any set of institutions, policies, and practices does is to see it from the standpoint of those who have the least power (Harding, 1991; Lukacs, 1971). That is, every institution, policy, and practice – and especially those that now dominate education and the larger society – establish relations of power in which some voices are heard and some are not. While it is not preordained that those voices that will be heard most clearly are also those who have the most economic, cultural, and social capital, it is most likely that this will be the case. After all, we do not exist on a level playing field. Many economic, social, and educational policies when actually put in place tend to benefit those who already have advantages.

This account resonates with my own journey to FST as I worked initially from postmodernism, to Marx, to Lukacs (1971), to Harding (1986) amongst others regarded as the founders of FST,[3] before learning of critical pedagogy.

Gerrard (2013, 189) poses the question, "[on] whose authority does a pedagogue proclaim the emancipatory potential of their education?" Similarly, students question my authority to teach Marxism, Feminisms and critical race theories. They do so for two reasons. One reason is that these perspectives are seen as unnecessary to a career in law, and another is that these perspectives are derided as alien to their experience of the world. I have written elsewhere (Ardill 2017) about why those perspectives are important for students reading law.

As to the second reason, I am able to engage students with the proposition that their individual experience of life may be real to them but it does not follow that it is a universal truth for everyone else especially for the good of the marginalised and oppressed. This is reinforced by a learning objective to critically assess the reasons for property inequality not by their own individual experience of it but by observing its historical and contested construction. Instead students learn about a history of ideas and their dialectical relationship with the shift from feudalism to capitalism - from theologies to positivism and from Hobbes to Locke to Hegel to Marx to postmodernism – students appreciate the partial nature of epistemological authority and legitimacy and its relationship with power and hegemony.

---

3   Often attributed to Dorothy Smith and Sandra Harding, but see generally Haraway 1988, Harding 1986, Hartsock 1983, and Smith 1987.

Crucially, students see that property doctrines cannot account for property inequality despite all the detailed tradition, jargon, and the pretence of legitimacy and authority. What Rose (1998, 605, 630) refers to as "Ownership Anxiety" which arises because of either a legal "indifference toward specific distributions" or an inability to justify any "distributional foundations of existing property rights." With the reality that property has been concentrated less by "reaping what you sow" than privilege, and inequality is unable to be justified by law or philosophy, the student gains a deeper understanding of law and their place in it. They are freed from the solipsism that chokes learning and are able to step into the shoes with those who do not have property.

Deep critique means that compulsory property doctrine is historicised and critiqued using Marxism, Neo-Marxism, Feminisms, critical race theory, and Feminist Standpoint Theory. The course commences by noting that property has been concentrated historically on the basis of race, class and gender (recognising the constructed and contested significance of those categories). Students are taught that both knowledge and property are social constructions in which they play a crucial role, in their dialogical relationship with me, as future practitioners, leaders, policy-makers and so on. They are expected to critically reflect on themselves as they study the way doctrines of property have changed over time starting with feudalism through to the current world order. They are asked to reflect on this history of property as a continuous struggle over ownership and its boundaries – who makes these laws and who benefits from them, and who loses out? They are invited to discuss in class and in reflective diaries how their experience of the world might influence their view of the concentration of property and its effects.

In this way students work with and reconsider technical doctrine not merely as an abstraction, but as something shaped by particular interests and impacting on human life. It is understood as a process of continuous reproduction (of past and present inequality) in which they play a part. They see the concentration of property not as natural and inevitable but as the result of complex struggles between classes over time, over technology old and new, and over resources as classes are reconstituted. Students recognise the dependence of capitalism on the continuous privatisation of commons and the extraction of surplus value from wages, and through interest, prices, and rent. If the law recognises proprietorship, then it does so by denying First Australians any sovereignty over their land and affords them inferior property rights (native title). Similarly, women were deprived the status of proprietors and instead men have been their proprietors until very recently. Men wrote laws of primogeniture and coverture subordinating women and this control remains today over the right of women to own and control the means of reproduction (birth control, sexual and bodily autonomy, child-rearing, domestic labour and caring).

The final closed book exam asks students not to regurgitate what they remember of my lectures, rather to present their understanding of why property is concentrated on the indices of race, class and gender. The requires students to internalise and then build upon the proposition that property is unjust, it need not be that way, and that it is the result of complex historical and social struggles that continue today, and to see themselves within this arrangement. As new lawyers they master the rhetoric of the doctrines as much as the way doctrines mystify inequality.

In my 18 years of experience in the classroom the biggest intellectual hurdle as a human being is to be able to understand and contest the injustice of inequality, and with this, to reconcile through dialogue and action one's own privilege relative to someone/others oppressed by that privilege. This is why I refer to my teaching practice as deep critique. Deep critique is a small step toward an emancipatory education:

> The first step would be to see education as a crucial foundation for creating the agents necessary to live in, govern, and struggle for a radical democracy. Another task would be to recognize how education and pedagogy are connected to and implicated in the production not only of specific agents, a particular view of the present and future, but also how knowledge, values and desires, and social relations are always implicated in power.
> GIROUX 2013

It is for these reasons I teach deep critique featuring FST as my way of practising critical pedagogy. In sum, firstly because FST does not abandon Marxism, feminism and critical race theories and instead regards them as necessary for understanding oppression and conducting critique. Secondly, FST requires accountability to those most marginalised or oppressed by their class (economic, social, gender, race) as the starting point for that critique. It does so by rendering:

> ... dominant institutions in education and the larger society up to rigorous questioning and at the same time this questioning must deeply involve those who benefit least from the ways these institutions now function. Both conditions were necessary, since the first without the second was simply insufficient to the task of democratizing education.
> APPLE 2009, 94

It is also implicit here that critique in a pluralist sense is inadequate because pluralism is accountable to the notion of respect for all perspectives whether an oppressor or not. Pluralism is therefore necessarily tethered to the status quo as opposed to emancipation. Thirdly, essential to deep critique through the methods of FST is the ability to critically self-reflect as a social being and it is ultimately through that practice – not as narcissistic self help psychology – that the individual is reconnected to humanity and the structures that restrict and enable emancipation. Whether that means Adorno's defensive critical pedagogy aimed at preventing another Auschwitz or Freire's revolutionary version of critical pedagogy.

## 5 Conclusions

Critical pedagogy, or in my case deep critique, is a practice that is intrinsically part of who I am as a self-described Feminist Standpoint Theorist (Ardill 2008 and 2013). Deep critique is a work in progress informed dialogically with my students according to the critical self-reflection I engage in and as I do research. At the same time, I recognise that the corporate university aims to "meet the demand for 'an ideologically compliant but technically and hierarchically skilled workforce'" (Baron 2013, 275, quoting Hill and Kumar 2009, 3). Even the earlier more critical and liberal university had limited scope to prevent barbarianism or to emancipate humanity while working for the opposite possibility:

> [Their] insights sadly effected little societal transformation on the way out of the growing despair of poverty, the melanoma of racism (West, 1993), and the general malaise that attends a social system characterized as misanthropic and segregated by class, race, and gender.
> KANPOL 1997, X

Education has for the most part been about reproducing the system as Gerrard (2013, 186) writes:

> As much as education offers powerful possibilities for social action, systems of education have also played an unmistakable role in maintaining structures of inequality. Decades of work in the history and sociology of education clearly demonstrates that, in Basil Bernstein's (1970, 344–47) words, "education cannot compensate for society," and that in many cases it compounds existing inequalities, exclusions, and disadvantages.

Neo-liberalism creates the conditions where students must look out for themselves from an early age to function in that system. Before students arrive at the corporate university their understanding of the world is atomised leaving them with the belief that their existence in society is a product of their choice. For the majority of the middle-class students I get to work with, this may not be problematic for them in a relative sense, though it leads to malaise and a failure to understand inequality.

This makes it necessary to not only resist the constraints imposed on me and my students by the corporate university but also to make use of the opportunities and contradictions that arise as a result of neoliberal structures. It also requires working with students to reflect on what is best for them may not necessarily be best for everyone, in particular those who have a lot less. Deep critique is one way of empowering the student to unveil the possibility of a better world as they critically assess their place in it. Recognising as did Freire (1994, 150) that

> No one can, however, unveil the world *for* another. Although one Subject may initiate the unveiling on behalf of others, the others must also become Subjects of this act. The adherence of the people is made possible by this unveiling of the world and of themselves, in authentic praxis.

Deep critique embodying Marxism, Feminisms, Critical race Theory, and Feminist Standpoint Theory are making a mark on the lives of my property law students. Students are surprised when they first discover the extraction of surplus value and commodity fetishism, and then enthusiastically supply their own examples of the ways in which property obscures the nature of the exploitative and wasteful production relations that have brought commodities to market. They are both shocked and excited to discover that they themselves are commodified through the very same exploitative and wasteful production relations. For other students they never quite connect the dots and still see oppression as aberrations involving pockets of discrimination or alternatively blame the victim never a system.

As someone privileged by my whiteness, gender, place of birth, and recently by class, I believe the hardest achievement as a human being is to confront inequality and to reconcile through both dialogue and action one's own privilege relative to someone/others oppressed by that privilege. It follows from that belief I must work with my students to challenge privilege in the corporate classroom. Critical pedagogy is even more important in the corporate university because students become the next generation of leaders. If universities simply reinforce a desire in students to emulate those with power today, then the future is indeed grim. On the other hand if students are encouraged to reflect on who they are by critically assessing the circumstances that have produced their existence, hope for a better humanity becomes possible. Critical pedagogy is as relevant to an exploited Brazilian plantation worker (Freire) as it is to western university students (Adorno) and the global conditions sustaining inequality. Were Adorno and Freire to be wrong about this then the world would not be characterised by extremes in inequality and power.

## Bibliography

Adorno, Theodor (2005) *Critical Models: Interventions and Catchwords.* New York: Columbia University Press.

Apple, W. Michael (2009) "Some Ideas on Interrupting the Right: On Doing Critical Educational Work in Conservative Times." *Education, Citizenship, and Social Justice* 4, no. 2: 87–101.

Appleby, Gabrielle, Burdon, Peter, and Reilly, Alexander (2013) "Critical Thinking in Legal Education: Our Journey." *Legal Education Review* 23, no. 2: 345–377.

Ardill, Allan (2008) "Sociobiology and Law." PhD Diss., Griffith University. https://www120.secure.griffith.edu.au/rch/items/14656573-04df-f6f3-dab9-b37f50f0c65c/1/ or http://www.academia.edu/27192360/Sociobiology_and_Law.

Ardill, Allan (2013) "Australian Sovereignty, Indigenous Standpoint Theory and Feminist Standpoint Theory: Why First Peoples Sovereignties Matter." *Griffith Law Review* 22, no.2: 315–343.

Ardill, Allan (2017) "Critique in Legal Education: Another Journey." *Legal Education Review* 26, no. 1: 137–160. http://epublications.bond.edu.au/ler/vol26/iss1/7.

Baron, Paula (2013) "A Dangerous Cult: Response to 'The Effect of the Market on Legal Education.'" *Legal Education Review* 23, no. 2: 273–289.

Best, Steven and Kellner, Douglas (1998) "Postmodern Politics and the Battle for the Future." *New Political Science* 20: 283–299.

Cho, Daniel K. (2009) "Adorno on Education or, Can Critical Self-Reflection Prevent the Next Auschwitz?" *Historical Materialism* 17: 74–97.

Davies, Martin (2016) "What is critical thinking? And do universities really teach it?" The Conversation. Novembere 23, 2016. http://theconversation.com/what-is-critical-thinking-and-do-universities-really-teach-it-69046.

Freire, Paulo (1994) *Pedagogy of the Oppressed.* revised 20th ed. New York: Continuum.

Freire, Paulo (1998) *Pedagogy of the Heart.* New York: A & C Black Academic and Professional.

Gerrard, Jessica (2013) "Class Analysis and the Emancipatory Potential of Education." *Educational Theory* 63, no. 2: 185–201.

Giroux, Henry (2013) "Henry Giroux: The Necessity of Critical Pedagogy in Dark Times," interview by Jose Maria Barroso Tristan, Truth-out, February 6, 2013. http://www.truth-out.org/news/item/14331-a-critical-interview-with-henry-giroux.

Haraway, Donna (1988) "Situated Knowledges: The Science Question in Feminism and the Privilege of Partial Perspective." *Feminist Studies* 14, no. 3: 575–599.

Harding, Sandra (1986) *The Science Question in Feminism.* Ithaca: Cornell University Press.

Hartsock, Nancy (1983) "The Feminist Standpoint: Developing the Ground for a Specifically Feminist Historical Materialism." In *Discovering Reality: feminist Perspectives on Epistemology, Metaphysics, and Philosophy of Science,* eds. Harding, Sandra and Merrill Hintikka, 283–310, Dordrecht: Reidel.

Kanpol, Barry (1997) *Issues and Trends in Critical Pedagogy.* Cresskill, NJ: Hampton Press.

Kift, Sally, Israel, Mark, and Field, Rachel (2010) "Learning and Teaching Academic Standards Project, Bachelor of Laws, Learning and Teaching Academic Standards Statement," *Australian Learning and Teaching Council.* https://cald.asn.au/wp-content/uploads/2017/11/LLB-TLOsKiftetalLTASStandardsStatement2010-TLOs-LLB2.pdf.

Marx, Karl (1843) "Letter from Marx to Arnold Ruge." Kreuznach, September 1843. transcribed by Andy Blunden. Accessed July 13, 2018. https://www.marxists.org/archive/marx/works/1843/letters/43_09.htm.

Marx, Karl and Engels, Frederick (1998) *The Communist Manifesto & Its Relevance For Today.* 1888 English edition. Chippendale, NSW: Resistance Books.

McLaren, Peter (1998) "Revolutionary Pedagogy in Post-Revolutionary Times." *Educational Theory* 48, no. 4: 431–462.

McLaren, Peter (2000) *Che Guevara, Paulo Freire, and the Pedagogy of Revolution.* Lanham, MD: Rowman and Littlefield Publishers.

OECD (2015) *In It Together: Why Less Inequality Benefits All.* Paris: OECD Publishing, https://doi.org/10.1787/9789264235120-en.

Piketty, Thomas (2014) *Capital in the Twenty-First Century.* translated by Arthur Goldhammer. London: Bellknapp Press.

Rose, Carol (1998) "Canons of Property Talk, or, Blackstone's Anxiety." *Yale Law Journal* 108: 601–632.

Sengupta, Shuddhabrata (2006) "I/Me/Mine – Intersectional Identities as Negotiated Minefields." *Signs* 31, no. 3:629–639.

Singh, Paramjit (2017) "Understanding Marx's Capital." *Critique* 45, no. 3: 409–426.

Smith, Dorothy (1987) *The Everyday World as Problematic: A Feminist Sociology.* Boston: Northeastern University Press.

Traverso, Enzo (1999) *Understanding the Nazi Genocide: Marxism after Auschwitz.* International Institute for Research and Education. London: Pluto Press.

Žižek, Slavoj (2009) *First as Tragedy, Then as Farce.* London: Verso.

CHAPTER 8

# Pedagogies of Freedom: Exile, Courage, and Reflexivity in the Life of Paulo Freire

*Mauro J. Caraccioli*

1    Introduction

In the title essay of his collection *Reflections on Exile* (2000), Edward Said remarks on the political character of exile as a problem "produced by human beings for other human beings" (174). Though stories of exile have always spoken to a real and metaphorical sense of homelessness, the prevalence of exile today seems to lack any lessons in timeless wisdom. While Said offers some consolation that histories of exile have always given, and may yet continue to give, modern spectators something to ruminate on, the larger problem rests on what he perceives as our inability today to live the lessons that exile once proffered. "Exile," he concludes, "is never the state of being satisfied, placid, or secure. Exile…is 'a mind of winter' in which the pathos of summer and autumn as much as the potential of spring are nearby but unobtainable" (186). In the following pages, I argue that implicit in the weathered experience of exile is a relation between a thinker and their context that points towards the possibility of learning tragic, yet empowering lessons. I seek to offer here a broader grounding for the concept of exile and how its lived-experiences in the scholarly realm can offer insights regarding courage and scholarly reflexivity in the contemporary North American academy.

A recent wave of work on the role of narrativity and storytelling in International Relations has begun this difficult reconstruction of exile and its place in international theorizing (see: Beattie 2015; Solomon 2014; Dauphinee 2013; Inayatullah 2011). Following these readings, I intend to link the experiential character of exile to forms of courage that emerge in one thinker's encounter with political change. To do so, my analysis turns to the life of Paulo Freire as a contemporary example embodying the courage to risk exile and to use it as a staging ground for critical thought. Though Freire's own displacement was a product of his social and political activism at the frontlines of Cold War politics, his approach to education acts as a "pedagogy of freedom" that offers IR scholars an opportunity to re-think exile in light of contemporary academic challenges. By exploring Freire's resilience throughout multiple international encounters—global literacy campaigns, challenges to leftist authoritarianism, and the worldwide corporatization of higher education—I also use these experiences as an opportunity to speculate on IR scholarship's noticeable silence on Freire's endeavors.

The silence on Freire—as well as on the mechanisms of domination he found central to perpetuating what he termed as the "culture of silence" (Freire 2000, 71–86)—leads me to position the "intellectual-in-exile" as one that cultivates a mode of questioning essential to living and thinking in the midst of crisis. Freire's lessons on education and pedagogy may not fit the paradigmatic mold of conventional approaches to the study of global politics. However, they do offer a tactical response aimed at unpacking how the study of world politics is constituted and reproduced in everyday spaces wrapped-up in those same politics (see: de Certeau 1984; Caraccioli 2011). In particular, I look to Freire's concern with the ideological nature of all education as being a central dilemma of contemporary IR scholarship. The embodied character of Freire's pedagogy of freedom, I maintain, serves to acknowledge the often silent (though no less polemical) elitism facing scholars within the neoliberal university today. IR scholars can thus specifically draw from Freire the questioning attitude at the heart of all of exiles: a reflexive attitude at once indebted to, and positioned against, the arbitrary exercise of political power.

I conclude the chapter by looking at the implications of Freire's critical pedagogy on the problem of courage in the scholar's negotiations with "the Ivory Tower." While IR scholars today have recently taken up reflexivity and *parrhesia* (i.e., frank speech, truth-telling) as acts to be employed with both courage and caution, many of these efforts continue to treat central analytic features of exile as either internal or external phenomena, where courage acts as a kind of internal response on the part of she who is exiled (Steele 2010; Oren 2006). Building on the work of scholars employing the concept of reflexivity, I instead position exile as a co-extensive feature of the courage and reflexivity that shape the life of international scholars at three levels: personal journeys, higher education training, and the visions scholars impart through teaching. By engaging with exile as an inherent feature of IR theorizing, I see the challenge facing contemporary IR scholars as how to understand exile as *both* a theory and practice of human freedom, a path modeled by Freire that counters the notion of education as a form of domination.

My intentions are therefore not to diminish the everyday courage and relevance that refugees and other exiles face on a daily basis. Rather, my concern is with the ways that IR scholars adopt the question of exile as an exhortation for courage in the struggles of scholarly work. In this sense, the chapter acts as a political ethnography of exile: a reflexive inventory of the discipline's attitude towards what is in effect more than just an empirical problem (see: Wedeen 2009). In brief, there is a kind of exile that pervades the academy, especially vivid in the marginalization of reflexive scholarship, which I find IR scholarship ill-equipped to talk about. Yet as Freire describes it, exile is a problem that "touches you existentially. It envelops you as a being. It shakes you up physically and mentally…magnifies your virtues and your faults. And this is what exile did to me" (1985, 181). To describe the spaces of exile—both as practical endeavor in reshaping one's life, but also as a means of speaking truth to power—requires a form of courage that emerges from uncertainty and loss, elements highly under-theorized in IR.

The distinction between "exile as a feature" of politics and "exile as constitutive" of a critical disposition is crucial here because it highlights key opportunities for IR scholars to develop and employ new forms of political courage from a world that many of us often claim to want to save, but just as often use to save ourselves (see: Patterson 2000; Mignolo 2002; Drainville 2003; Tickner 2006). As I will argue below, one pertinent way in which IR as a discipline may benefit from an experiential analysis of exile is through the grounding of contemporary pedagogical debates within the space of "professionalization." Reflexivity in our professional biographies has an explicitly intersubjective component, shifting the "global knowledge" ethos of the discipline towards the "local knowledge" of everyday circumstances. By acknowledging the role of lived-experiences in education and teaching, IR scholars may convey, in Löwenheim's (2010) words, "the humanity and intrinsic worth and distinctiveness of other individuals" (1028).[1] In this spirit, IR scholars can develop more communal attempts—both within and outside of the field—to rethink and theorize courage in today's academic landscape.

## 2  The Intellectual-in-Exile: A Critical Portrait of Paulo Freire

Few disciplines have perhaps been as richly influenced by political exiles as IR. Both classical and contemporary schools of thought can trace their lineage to the experience of expulsion, escape, or as a result of the contradictions generated by capitalism and communism alike. Yet why have IR scholars neglected to take up the question of exile and what it can teach us about studying global politics? While there are predecessors in the history of IR that help convey

---

[1] Given the increasing attention to the problem of "paradigmatism" on the study of IR, works focusing on the trajectories of scholars themselves offer crucial insights on the analytic value of biographical knowledge. See: Kruzel and Rosenau, 1989; Jacobi et al., 2011.

the co-constitutive relation between the concept and experience of exile (for example, E.H. Carr's (1964) concern with the relation between utopia and reality in the face of his own disenchantment with Liberalism and Hans Morgenthau's own "middle-road" approach to navigating the ideological extremes of his time), IR scholarship today seems to miss the importance of exile as a mode of self- and collective critique.[2]

In the following section, I turn to the life and work of Paulo Freire as a response to attempts at theorizing exile's role as a courageous and reflexive facet of challenging political power. While Freire's life and work were highly impacted by the experience of exile, his deeds and methods were far removed from the image of the exile as being "homeless" (Said 2000), or, exile as some kind of causal mechanism for changing societies (Sznajder and Roniger 2009).[3] Rather than viewing his sojourn as a source of alienation, Freire conceptualizes exile as an opportunity to be both free and "at home" in the broader world. Within the broader history of Latin American exiles, his experience offers timely lessons for an allegedly timeless problem.

To begin, what does Freire's trajectory look like? A small set of highlights should help frame the present discussion: born into a middleclass family, Freire grew up in almost abject poverty after his father died in the middle of the Great Depression. His first encounters with education were less than encouraging, but by his own account, these helped to frame the great challenge of educating the forgotten masses of the world. "Thought and study alone did not produce" his studies and texts, he notes in one of the prefaces to *Pedagogy of the Oppressed*; rather, these are "rooted in concrete situations and…the reactions of laborers (peasant or urban) and of middle-class persons whom I have observed directly or indirectly during the course of my educative work" (Freire 2000, 37). That direct engagement would be central to Freire's own sense of learning and discovery, as well as how he would implement these in practice.

First a lawyer and later an educator by training, Freire was influenced by a cocktail of intellectual currents ranging from Marxism, to phenomenology, and liberation theology, among others (see: Rivera 2004). His early pedagogical and activist work with the peasant communities of the Brazilian Northeast, as

---

2   Recent efforts have attempted to clarify the role that exile played in Carr and Morgenthau's formative periods. Yet such histories have so far single out the problematic nature of exile and its limits on studying international political theorizing, rather than its possibilities. See: Frei, 2001; Williams, 2004; and Nishimura, 2011; Williams, 2005.
3   Although Sznajder and Roniger's efforts are to be commended—particularly in their reading of exile as "both the result of political processes and a constitutive factor of political systems" (2009: 5)—my aim here is to go beyond the macro-political effects of exile as an explanatory model, to the reflexive elements of exile that contribute to a pedagogical understanding.

an official of Pernambuco state, focused on developing a dialogical pedagogy that emphasized local history and human freedom as understood in the locals' own terms. He observed how, "labor in the fields, meetings of a local association (noting the behavior of the participants, the language used, and the relations between the officers and the members), the role played by women and by young people, leisure hours, games and sports, conversations with people in their homes (noting examples of husband-wife and parent-child relationships)" all formed part of the spectrum under which adult education teams, for example, should observe the "life of an area" (Freire 2000, 111–112). It quickly becomes evident how these strategies put Freire in the left-wing of the Brazilian ideological spectrum, often raising accusations of attempts to deploy Cuban-inspired efforts at fomenting populist revolution, not educational reform.

In the lead-up to the 1964 U.S.-backed coup against the democratic government of João Goulart, the provocatively political and nationalist illustrations that Freire developed for teaching peasants to read—including images of daily toils and struggles, of civic participation and voting, of collective solidarity and support—were singled out by both right-wing propaganda groups, as well as U.S. government officials responsible for dispersing USAID funds, as "disseminating anti-U.S. or Marxist doctrine in adult education programs" (Kirkendall 2010, 51). His exposure to the region's poverty and the lack of alternatives available to its peoples (e.g., literacy was a voting requirement in Brazil) led Freire to enact education projects dedicated to bring the working classes closer to understanding their own context and situations. In his book *Pedagogy of Hope*, for instance, Freire emphasized how important visual and popular media in particular could be when used to convey a person's positionality within their broader society:

> Never does an event, a fact, a deed, a gesture of rage or love, a poem, a painting, a song, a book, have one reason behind it. In fact a deep gesture, a poem, a painting, a song, a book are always wrapped in thick wrappers. They have been touched by manifold whys. Only some of these are close enough to the event or the creation to be visible as whys. And so I have always been more interested in understanding the process in and by which things come about than in the product itself.
> FREIRE 1994, 10

For Freire, these moments of discovery were critical tools for the educator to use in empowering their students through self-conscious acts of contextualization. That these tactics linked Brazilian struggles against underdevelopment with the broader global struggles of decolonization through education did not seem to be explicit Freire's doing. Rather, it was perhaps the recognition from his contemporaries of the larger global context in which underdevelopment and colonial domination operated. In an increasingly tense climate of revolution and dictatorship, Freire was arrested as a traitor in 1964 and later forced into exile for approximately sixteen years. An ironic side-effect of Freire's exile was the worldwide impact of his methods stretching across the Western Hemisphere and into the African and Middle Eastern contexts (Gadotti 1994, 35–48).

Freire traveled in the late-1960s to Bolivia and Chile, where he first put his methods to international scrutiny through his work with the UN's Food and Agricultural Organization. Between 1967 and 1968 he published two key texts, *Education as the Practice of Freedom* (1967) and *Pedagogy of the Oppressed* (1968), of which the latter would push his name to international renown. Both these texts focused on the transformation of society through popular education and in particular the role of literacy in civic participation. The experience in Chile made Freire's name known across Latin America, particularly since his efforts were the hallmarks of both radical efforts at empowering the powerless, as well as burgeoning land reform programs enacted by the ruling Christian Democrat party. These experiences also helped to frame a wide field of differences for Freire, as he became increasingly concerned with the question of national culture, and how concepts, ideas, and values traveled between nations.

After being invited to a visiting professorship position at Harvard in 1969, Freire spent the following decade working as a special education advisor with the World Council of Churches and its literacy campaigns in Guinea Bissau and Mozambique. It was in his experience in Africa that we find one of Freire's most interesting contradictions, as seen in his optimism regarding a one-party state's abilities to enact a national literacy campaign and the subsequent inadequacy of the literacy program enacted there. Freire's own role in the failure of the Guinea-Bissau and Mozambique projects can be tied to a misperception on his part of the political consciousness of the Guinean peasantry and the commitment of a militaristic state to a democratic endeavor (see: Freire 1978). As Freire recognized, these failures would have a profound effect on his earlier assumptions about a certain existential universalism informing political and educational endeavors. Freire returned to Brazil in 1979 and subsequently joined the *Partido dos Trabalhadores* (Worker's Party of Brazil), enacting dozens of adult literacy campaigns in the city of Sao Paulo, while continuing to advise multiple educational efforts in Nicaragua and inner-city schools in the U.S. Noteworthy across Freire's development as a pedagogical and international thinker was his focus on the experience of the poor.

In his *Pedagogy of the Oppressed* (2000), for example, Freire traced the notorious problem of the "banking notion of education" to two elements: the prevalence of the Liberal notion of the individual as a *tabula rasa* and the central role a dialectical sense of history played in individual and collective liberation (71–86). His last statement on this issue came in a series of lecture notes compiled for a seminar on liberation pedagogy at the Harvard Graduate School of Education in the late 1990s. Freire died in May 1997 before the course could begin, but his lecture notes were published in 1998 under the title *Pedagogy of Freedom*.

In this course, Freire frames the core of his life's trajectory and pedagogical concerns in a characteristically unconventional fashion, channeling the spirit of multiple critical (and future) observations on the corporatization of the university, while remaining an unrepentant humanist:

> I cannot avoid a permanently critical attitude towards what I consider to be the source of neoliberalism, with its cynical fatalism and its inflexible negation of the right to dream differently, to dream of utopia. My abhorrence of neoliberalism helps to explain my legitimate anger when I speak of the injustices to which the ragpickers among humanity are condemned. It also explains my total lack of interest in any pretension of impartiality. I am not impartial or objective, not a fixed observer of facts and happenings. I never was able to be an adherent of the traits that falsely claim impartiality or objectivity. That did not prevent me, however, from holding always a rigorously ethical position. Whoever really observes, does so from a given point of view. (1998, 22)

By Freire's account, many of the positivist assumptions and "pretensions of impartiality" about the nature of knowledge do great violence to human experience. If there is at least one thing that exile taught him in this regard, it is that life is fluid and impermanent; our insights and concepts are not those of a "fixed observer," but rather always "from a given point of view." Freire himself traces this critical disposition directly to what exile taught him: first, that exile is never "peaceful"; second, that "nobody goes into exile by choice"; and lastly, that while in exile he realized his true interest in learning, as an opportunity to "each day be open to the world, be ready to think; each day be ready not to accept what is said just because it is said, be predisposed to reread what is read; each day investigate, question, and doubt" (1985, 181).

While tempting for those who are critical of his approach to see Freire as too much a product of his time—a remnant of the post-Cuban Revolution radicalism that informed the 1960s and 1970s—such a critique may be more the result of the tenacity of a neoliberal individualist ideology than any concrete theoretical or pedagogical critique of Freire's method. Freire is quite upfront about how his experience affected his role as a teacher, scholar, and participant in the dynamics of international politics. The very act of teaching, for Freire, is part of the human individual's experiential relation to the world around her, and the space where both "teacher" and "student" learn embodies a process of self-discovery and engagement with that which is different.

Sandra Harding, among other prominent feminist theorists and historians of science, has echoed these same sentiments concerning the hegemony of objectivity over the lived-experiences of academic production, person-to-person relations, and human-nonhuman encounters. "The problem with the conventional conception of objectivity is not that it is too rigorous or too 'objectifying,'" she argues, "but that it is *not rigorous or objectifying enough*; it is too weak to accomplish even the goals for which it has been designed, let along the more difficult projects called for by feminisms and other new social movements" (Harding 1993, 50–51). For Harding, like for Freire, what conventional notions of science, learning, education, and theoretical thought fail to account for the great resource that reflexivity—as a critical form of subject positionality—has become in reminding scholars that "[observers] do change the world that they observe" (Harding 1993, 73), how else is the conviction of one's beliefs about the world put into action?

The intersubjective and context-bound nature of teaching is thus for Freire an act that "cannot be reduced to a superficial or externalized contact with the object or its content but extends to the production of the conditions on which critical learning is possible" (1998, 33). The development of Freire's life can be read along similar lines, where the transformations and transitions he embodied formed part of a broader array of changes and challenges faced by an entire generation of Latin American exiles (see: Dorfman 2011). Freire's life illustrates both the journey and return from exile, offering a vivid description of the tensions between experiences and future endeavors, as well as how these can critically shape one's path—an exilic reflexivity.

None of this suggests that one could not criticize Freire's efforts or the meaning of his work for understanding exile. In fact, he saw such a confrontation as a necessary element of what he termed human *"unfinishedness"* and the responsibility of any teacher to encourage the search for the "support networks" of human life (1998, 51–54). As mentioned above, Freire himself acknowledges the threat of ahistorical reasoning and the alleged "end of history" as products of the creeping prevalence of neoliberal ideologies. The challenge here is to retain the ability to generate forms of history whose champions are people themselves. The objectives of a critical pedagogy therefore lie in the attempt to establish a kind of *conscientization* of both the environment in which teaching and learning take place (geographically, historically, and intersubjectively) and who scholars are as intellectuals, teachers, and ultimately political agents.

## 3 Learning From Freire: The *Conscientization* of International Relations

The notion of *conscientization* has often raised several alarms amongst scholars, particularly through its paternalistic connotations of enlightened individuals reaching down to unenlightened masses. It is often presented as a kind of universalism that is guilty of not giving enough attention to historical specificities and possibilities for difference and interaction. Rightfully, the concept needs to be interrogated for its ambiguous theoretical underpinnings. This lack, however, should not dissuade scholars and theorists from taking Freire's challenge of acknowledging the unfinished nature of human life and that critical scholarly work must always be embodied in the struggles of communicating, teaching, and learning from our communities (see: Glass 2001). Conscientization therefore continues to play an important role today as a dialogical challenge to the growing corporate elitism of higher education. The myth behind the objectivity of teaching and research falls flat, according to Freire, once we acknowledge the hidden relationship between past and future that neoliberal institutions embody, the experiences such institutions privilege, and the kinds of scholarship deemed worthwhile within them.

To ignore the extent to which the university today is becoming a neoliberal institution is to ignore the challenge faced by entire throngs of junior and budding scholars alike. That the "death of tenure" has become a mandatory theme in graduate seminar discussions on the political economy or future of the academy is no mere exercise in curiosity. Often, the tension and anxiety generated by such discussions assume the theory-practice divide with alarming alacrity, prompting a necessary discussion on the contemporary role of courage. More specifically, one of the reasons why present economic and institutional changes in the professorate are so alarming rests on the absence of discussions pertaining to notions of dignity, relevance, and commitment within academic work (see: Schmidt 2001; Deresiewicz 2011; Caraccioli and Hozic 2015). Freire highlighted such tensions and in the process made, but also lost, many friends. To be clear, the critique of the ideological nature of education is itself an ideological statement. Yet Freire never denied that, often noting how "for this reason...I, as a teacher, ought to be aware of the power of ideological discourse, beginning with discourse that proclaims the death of all ideologies" (1998, 117). In this regard, Freire's borrowings from Marxism and existentialism display his ability to draw insights from dominant and counter-hegemonic narratives, while still resisting their fatalistic excesses. Such grand narratives have been central to mediating change within society (and the academy) for much of modern history. Renewed calls for "living wages" or "niceness" are equally part of this trend. And while Freire never shied away from acknowledging this reality, the silence among IR scholars on his concrete global contributions, as well as his philosophical insights on the profession, become all the more salient.[4]

Within IR, what we find in many of the unquestioned ideologies of globalization is nothing more than the extension of the neoliberal and modernization projects Freire was fighting against in the Cold War: ideologies that reproduce a corporate structure of competition into the classrooms and landscape of social life. Even self-proclaimed "critical" approaches have become increasingly characterized by their reliance on Western rationalities and a mastery of self-preservation in the social world (see: Odysseos 2007; Odysseos and Pal 2017). From the textbooks, schools of thought, and case studies used in the classroom environment, there is a peculiar elitism to the study of IR that allows intellectuals and politicians alike to disconnect their thought from the broader experiences of everyday life that makes the international possible.

As Freire's notion of conscientization highlights, education requires a critical awareness of history and the obstacles that intervene to make pedagogy an intersubjective task, demanding from scholars the recognition of how our environment shapes (and is shaped by) the international realm. Such an act of recognition not only demands that we rethink pedagogic practices, but that we rethink them in the context of a broader assessment of everyday patterns of capitalist consumption, the standardized modes of accounting for scholarly productivity, and the analytic character of the exile's experience. Although the commodification of education may be quite a self-evident observation to the scholar who is well-positioned within the widening hierarchy of higher education, the dispossession and resentment of students and scholars alike is experienced quite differently across the spectrum. Indeed, the exilic reflexivity that Freire conveys shows how the largest threat of the contemporary capitalization of higher education is not the creative destruction of old rituals, or, the proliferation of new subjectivities of the student as consumer. Rather, the most scandalous dimension of such transformations is that scholarly conceptions of "diversity" and "excellence" may actually benefit from such developments.

As I will develop in the following section of this chapter, a reflexive and experiential engagement with this question begins with a much more radical turn than that found in contemporary (even critical) IR approaches. Indeed, there is a powerfully intersubjective dimension to exile that makes its character as both a metaphor and experience central to the academic profession as a

---

4  A single, though poignant, footnote in one IR theorist's work points to the lamentable effects of this silence. See: Neufeld, 1995, 161.

community. Recognizing the presence of another person as being *somewhere-else* from our point of view, as inhabiting a particular place *already-there* prior to our arrival, and not just merely "inside" or "outside" of my reach, is in part the ground on which an epistemic transformation can occur. The everyday interaction with people in spaces and places different from our own help illuminate the different styles and modalities through which human life is experienced. This dissonance between "inside" and "outside," as R.B.J. Walker long ago pointed out, continues to plague IR theorizing. Yet this is not a result of territorial states, the relative merits of one approach over the other, or, of the evolutionary narratives shaping inter-paradigm warfare. Rather, as Walker (1993) concludes, it is about the fact that for "all its ambition to explain the world," contemporary IR, "remains intensely parochial, and not just because it has been developed primarily in relation to the interests of hegemonic states" (180).

Freire's thoughts here are doubly useful: on the one hand, his intellectual program parallels that of the phenomenological tradition, itself a geographically contested tradition (see: Caraccioli 2015). Particularly key for Freire is the way in which the seemingly mundane and "normal" encounters carry the weight and *sedimentation* of a myriad histories. As the philosopher Maurice Merleau-Ponty (1962) put it before him, where "what is acquired is truly acquired only if it is taken up again in a fresh momentum of thought" (113). For Merleau-Ponty, as for Freire, consciousness "[provides] itself with one or several worlds, to bring into being its own thoughts before itself, as if they were things...[demonstrating] its vitality indivisibly by outlining these landscapes for itself and then by abandoning them" (114). Re-thinking the role of perception is therefore central in the development of a critical consciousness, one that recognizes and challenges the extent to which only ideas or abstracted rationalities pervade our identity.

Yet on the other hand, Freire (1998) also employs in his writings insights grounded within the context of his own history, Latin American history, resembling a conversation through which "the subjects in dialogue learn and grow by confronting their difference" (59). As seen in his reflections from Guinea Bissau and Mozambique, he questions his own actions, judgments, and preconceptions as an exhortation for scholars and teachers to acknowledge their participation in a shared, though certainly contested, world of interpenetrations. The goal is not merely to be critical about actions, ideas, and emotions; rather, more positively (and more inclusive of the possibility of learning from others' differences), the everyday workings of a given culture must form part of a tapestry of meanings often elided from scholarly visions, but just as constitutive: "they involve our whole lives, our cultures, the distinctive features that distinguish man from other animals" (1985, 182).

In Freire's work, culture "extends history to the praxis of people" and thus the more one experiences and learns from the everyday lives of the world around them, "the more they help me keep in touch with myself, while learning and reflecting" (1985, 182). It is important to point out here that Freire's method implies more than sitting down with our feelings, forcing ourselves to acknowledge a bigger world. He is concerned with employing an *analectical* method (see: Dussel 1985, 158–59) where the space of encounter (whether anecdotal or directly experienced) is re-constituted through an explicit denunciation of the structures of privilege and power that marginalize the poor and disenfranchised. The absence and presence of others—especially the conquered and dominated, who through Freire's method can be in effect empowered to achieve their own liberation—are acknowledged as constitutive of the power-relation and not a mere passive object of consumption.

Freire's experiences as a national educator in the poorest towns of Northeast Brazil portray the force, fragility, and implications of these kinds of dialogue with great clarity. The posture of conviction and openness that motivated his efforts was further coalesced through his exile and transformation into an international educator in both the Third World and the U.S. His experience of exile became an attempt to interrogate the ways spaces, homes, and sites, are thought of, particularly as having an impact on one's thoughts and actions. While a much broader reflection on the relation between space, place, and perception would be useful here, suffice it for now to suggest that, for Freire, these elements play central roles in the construction of human identity, especially in the scholar's response to the oppression of state-sanctioned international violence and the cultural transformations that have shaped global politics.

Where then does Freire leave us on the question of exile? I point here to the possibility of re-envisioning exile as a mode of questioning that is rooted in two realms: first, that of the existential, as it seeks not only to see the spatiality and experience of human displacement, but also to discover its intersubjective character; and second, that of the temporal, as that mode of questioning and probing that allows for intellectual queries to provoke further questions, attempting to clarify alternate visions and dimensions of reality.

The exile is perpetually in search of ways through which to can create and engage *places-to-be*: spaces that allow them to live, to express ideas, and to exchange agency in their given environments. However, the parallels with how teachers and students may be shaped by their shared encounters, particularly within an international environment, are not self-evident. To interpret human relations from an experiential lens may provide alternative forms of expression that resist conceptual or political domination, but they are always constructed in dialogue with others, never solely in isolation, and rarely at a distance. Thus, the revolutionary character of Freire's thought lies in coming back from exile right into the very heart of an institution's oppressive ideologies. That return need not be as a drastic as Freire's exile, but can be mirrored in our ongoing return to the shared spaces of the classroom and scholarly communities.

A common feature of contemporary undergraduate education, for example, remains the naturalization of phenomena such as competition, financial austerity, ethnocentrism (i.e., "Western" civilization) through the inductive mechanism of the natural sciences. While the lack of a consensus over the discipline's epistemology has led to vibrant debate in both graduate and professional settings, "practical" concerns in the changing structure of undergraduate education leave no room for such questioning and remain the norm. Most common remains the conception of education (and teaching) as an act of consumption and of services rendered, where the standardization of facts, methods, and data are directed towards the diffusion of a university's (or a state's) political and corporate interests. By privileging a corporate conception of the role of education in both national and international life—one that sees education as part of a banking system of "authoritative" forms of knowledge—the space for dialogue and exchange that lies at the heart of learning is reduced to the reproduction of pre-conceived ideologies.

I would suggest here, however, that Freire's intervention into the world of international politics puts IR scholars at a disadvantage. His preferential option for the poor is not merely a pedagogical exhortation, but rather a structural challenge that he asks of all self-proclaimed teachers to take up, weigh, and choose for themselves. In this sense, Freire is both an activist scholar, as well as a prophetic thinker, offering a challenge for scholars in the stark terms of the liberation of the oppressed, but also the alleged salvation and possibility of a certain *kind* of civilization. Indeed, the canonization of Freire as a figure to be emulated has been the subject of several criticisms regarding Freire's legacy and whether his approach is truly as universal as he often claimed. Kirkendall (2010), for example, suggests that similar to the corporate models they were struggling against, "the Latin American Left, as personified by Freire, had its own illusions, its own impatience, and its own inability to stay true to its democratic beliefs...Freire's historical experiences suggest that he should have embraced political pluralism more readily and more consistently, but the Left's disdain for "bourgeois democracy" and enthusiasm for the one-party state were slow to wane" (167). Additionally, as it concerns the transformation of the everyday into a "teachable moment," Carlos Alberto Torres (1993) has pointed out that "there is a tendency in Freire to overturn everyday situations so that they become pedagogical...While his initial point of reference might be non-formal, the educational encounters he explores remain formal" and thus, in a sense, works against the notion of dialogue (127).

While these criticisms reveal important gaps in Freirean scholarship, their intention, as Freire often admitted in later years, reveal the importance of challenging educators to take up their own methods to social and political liberation. The point here is not to criticize Freire's person, deeds, or methods (though these points have their own advocates, such as: Facundo 1984; Ohliger 1992); rather, I would like to pose here the problem of how we transform the everyday, especially concerning IR, into a critical pedagogical encounter. What "teachable moments" do we privilege in our discipline? What limitations do we draw for ourselves in negotiating the changing structures of the academy? And finally, in regards to Freire himself, why should we turn to such a paradoxical figure in clarifying our understanding of reflexivity and courage? Such questions lead to my claim that the IR scholar today faces a kind of existential exile with similar implications for our political and international life. In the section that follows, I address where such an exile comes from.

## 4    The Inversion of Exile: Coming Home in a Place-less World

In asking what exile teaches us about IR, we should also ask what IR teaches us about coming home. In his classic book, *The Hero with a Thousand Faces* (1949), Joseph Campbell suggests that "the place of the hero's birth, or the remote land of exile from which he returns to perform his adult deeds among men, is the mid-point or navel of the world" (334). Campbell's work was an attempt to situate the broader facets of myth and history within a world that was politically and ideologically unravelling. More specifically, in Campbell we find a broader engagement with the functions of myth in modern society: how the hero today, beyond the conscious effort to face the things that are unjust, is always already an exile.

For she who is banished, Campbell tells us, "exile is the first step of the quest," where individuals take within themselves their communities, their practices, their values towards other lands, realities, and ways of being; exile "brings the hero to the Self in all" (385–86). But if exile is to be understood as a form of banishment from what one thinks of as home, any return could only ever be a deficient one. To "come back," even under laudatory circumstances, is an act fundamentally imbued with both a sense of loss, as well as opportunity. Is such a return possible in today's world of corporate education? Do we need more heroes today in the academy? Why do we yearn for them, if not as a projection of our desire to save the world, or, save ourselves?

Throughout this chapter, I have emphasized the pedagogical exchange that takes place in the experience of exile and how a kind of exilic reflexivity may emerge from such moments. While exile generates lessons that emphasize the changing character of politics and education, it also represents the banishment of dissent. For example, rather than acknowledging "science" as part of a long process of pedagogical and intellectual transformation, scholars today continue to battle over one ready-made version of "science" (e.g., positivist, critical, or, pluralist) with often disturbing animosity against demonized others. No doubt the material and political character of the "science wars" is important. What is often missed or elided, however, is the wider existential and experiential horizon of students, amateurs, professionals, and publics that partake in the co-constitution of ideas. IR is no different in this regard, particularly if we eschew the difficult work of tracing the field's origins in colonial administration to our undergraduate students, normalize the political economy of adjunct and graduate exploitation, or, ignore our everyday complicity as members of the U.S. imperium while we wax poetic about the virtues of a humanities education.

In this sense, Brent Steele (2010) is right when he says, while writing about the marginalization of Liberal theorist-turned-critic Tony Smith, that the "status that gives purchase to the academic in their own scholarly community has an inverse quality in the political sphere" (52). The less "political" our research the more it seems celebrated; the more engaged with politics in becomes the more we risk being ostracized. The inverse of Steele's statement is also true: the social and political qualities that we inherit from the world often have the inverse effect when embraced in academia. Our demand on high rates of productivity isolates, rather than socializes our students; community is often built through antagonistic competition, rather than the cultivation of mutual intellectual interests; administrative and pedagogical dissent is reduced to personal quirks, rather than negotiated to properly reflect the material (and affective) capacities of our epistemic and learning communities. These three points are crucial as I illustrate the possible spaces generated by our personal journeys, and how the sites of our education inform the visions our discipline is capable of imparting to future generations.

Steele's comment regarding the inversion of scholarly and political goals is also tied to his broader analysis of the sociological vectors scholars face in speaking truth (*parrhesia*) to our broader scholarly communities. For Steele (2010), the prospects of *parrhesia* are most vivid today in the transition of IR from an active to a passive enterprise of scholarly involvement in the political (59–63). Central to his argument is the rise of neoconservatism in the U.S., and the overt endorsement or silence of IR scholars in the face of politicizing a national sentiment of mourning and loss around the attacks of September 11, 2001, and the justification of war in the name of spreading democracy. Steele's analysis asks for reflection on two points: first, the function of academic employment, or lack thereof, as being a primary obstacle to speaking truth to power; and second, the emotional and analytic distance that informs a scholar's generational vector.

In the first point, it is clearly those scholars without institutional affiliation to participate in the seasonal gatherings of the discipline that do not have their concerns or stories heard. But does that mean they have no stories? Inversely, the fear of unemployment (an increasingly insidious feature of the corporate university model of high production and low opportunity) puts the onus of being exiled from the discipline back on scholars themselves. We self-censor, we self-insulate, and though some scholars find outlets, or even families, of mutual dissent, others keep vitriolic and resentful sentiments within. In critical pedagogy circles, this amounts to the difference between "burning-out" and "burning-in," where some scholars drop out of the system of higher education, while others lose their sense of purpose in it (Higgins 2010; Beattie 2015).

It often seems inconsequential, if not narcissistic, to reflect on the exiled scholar of higher education. Yet professional venues such as the *Chronicle of Higher Education* and *Inside HigherEd* have increasingly drawn our attention to some recurring existential concerns: What are a department and university's scholarly relations built on? How well are graduate programs socializing their students for the challenges of both the academic job market and new tenure-granting metrics? How much is higher education still, if ever, about intellectual growth and maturity? Or, more pertinently, how much of it is about filling a teaching "need" or research trend? It seems unfair to frame the contemporary economic and generational dilemma of academia in purely career-oriented terms; however, the silence regarding so many of the above queries makes the failure to speak out all the more conspicuous. Indeed, the trade-off haunting the present academic generation may be less about relations between our colleagues, but rather which of them will I speak for as they are expelled, for either economic or political reasons.

Steele's (2010) second point regarding generational distance appropriately parallels the possibility of finding courage within this contemporary form of scholarly exile. In comparing the responses (or lack thereof) to both Hans Morgenthau and Tony Smith's criticisms of the Vietnam and Iraq wars, Steele brings up the problem of silence as a disciplining factor in both public and scholarly reactions. Key to his analysis is not so much that lack of acknowledgment punishes or teaches some kind of lesson to the *parrhesiastic* scholar. Rather, Steele's point is to emphasize the two-pronged effects of silence on theory formation as a form of dissent. Silence, he tells us, "can be a compelling form of discipline," not least because it is often expressed in the interest and attention a scholarly community grants an argument (52).

Additionally, and here Steele is less explicit, silence is a regulatory tool of "knowing your place." More specifically, he says, "[regardless] of what is intended by a theorist, we should ask if the construction and 'rules' of theory themselves are doing something that would make the theory attractive to those in power" (61). This is especially salient when theory formation elides the role of self-awareness in the process of "[abetting] those in power with a sense of legitimacy, scientific validity or authority" (64). For Morgenthau and Smith, this conflict was embodied in their role as leading intellectual figures in the study of global politics, while residing in the heart of American empire. Contemporary IR scholars live in a context that has not changed much since the Vietnam and Iraq Wars, not least in the prevalence of imperialist war-making. In terms of what we as a scholarly community do, however, many things have change and it is useful here to bring Freire back into the conversation. For Freire (1998), education is first and foremost a "specifically human act of intervening in the world" (99), yet one with an unequivocal target:

> When I speak of education as intervention, I refer both to the aspiration for radical changes in society in such areas as economics, human relations, property, the right to employment, to land, to education, and to health, and to the reactionary position whose aim is to immobilize history and maintain an unjust socio-economic and cultural order. (2000, 99)

Indeed, as Steele goes on, since this kind of self-awareness in our actions is "the most difficult of the practices to inhabit as a scholar" (64). He concludes with a set of alternatives that, while productive, also assume a previous theoretical move. Both the kind of reflexivity that Steele draws attention to, as well as the kinds of scholarly interrogation that he admits would generate greater forms of courage (but at higher personal costs), assume that IR scholars know what kind of "IR self" one embodies. Steele assumes we can know who we are without ever asking and looking at who we share our worlds with, and who (by virtue of generational, physical, or emotional distance) we do *not* share this world with. Such a portrait of reflexivity risks bordering on the self-indulgent, assuming we can know ourselves in the absence of how we look to others. It forgets, again in Merleau-Ponty's (1968) phrasing, that it is always "through other eyes that we become for ourselves fully visible" (143).

It seems at this point that greater discussion on the intentions of scholars and their theories is called for. More specifically, the courage that such intentions demand today in the face of silence, being publicly ostracized, and even denied tenure, require a closer look at the way exile pervades our daily lives. There is great potential here for IR scholars to look both within and outside of the discipline for the stories and examples that for centuries have shaped the experience of speaking truth to power. While I have offered a brief sketch of just one such example in the life of Paulo Freire, I will add that it is those stories that overlap the most with our own situations that should also be sought out. Steele (2015) has more recently been more vocal about these stories, increasingly referring in his works to the need for "documentary provocation" as a mode of reflexivity. As a kind of inventory of our work, documentary provocation "[holds] scholars responsible to a variety of outcomes linked to their scholarship—outcomes planned, unplanned, seen, and unforeseen" (62). That such an approach will generate discomfort among neopositivist scholars is precisely Steele's intent, an aim that Freire himself would recognize as part of the "ethics of human solidarity" (1998, 116).

The present article, then, is part of a similarly situated web of scholarly activities, taking aim at the institutionalized silos that treat the goal of human solidarity as an ancillary concern of proper social science. More specifically, it is a story written in the midst of a broader crisis in the production of knowledge, one tied to public defunding of universities, the use of corporate metrics for intellectual activity, and the individualizing of scholarly work away from politics itself (see: Sclofsky and Funk 2018 [and Chapter 1 in this volume]). Although multiple challenges to how highly industrialized societies think, work, and live have emerged as a result of the ongoing global economic crisis, substantive analysis of how higher education is coping (or not) with these material changes remains scant. What the systematic analysis of exile brings to scholarly discussions in these times is a reflexivity that informs the daily encounter with the world, not least in spaces where we have the opportunity to reflect on education, but perhaps only occasionally pursue it.

Indeed, much of the romanticism surrounding the current state of academic life forgets that no "golden era" of higher education truly ever existed. Rather, there are more or less extreme rearrangements of public money and institutions in the service of various facets of state power. At some times these facets were about greater public empowerment, at others they have been about militarism, racism, and the bulwarking of global capitalism. What is new today in these institutional dynamics is a defanged public sector open for greater market exploitation than ever before. Our reminiscence of past times may then just be a symptom of a de-politicized present.

## 5 Conclusion: The Changing Face of IR Scholarship

Exile is such a human component of contemporary life that it produces both nostalgia and disenchantment in the larger constellation of the twentieth century. More than this, exile also produces a different temporality that speaks to other ways of recovering the past in light of the theoretical poverty of our language. One of these ways is the narratives about the world we live in and the world to come. Such utopian aspirations, however, must not only be for the future, but also for the past. Our aspirations must attempt to recover the experiences that have been erased by the sanctioned packages of "structural readjustment," "austerity," and particularly the ambiguities of career-oriented "credentialism." Exile demands a re-construction of who we were and who we are in light of the coming challenges we can see so clearly. Freire is testament to this changing temporality, oscillating between a hope in the power of education to save the individual and the existential angst of questioning our differences as a lesson in plurality. To trace and conceptualize this effort takes searching for a new language. And while today's scholarship may be poor in new concepts (and perhaps even poorer in capturing the experiences of exile), one is never alone in the perpetual search for a scholarly home.

I conclude here with the object of our analysis: exile and courage in the study of international politics. Generations of students restlessly await the originality, creativity, and conviction that so many of us have been taught are crucial for our future of the discipline. IR today does them a great disservice by failing to acknowledge the context and implications of the larger crises of exile shared worldwide. For Freire, courage is only possible as an attitude that replaces—by way of human intervention into our existential and material conditions—the fear and insecurity that are inherent to the activities of learning. This is true within experiences of personal and collective questioning, but even more so in a context of indifference and injustice. As it concerns IR, the last decade has been marked by a simultaneous return and retreat from the question of courage via a turn towards epistemology and the space of "qualitative" analyses. This turn speaks powerfully to Freire's concern with teaching as being more than "the mechanical repetition of this or that gesture," but rather "a comprehension of the value of sentiments, emotions, and desires" (1998, 48). There is a risk in these turns of closing the space that generated indignation and the courage to revolt to begin with, making the spirit of inquiry a thing to be reproduced objectively, rather than reenacted personally and contextually.

If one considers the experiences that inform a scholar's trajectories, we will often find that both great teachers, but also great struggles, have made the particular moments of an education truly memorable. The spaces that inform educational experiences are always contentious and contested. I think this much should be true of the classroom today, as well as how we conceive of education in our discipline as part of the larger classroom of the world. Sadly, the world we inhabit is one of tragedy and strife, hardship and injustice, abandonment and exile. I say this not only for IR and study of politics, but also for our personal worlds as thinkers and scholars. The common link here is that both are human worlds; yet in these worlds lay the visions of other worlds long gone and many still to come. Courage, it seems, lies in the acknowledgment of that space of inclusion/exclusion, diligence/capitulation, and indignation/humility that makes waking up a struggle and a privilege.

More specifically, if there is anything that the contemporary crisis of academia should do—particularly as it has been experienced in North America—is convince us of the need for deeper engagement with the reasons scholars choose their craft and the questions that emerge when they are threatened with dissolution, punishment, indifference, or even exile. The question of exile is a way of articulating an experiential attitude that is rooted not just in physical displacement, but also personal acknowledgment. It ultimately points to an interrogation of context and motive that almost always reveals hidden possibilities. For the sake of our discipline, it may be time IR scholars realize that the place for those opportunities to magnify our virtues and our faults may be right where it always was: inside ourselves and our communities.

### Acknowledgements

The long life of this article has benefitted from feedback across three institutions, the 2011 Millennium Conference, and participation in the "Pedagogies of the 'International': Displacement, Emancipation, Reification" panel at the 2015 International Studies Association meeting in New Orleans. I wish to acknowledge the incisive support of François Debrix, Aida Hozic, Wanda Vrasti, Evgenia Ilieva, Manu Samnotra, Ty Solomon, Louiza Odysseos, Anna Selmeczi, Erzsebet Strausz, Kim Hutchings, Eric Selbin, and the editors at *International Studies Perspectives* for their permission to reprint it here.

### Bibliography

Beattie, A. (2015) "Exile as Reflexive Engagement: IR as Everyday Practice." In *Reflexivity and International Relations: Positionality, Practice, and Critique*, edited by B.J. Steele and J. Amoureux, pp. 160–176. New York: Routledge.

Campbell, J. (1949) *The Hero With a Thousand Faces*. New York: Meridian Books.

Caraccioli, M.J. (2011) "Spatial Structures and the Phenomenology of Inter-National Identity." *International Political Sociology* 5(1): 98–101.

Caraccioli, M.J. (2015) "A Global Human Condition." In *Human Beings and International Relations*, edited by Daniel Jacobi and Annette Freyberg-Inan, pp. 212–228. Cambridge: Cambridge University Press.

Caraccioli, M.J. and Hozic, A. (2015) "Reflexivity @ Disney U: 11 Theses on Living in IR." In *Reflexivity and International Relations: Positionality, Practice, and Critique*, edited by B.J. Steele and J. Amoureux, pp. 142–159. New York: Routledge.

Carr, E.H. (1964) *The Twenty Years' Crisis, 1919–1939: An Introduction to the Study of International Relations*. New York: HarperCollins Publishers, Inc.

Dauphinee, E. (2013) *The Politics of Exile*. London: Routledge.

De Certeau, M. (1984) *The Practice of Everyday Life*, trans. by S. Rendall. Berkeley: University of California Press.

Deresiewicz, W. (2011) "Faulty Towers: The Crisis in Higher Education." In *The Nation* 23. Available at: http://www.thenation.com/article/160410/faulty-towers-crisis-higher-education.

Dorfman, A. (2011) *Feeding on Dreams: Confessions of an Unrepentant Exile*. New York: Houghton Mifflin Harcourt.

Drainville, A.C. (2003) "Critical Pedagogy for the Present Moment: Learning from the Avant-Garde to Teach Globalization from Experiences." *International Studies Perspectives* 4(3): 231–249.

Dussel, E. (1985) *Philosophy of Liberation*. Mary Knoll: Orbis Books.

Facundo, B. (1984) *Freire-Inspired programs in the United States and Puerto Rico: A Critical Evaluation*. Washington, D.C.: Latino Institute. Available at: http://www.bmartin.cc/dissent/documents/Facundo/Facundo.html.

Frei, C. (2001) *Hans J. Morgenthau: An Intellectual Biography*. Baton Rouge: Louisiana State University Press.

Freire, P. (1978) *Pedagogy in Process: The Letters to Guinea-Bissau*. New York: Seabury Press.

Freire, P. (1985) *The Politics of Education: Culture, Power and Liberation*. Westport: Bergin & Garvey.

Freire, P. (1998) *Pedagogy of Freedom: Ethics, Democracy and Civic Courage*. Lanham: Rowman & Littlefield Publishers.

Freire, P. (2000) *Pedagogy of the Oppressed*. New York: Continuum Books.

Gadotti, M. (1994) *Reading Paulo Freire: His Life and Work*, trans. by J. Milton. Albany: New York: State University of New York Press.

Glass, R.D. (2001) On Paulo Freire's Philosophy of Praxis and the Foundations of Liberation Education. *Educational Researcher* 30(2): 15–25.

Harding, Sandra (1993) Rethinking Standpoint Epistemology: What Is "Strong Objectivity"? In *Feminist Epistemologies*, edited by L.A. and E. Potter, pp. 49–82. New York: Routledge.

Higgins, C. (2010) The Hunger Artist: Pedagogy and the Paradox of Self-Interest. In *Journal of Philosophy of Education* 44 (2–3): 337–369.

Inayatullah, N. (2011) *Autobiographical International Relations: I, IR*. London: Routledge.

Jacobi, D., Kessler, O., Michel, T., Caraccioli, M.J., and Brighton, S. (2011) "'To the Things Themselves'...and Back! International Political Sociology and the Challenge of Phenomenology." *International Political Sociology* 5(1): 87–105.

Kirkendall, A. (2010) *Paulo Freire and the Cold War Politics of Literacy*. Chapel Hill: University of North Carolina Press.

Kruzel, J. and Rosenau, J.N. (1989) *Journeys Through World Politics: Autobiographical Reflections of Thirty-Four Academic Travelers*. Lexington: Lexington Books.

Löwenheim, O. (2010) "The 'I' in IR: An Autoethnographic Account." *Review of International Studies* 36(4): 1023–1045.

Merleau-Ponty, M. (1962) *Phenomenology of Perception*. London: Routledge & Kegan Paul.

Merleau-Ponty, M. (1968) *The Visible and the Invisible*. Evanston: Northwestern University Press.

Mignolo, W.D. (2002) "The Geopolitics of Knowledge and the Colonial Difference." In *The South Atlantic Quarterly* 101(1): 57–96.

Neufeld, M.A. (1995) *The Restructuring of International Relations Theory*. Cambridge: Cambridge University Press.

Nishimura, K. (2011) "E.H. Carr, Dostoevsky, and the Problem of Irrationality in Modern Europe." *International Relations* 25(1): 45–64.

Odysseos, L. (2007) *The Subject of Coexistence: Otherness in International Relations*. Minneapolis: University of Minnesota Press.

Odysseos, L. and Pal, M. (2017) "Towards Critical Pedagogies of the International? Student Resistance, Other-Regardedness and Self-Formation in the Neoliberal University." Forthcoming in *International Studies Perspectives*. DOI: https://doi.org/10.1093/isp/ekx006.

Ohliger, J. (1992) "What Is Radical Adult Education?" *Adult & Continuing Education Today*. Available at: http://www.bmartin.cc/dissent/documents/Facundo/index.html

Oren, I. (2006) "Can Political Science Emulate the Natural Sciences? The Problem of Self-Disconfirming Analysis." *Polity* 39(1): 72–100.

Patterson, A.S. (2000) "It's a Small World: Incorporating Service Learning into International Relations Courses." *PS: Political Science and Politics* 33(4): 817–822.

Rivera, R. (2004) *A Study of Liberation Discourse: The Semantics of Opposition in Freire and Gutierrez*. New York: Peter Lang.

Said, E. (2000) *Reflections on Exile and Other Essays*. Cambridge: Harvard University Press.

Schmidt, J. (2001) *Disciplined Minds: A Critical Look at Salaried Professionals and the Soul-Battering System That Shapes Their Lives*. Lanham: Rowman & Littlefield Publishers, Inc.

Sclofsky, S. and Funk, K. (2018) "The Specter that Haunts Political Science: A Ruthless Criticism of Neglect and Misreadings of Marx in International Relations and Comparative Politics." *International Studies Perspectives* 19(1): 44–66.

Solomon, T. (2014) "Time and Subjectivity in World Politics." *International Studies Quarterly* 58(4): 671–681.

Steele, B.J. (2010) "Of 'Witches Brew' and Scholarly Communities: The Dangers and Promise of Academic Parrhesia." *Cambridge Review of International Affairs* 23(1): 49–68.

Steele, B.J. (2015) "Whistle Disruption: Reflexivity and Documentary Provocation." In *Reflexivity and International Relations: Positionality, Practice, and Critique*, edited by B.J. Steele and J. Amoureux, pp. 61–80. New York: Routledge.

Sznajder, M. and Roniger, L. (2009) *The Politics of Exile in Latin America*. New York: Cambridge University Press.

Tickner, J.A. (2006) "On The Frontlines or Sidelines of Knowledge and Power? Feminist Practices of Responsible Scholarship." *International Studies Review* 8(3): 383–395.

Torres, C.A. (1993) "From the 'Pedagogy of the Oppressed' to 'A Luta Continua': The Political Pedagogy of Paulo Freire." In *Freire: A Critical Encounter*, edited by P. McLaren and P. Leonard, pp. 119–145. London: Routledge.

Walker, R.B.J. (1993) *Inside/Outside: International Relations as Political Theory*. New York: Cambridge University Press.

Wedeen, L. (2009) "Ethnography as Interpretive Enterprise." In *Political Ethnography: What Immersion Contributes to the Study of Power*, edited by Edward Schatz, pp. 75–94. Chicago: University of Chicago Press.

Williams, M.C. (2004) "Why Ideas Matter in International Relations: Hans Morgenthau, Classical Realism, and the Moral Construction of Power Politics." *International Organization* 58(4): 633–665.

Williams, M.C. (2005) *The Realist Tradition and the Limits of International Relations*. New York: Cambridge University Press.

CHAPTER 9

# The Materiality of Proletarian Subjectivity: Anticapitalist Antiracist Pedagogies for the 21st Century

*Zachary A. Casey*

> *They know that property, capital, money, wage-labour and the like are no ideal figments of the brain but very practical, very objective sources of their self-estrangement and that they must be abolished in a practical, objective way for man to become man not only in thinking, in consciousness, but in mass being, in life.*
> KARL MARX—THE HOLY FAMILY

∴

In many ways it feels today like we are in a kind of "era of identity" on the Left.[1] That is, in 2018, particularly here in the United States, it seems as though the first and most important starting point for anti-oppressive work is with one's self and the different identities one can make meaningful claims to. We hear more and more claims of "intersectional identities" from those on the Left, a reworking (and appropriation) of Crenshaw's (1992) critical black feminist insight that multiple forms or systems of oppression enmesh and inform one another—so much so that one cannot meaningfully distinguish, in the context of a black woman in the U.S. for instance, where the oppressions that stem from white supremacy begin-end and those from heteropatriarchy begin-end. Heteropatriarchy is supported by white supremacy, and vice versa, so much so that to understand either system of exploitation one must take the other seriously and examine the ways in which approaches to antiracism, for instance,

---

[1] Portions of this chapter are adapted from my book, *A Pedagogy of Anticapitalist Antiracism: Whiteness, Neoliberalism, and Resistance in Education*, published by State University of New York Press.

will always run the risk of re-centering cis-male privilege. All identities then are always in relationship to the structural forces that produce those identities, revealing ways that systems of oppression create intersections that must be taken into account when we aim to mobilize the assets of our identities for anti-oppressive praxis.

But increasingly we aren't hearing about intersectional identities as being materially determined (in the Marxist sense, which is discussed below) by oppressive systems, but rather as a stand in for something like "multiple identities." My "intersectional" identities in this context might include my identifications as cis-male, white, English speaking, from the U.S., middle class, and so on. But such a listing, though certainly satisfying the criteria of being "multiple," erases the material determinisms that function to limit and contort our social reality for the needs of the owners of capital. They aren't *intersectional* at all, and as a result we find an absence in such projects of material redistributions—of ways that commitments to justice become realized capacities for historically marginalized social actors to have greater access to social goods, services, and opportunities. These projects towards justice seem mostly about emotional solidarities and discoursal redistribution: referring to others in more inclusive ways in lieu of actually redistributing capital in such ways that all peoples have access to meaningful unalienating labor, housing, health care, food, and so forth. If everyone is included in discourse, so this logic goes, we will realize the kinds of just social practices we seek. This, for any Marxists, is usually coded as an instance of "false consciousness." But too few Marxists, I argue, recognize this moment as a *pedagogical* challenge—as a call for a different set of approaches to teaching and learning about capitalism as it informs and produces other forms of oppression.

This chapter is about ways of imagining this pedagogical challenge particularly towards the links between white supremacy and capitalism. Here I articulate a Marxian approach to the problem of identity/identities as a pedagogical challenge in three parts. In part one, I juxtapose the concepts of proletarian subjectivity with identity. I work to connect the works of Paulo Freire with Teresa Ebert and Mas'ud Zavarzadeh to articulate a conception of proletarian subjectivity as being materially produced, offering ways of being in solidarity that present conceptions of identity make impossible. Next, I review what I have elaborated (see Casey 2016) as the primary frames for engaging in anticapitalist antiracist pedagogies, focusing on antiracist anticapitalist conceptions of learning, curriculum, and consciousness. Finally, I present four frames for thinking about how we might engage more fully with the praxis of critical pedagogy as we work to teach and learn Marx and Marxism in the 21st century.

## 1 Sectarianism and the Need for Proletarian Subjectivity

When we think of Marxism as a pedagogical project—as a call for politically conscious teaching and learning on the side of liberation and redistribution—the work and life of Paulo Freire comes to mind almost immediately. His most widely read and known text, *Pedagogy of the Oppressed,* can be read as a pedagogical extension of Marx, as a way of "reinventing" critical components of Marx's thinking, especially dialectical materialism and the dialectical conditions of oppression (oppressors who actively oppress those who are then constructed as the oppressed, defined in relation to those who oppress them) (Freire 2000). Freire's work centers praxis: action and reflection in equal measure on the world in order to transform it. Such a praxis calls on us to "read" both "the word" and "the world" in order to name for ourselves and with others the conditions of our dehumanization and how we can organize our lives and efforts to be on the side of humanization. In Freire's (2000) terms, this requires developing a critical capacity for *conscientização:* "learning to perceive social, political, and economic contradictions, and to take action against the oppressive elements of reality (35). While we will return to a more detailed account of consciousness as part of the pedagogical project of anticapitalist antiracism, for now we can focus on the curricular directionality of Freire's definition of conscientização. Perceiving the social, political, and economic contradictions that make up our social reality can be read as a call for the content of our critical study: it can be read as that which we ought to teach and learn about, if our pedagogical activity aims to be on the side of humanization.

Such activity must be diligent to avoid what Freire calls "sectarianism," the propensity for many to advocate for narrow and partial projects based on reactionary responses to social conditions. Freire is clear that such sectarianism often emerges from the Right, by means of appeals to the supposed "commonsense" of radical self-interest and the maintenance of the oppressive status quo. However, too often those advocating for humanization and liberation find themselves taking up equally sectarian positions as those who oppose their/our visions for justice and social transformation. For Freire, "Not infrequently, revolutionaries themselves become reactionary by falling into sectarianism in the process of responding to the sectarianism of the Right... Sectarianism in any quarter is an obstacle to the emancipation of mankind" (37). We can think of examples of Left sectarianisms if we think of the various identity-based appeals to social movements that fail to even mention the exploitative conditions of capitalism. Two examples of this should suffice to make the point.

First, we can look to the ways we often explain evidence of patriarchy and sexism in our present social reality. Most commonly, we point to data that shows the "wage gap" between men and women, regularly finding that women with the same professional experiences and qualifications as their male counterparts make 80 cents for every dollar made by men in the same position (National Committee on Pay Equity). Another, similar, example comes in the form of the racialized differences in unemployment experiences. While there has been much discussion in recent months of the United States' historically low unemployment rate, under 4% overall, African American unemployment stands at almost double this national average (Bureau of Labor Statistics). In other words, African Americans in the United States experience unemployment at a much greater rate than other racial groups. For both examples, we can see the ways in which the capitalist system itself is treated as a taken for granted natural condition of being—as a fair and objective barometer in order to understand the relative oppressions and discriminations that manifest in our present social reality. Arguing narrowly for an end to the wage gap, or to no longer see disproportionate overrepresentation for black folks in unemployment, without attention to the structures that condition and determine our economic reality, can only ever be sectarian. Thinking in particular about the unemployment example, we can imagine easily the ways in which the maintenance of a broader system of white supremacy functions within capitalism to produce unequitable hiring practices—but narrowly working only to redress this disproportionality cannot actually transform any of the determining conditions that keep this reality in place. That is, even full employment for black folks would not automatically redress broader wealth gaps, historically accrued wealth by dispossession, or combat the exploitative and dehumanizing conditions of wage labor in capitalism. Yet the draw to a sectarian position narrowly arguing for greater employment opportunities is great—and likely for most readers, we would have an easier time thinking of existing community organizations and programs that combat unemployment than those that explicitly seek to combat capitalism.

There are of course many more examples of Left sectarianisms we might list here, but the critical point for the present argument is that we understand the failures of sectarian approaches from the beginning: that positions that do not place social actors in social contexts—in *full* context—are sectarian and incapable of eliminating the determining mechanisms of oppression. The reflexive and Freirean call for engagement with the contradictions that make up our social conditions here asks us to position all instances of oppression and dehumanization in context and in relation to other systems and forms. We must work to realize the connections and intersections of different manifestations of oppression—not so that we can create isolated and reactionary responses to each different instance, but rather so that we can understand these relationships and articulate a praxis that can carry us forward in ways that grow the scope of our project—to interrogate and re-interrogate that which we are studying to better articulate the connections to other injustices so that we might better articulate a shared project of humanization: a praxis.

There is perhaps a way to think of sectarianisms as resulting from a feeling of pragmatic expediency: "we must center our struggle for recognition and humanization in reactionary ways because there is no other alternative" this perspective insists. Ebert and Zavarzadeh (2007) approach this philosophically, but the implications for pedagogical projects and others abound, in their treatment of the ways we too often misrecognize the ways that class is materially determined. This material determination marks it as a social category and lived experience that stands in tension with contemporary notions of culture—shared systems of meanings, thoughts, activities, and behaviors passed generationally in communities. Class is made, produced, and as such functions to produce particular subjectivities that can be understood as deriving meaning from their conflict and contradiction. For Marxists, these are the social categories of bourgeoisie and proletariat, those who own the means of production and those who must sell their labor to subsist.

Ebert and Zavarzadeh (2007) point us to the ways that sectarianisms have resulted in a Left that seems more critical of essentialisms than capitalism. These forms of sectarianism take on the position that developments in late capitalism have produced culture as a material reality and that consumption and production (of culture) are "no longer distinguishable" (38). Everything, in other words, is now cultural, and so any claims about objective reality are seen as mediated by a particular culture—and to not name that particularity is to run the risk of essentialism. The collapsing of cultures into a single objective reality, like the Marxist notion of class, functions to ignore cultural differences and thus essentializes all peoples into a taken for granted Eurocentric epistemology, so this critique goes. However, this argument obscures the material ways that class position (relation to the means of production) functions to *produce* culture. Yes, culture has *and ought to have* significant meaning for peoples and communities. But it would appear that in our contemporary social reality culture has replaced class as the most impactful condition for peoples' material condition—for what animates and explains the reasons for the ways they live their lives. This position functions to normalize capitalism and capitalist exploitation as they impact both identity formation and a person's material reality. Ebert and Zavarzadeh reason that if this is the case, that culture really is more impactful than social class for people living today in the 21st century, then there is no need for any further discussion of anticapitalism. They write,

> Class... is a property relation; this means class differences are produced at the point of production where surplus labor is extracted from workers and not in the market. The market does not produce wealth; it simply distributes what is produced elsewhere, and the elsewhere is where labor power produces surplus labor. (xvii)

Ebert and Zavarzadeh thus work to show that class cannot be reduced to culture, and that such a practice, making class cultural, obscures the material relations of owners and workers—we lose sight of distribution and fall back on taken for granted seemingly "natural" ways of thinking and knowing about the material conditions of our lives. Owning a home, or an Xbox, as Ebert and Zavarzadeh discuss, does not make one a capitalist. Owning, buying, and selling the labor of others does. We cannot fall back on thinking of class as an attitude (Eagleton 2011) as though classism were the sectarian area we sought to challenge. Marxism is not a critique of snobbery, treating working class people with kindness and empathy without abolishing the conditions for their precarious class position will not transform our social order. It is thus not essentializing to say someone sells their labor in order to live if it is objectively true, and one's class position has little to do with how one *feels* about—or the language they use to describe—said class position. The abolition of capitalism must be understood as a project that exceeds and exists outside of identity claims because class is an objective reality that cuts across cultures.

Such an understanding, drawn from Ebert and Zavarzadeh, can be read alongside Freire's conception of sectarianism to produce a concept of *proletarian subjectivity*. Conceptually, proletarian subjectivity works to reconcile the problem of sectarianism that seemingly all forms of identity-based Left struggles fall into. The descriptor "proletarian" works citationally to name the Marxist orientation to the ways in which our social realities are determined—produced—through the exchange and distribution of capitalism as it works to shape, control, and contort any and all areas of social existence. "Subjectivity" adds the Freirean dimension, working to name the ways that while class positions are materially determined and produced, human beings are not reducible to the status of *objects*. Subjectivity also carries with it the connotation of referring to a shared category or group yet avoids the sectarian position of centering the individual as a completely cultural being, comprised of multiple cultural impacts and influences, unlike any and every other confluence of identities, and so forth. Proletarian subjectivity then denotes a shared material condition of oppression within capitalism capable of transcending the various snares of sectarianism that function to pit proletarian subjects against one another. One further word about proletarian subjectivity is needed before turning to a summary of the major elements of anticapitalist antiracist pedagogy; namely, a way of placing identity with/in this work given the above.

Identities certainly retain value, meaning, and potency as they help us name our realities. They offer sources of comfort and membership, of belonging and history, that proletarian subjectivity cannot and should not aim to erase. What a reading of Freire alongside Ebert and Zavarzadeh offers is a way of acting in solidarity that is not premised on competing identities. Take for instance the question of a white person advocating for antiracism. From a sectarian perspective the white person is hoping to help people of color in *their* struggle against racism: the white person's identity does not place them within the group of those who are marked as other and thus discriminated against, and so the white person's identity is foregrounded and largely gets in the way. Their whiteness becomes all of who they are: in the context of antiracism they are *only* white, and thus always already prefigured in a hierarchical relationship with peoples of color in terms of fitness for antiracist work, or proximity and complicity with the owners of the means of oppression. Proletarian subjectivity does not make anyone no longer marked and identified by race, class, gender, sexuality, nationality, and so forth—nor is this desirable. Old clichés of Marxists considering race merely another example of false consciousness might come to mind and bring with them the caution that in our desires to articulate solidarities across perceived differences we can further exacerbate the cultural differences that capitalism has made part of its operating ethos: we can spend our time fighting one another rather than fighting for redistribution and equity. We can then think of proletarian subjectivity as a source of shared experience that can function to help us on the Left avoid the pitfalls that identity-based work has produced. Our shared proletarian subjectivity becomes the means by which we can understand the Freirean concepts that it is both the oppressors and the oppressed who are dehumanized via the act of oppression, and the means by which one who has been solidary with the oppressors can, by learning with and from the oppressed, transform their consciousness and act on that transformation to engage in praxis. Such positionalities seem foreclosed from the starting place of identity—from the perspective of proletarian subjectivity they become means by which we can act pedagogically on the side of humanization.

## 2   Frames for the Teaching and Learning of Anticapitalist Antiracist Pedagogies

In other writing I have worked to articulate a detailed account of anticapitalist antiracist pedagogy and its implications for teaching, learning, and teacher education (see Casey 2016). It is not my intention to repeat myself here, but rather to place the above discussion of proletarian subjectivity in a pedagogical context. Returning to the introduction of this chapter, reading Marx as a pedagogical challenge of the 21st century offers ways of resisting various overdetermined, reactionary, and sectarian responses to Marx and Marxism. Marxism is a pedagogical project devoid of a completely known and pre-articulated end point: Marx is not interested in, nor does he ever explicitly state how it is he thinks people ought to live after capitalism and private property have been abolished. Thus, it is not actually possible to "backwards design" a Marxian project of proletarian subjectivity.

Backwards design refers to the work of Wiggins and McTighe (2008) to offer a practical set of strategies for curriculum makers to ensure that students are able to be productive with content in context, not to just simply memorize what they need to for a set assignment or exam and move on. A simplified version of their method is this: start at the end point, when students will be acting on and using the content that they have learned with us and use *that* as the basis of designing the lesson. If we know where we want to get to, the end point, we can then think of steps and ways of understanding our progress in order to create activities and assessments that will support us in getting there. While there is no *there* that Marx articulates fully as the destination of proletarian struggle, certainly we have a great sense of the conditions of *there*, even if no clear and universal endpoint is possible. Still, we need a criterion to understand how we ought to build curriculum on the side of humanization. Once again, Freire's work can serve as such a guide.

Freire's Chapter Two of *Pedagogy of the Oppressed* ends with a warning that speaks directly to the impossibility of backwards designing life after capitalism and private property. Freire (2000) writes, "In the revolutionary process, the leaders cannot utilize the banking method as an interim measure, justified on grounds of expediency, with the intention of *later* behaving in a genuinely revolutionary fashion" (86). The banking method he refers to should be read metaphorically, but in a literal way. Banking education means making deposits, with the teacher depositing into students' minds with the aim of reaping a return on their investment. This return might be in the form of docile behavior, scoring well enough on tests to demonstrate competence, acceptance of the status quo, and so forth. Freire's warning then is that even if we knew the exact destination of our journey toward humanization, we cannot utilize oppressive means of teaching and learning in order to help reach this destination faster. We cannot allow liberatory ends to justify oppressive means, and thus we need a way of understanding and naming the constituent elements of a pedagogical project of proletarian subjectivity. To accomplish this, I next focus on anticapitalist antiracist conceptions of learning, curriculum, and consciousness.

Learning in anticapitalist antiracist ways necessitates what Carl Rogers (1989) called "self-appropriated" knowledge. For Rogers, what we know best is knowledge that we have worked for ourselves, that we have been active and invested in constructing and building meaning, and thus learned. He writes, "My experience has been that I cannot teach another person how to teach. To attempt it is for me, in the long run futile" (301). Rogers makes this conclusion based on two principles: the most important learning is basically impossible to communicate and can only be experienced, and much of what is taught is inconsequential. Rogers' notion that teaching is too often inconsequential is connected to the Freirean (1998) notion that "there is no teaching without learning" (29). If someone stands in front of a group of people who are younger than them, and explains something, it is only teaching if the students are learning from it. If what is being delivered does not hold their interest and does not produce the conditions for the self-appropriation of learning, for Rogers, it is inconsequential. For Freire, it isn't even teaching.

The trouble of communicating how to teach for Rogers stems from his desire to learn more than anything else—to learn with and from others, for him, is far more impactful on our behaviors. Rogers sees behavior as the most meaningful assessment of learning: if it does not change our behavior, it is inconsequential. This again connects to Freire, largely in the ways that Freire's work aims to blur distinctions between teachers and students. The aim of such blurring is to center learning: to make learning with and from one another the primary activity of our work in classrooms, rather than the un-learning teaching that is banking. An example I have used many times in discussions of banking education, about a young person learning to tie their shoes, can help make the more abstract qualities of Rogers' and Freire's arguments more grounded.

If we think of a moment wherein a young person asks us to show them how to tie their shoes, and then we do, this is not an instance of banking education. Why? Because the young person *wants* to know how to tie their shoes. If we know something, in this case, about tying shoes, and another would like to access that same knowledge, and we share it, we are not complicit in the oppression of the young person. And further, even though we are showing them how to tie their shoes, they are still actively building and constructing meaning, because of their desire to learn how to tie their shoes. Our teaching of the young person then has a very practical outcome: we hope they are able to tie their shoes. Since they desire that too, we can work together, to build whatever scaffolding we need to, in order to support the young person to self-appropriate the knowledge of how to tie their shoes.

If someone stands and lectures and their students learn nothing, they are not teaching. And thus, in an anticapitalist antiracist pedagogy, self-appropriated learning must be the central aim and focus. This self-appropriation carries with it conditions that mark learning as authentic: as not conditional on an outside or capitalistic desire for the commodity-student to "master." Learning must be of and for those engaged in the learning, connecting the learner and their wealth of knowledge and experiences regardless of age—their "funds of knowledge" (Gonzalez & Moll 2002)—to the material conditions that constitute and determine their social reality.

*Curriculum* can be thought of abstractly as "the what" of teaching and learning: the content. In the Freirean sense, curriculum is anything we can "read." Thus, if we are reading the world, the world can be understood as a curriculum. While we often approach curriculum from the starting point of what Michael Apple (2000) has called "official knowledge"—examples include state content area standards, Pearson textbooks, and so on—anticapitalist antiracist pedagogies must consider the full range of curricular possibilities for humanizing learning. Anything we can learn from is curricular. Our various readings of different curricular artifacts and "texts" do not start and stop with the bells that signal particular moments of the school day, but rather are always ongoing. We are always making meaning from our experiences, and always experiencing elements of social reality that we learn from.

For the project of proletarian subjectivity as an animating shared material condition, anticapitalist antiracist pedagogies insist on a broad and elastic conception of curriculum. But this conception also insists that curriculum not be seen as an end in itself, as though mastery of a particular curriculum can guarantee particular outcomes. Reading Marx, as incredibly important to my life and my work as it has been, is empty if it begins and ends only as curriculum. Freire insisted that literacy is not an end in itself, that being able to read and write for the sake of reading and writing is meaningless if the activity of literacy cannot be directed towards greater realization of humanization. For Freire, voting literacy laws that disenfranchised millions of people made literacy inherently political—but even in the absence of voting literacy laws and juridical requirements for particular literacies, literacy is always-already political because of the political nature of our social reality. This means that there is no set of texts or experiences, a set curriculum, that can guarantee the same particular results over and over—and it also means that curriculum must be seen as a tool. The pedagogical challenge is to make curriculum a tool of liberation, rather than a tool that thwarts critical consciousness.

*Consciousness* is central to Freire's pedagogical Marxism, as it is central to Marx's (1981) sense of proletarian subjectivity and revolutionary activity. Teacher educator Gloria Ladson-Billings (1995) has detailed what she has termed "culturally relevant pedagogy." In her work, she insists that sociopolitical consciousness is a prerequisite for engaged and impactful teaching and learning. She writes,

> The first thing teachers must do is educate themselves about both the local sociopolitical issues of their school community (e.g., school board policy, community events) and the larger sociopolitical issues (e.g., unemployment, healthcare, housing) that impinge upon their students' lives. (37)

Consciousness can thus be understood here as working to connect the local and the universal, both what is close and visible as well as the structures, systems, and frames that inform and act on both individuals and groups. For Marx, revolutionary consciousness is tied to understanding one's position in relation to the means of production. When workers understand that the owners of the means of production alienate and dehumanize in the pursuit of profits they can then articulate their proletarian subjectivity with the understanding that the present economic system denies them their capacity to be fully human.

For anticapitalist antiracist pedagogy, this consciousness is premised on the ability to see, in both local and global contexts, the present realities of white supremacy and the ways in which the logics of white supremacy function to legitimate capitalist exploitation, and vice versa, the ways capitalism normalizes white supremacy as simply part of the meritocratic social hierarchy. It is this ability to see that consciousness offers, not merely having an abstract principle, but rather a self-appropriated ability to read both the word and world in critical ways.

Anticapitalist antiracist pedagogies approach learning, curriculum, and consciousness through the lens of proletarian subjectivity in order to advance a means of working across difference on the side of humanization. By privileging learning above all other aims for work in formal educational spaces, students and teachers can better work together to name their reality and work dialogically to get smarter about the ways they can struggle together for justice. Curricula can be drawn from across disciplines, fields, and styles and make space for the full breadth of knowledge and experience present in any group of people, regardless of their ages. We can learn from anything, but this is not an argument that relativizes content and curriculum. Critical readings of reactionary and sectarian texts can offer powerful learning experiences. Most critically, we cannot select a rigorous and humanizing curriculum and then think that what follows will automatically be just and liberatory. Curriculum is a tool that can be used instrumentally for just and unjust ends. It must be mediated, by a consciousness that works to connect the local and the systemic and understands the social relations imbedded therein. Consciousness of the sociopolitical contexts of our work, of the ways in which our lives are determined in and by capitalism, offer a directionality to what it is we ought to strive to learn and the means by which we take up that learning. In the final section of this chapter, I offer four frames for thinking about anticapitalist antiracist pedagogies that center proletarian subjectivities.

## 3   Four Frames for Praxis in Learning Marxism in the 21st Century

The concept of frames and framing comes from the work of cognitive linguist George Lakoff (2002, 2004). Lakoff (2004) tells us that, "frames are mental structures that shape the way we see the world" (p. xv). Frames are always-already political, because they conjure particular inclusions and exclusions that structure the ways in which ideas move in discourse. These discourses then impact material outcomes, in the form of social policies, projects, and institutions that act on and in frames. For examples we can look to Kumashiro's (2008) work to articulate Rightist frames that dominate education in the United States. His analysis centers on "standards, accountability, sanctions, and school choice" to demonstrate how these frames "become linked together by a metaphor (the strict-father model) that makes the four frames inseparable from one another" (35). The "strict-father model" is a concept drawn from Lakoff (2002, 2004) to name the primary logic of conservative interests with regard to national politics. A strict-father model employs the frames of "family, self-sufficiency, and meritocracy" to argue that those who have not been successful in our capitalist society have failed because of their own moral failures and inability to work hard (Kumashiro, 2008, 35).

Frames can be thought of as particular lenses, ways of viewing something that are conditioned by the mediation of the contexts said viewing is happening in. Proletarian subjectivity, while it certainly can function as a frame on its own, can be articulated further by thinking through four frames that focus in on particular elements and possibilities for praxis. These four frames are *audience(s)*, *resistance(s)*, *discourse(s)*, and *hope(s)*. I discuss each frame here to conclude the chapter, with the hope of inviting others to think with me and reinvent these ideas, in the Freirean sense, on the side of humanization.

The frame of *audience(s)* for proletarian subjectivity asks us to think about who we see as included in the conception detailed above of proletarian subjects. While my aim in this work has been to be as inclusive as possible, there are perhaps difficulties in thinking of such a broad project inclusive of all peoples and identities that can be understood as working class. There are, of course, deep schisms and divisions on the Left that make solidarities complex and at times seemingly impossible. Ebert and Zavarzadeh have connected these schisms to the philosophical project of poststructuralism, and the attention to essentialism coming to replace attention to capitalist exploitation in philosophical inquiry. Their conclusions that class is a material production, marking it as distinct from other kinds of cultural formations and groups, offer theoretical terrain that must be taken up and acted on in order to be made practical by those engaged in practice. Thinking about the ways that different historically marginalized groups, for instance black and Latinx peoples in the United States, have been pitted against one another for the needs and demands of capitalism might offer different ways to engage these groups in conversation together about their shared sense of proletarianism coupled with the important differences that separate them from others. Too often such intercultural work relies on a taken for granted and untheorized universalization of experience that asks participants to find what they have in common "with everyone" or "anyone." Such universalization is not what proletarian subjectivity advocates—it is *not* a universal subjectivity, but rather names the great majority of humanity in their material produced condition. Attention to audience(s) offers further ways of thinking through possibilities and limitations of proletarian subjectivity that connect to different kinds of resistance(s).

The frame of resistance(s) asks us to think about those who will be in opposition to the project of conscientizing around proletarian subjectivity. It is beyond the scope of this chapter to articulate the many reactionary and sectarian critiques and resistance(s) of/to Marx, Freire, critical pedagogy, and proletarian subjectivity. But we should be clear in our thinking on this matter: there will always be resistance(s) to counter-hegemonic praxis, resistance(s) from areas we expect, such as capitalists and avowed white supremacists, and from areas we might not, perhaps from queer and disabled communities. In such moments, Kumashiro's (2009) reminders about the paradoxical conditions for anti-oppressive work are important to keep in mind: any effort to center a particular form of oppression is simultaneously a lack of effort to center other forms of oppression. This offense by omission is impossible to avoid but can be addressed explicitly and discussed openly. Certainly, the abolition of capitalism will not result in the abolition of all forms of oppression. Said forms of oppression would take on an utterly new and different character, but we cannot pretend that we can collapse and combine *all* forms of oppression and then act on that singularity. We must know, and expect, that at every step of our anticapitalist antiracist work we will face resistance(s), some of which we can anticipate and respond to in real time, and others that we won't be able to be so proactive with. This is why attention to the ways we talk about proletarian subjectivity, as materially produced, are so critical.

The frame of discourse(s) for proletarian subjectivity asks us to think about the ways we think and talk, the languages we mobilize, and how we might think about using multiple discourses to work toward a shared aim. Much like culture, it sometimes feels like "discourse" has come to describe any and everything in our social reality. The politics of language are hyper visible in multiple contemporary justice struggles. Discoursal shifts might feel small and insignificant in the abstract, but when applied to the marking of one's gender on their I.D. or the experience of being "dead-named," to name just two examples from trans- struggles for equity and inclusion, the materiality of discourse can be understood. This frame also asks if there are perhaps other means of communicating and sharing across differences that will enable more social actors to read themselves into solidarities rooted in proletarian subjectivity. If we imagine a society that has abolished capitalism and private property, would we think a revolutionary society impossible if the discourse of bourgeoisies, proletariat, communism, and property did not appear in regular usage? In some ways this is begging the rhetorical "a rose by any other name" trope that is far more relativistic than the cautions I wish to make plain in this conclusion. The frame of discourse(s) here asks in what ways might we mobilize further to advocate for anticapitalist antiracism—and asks us to be self-critical and reflexive in our own discourse. It calls for greater theorizing and reinvention, and for greater revolutionary imagination.

The frame of hope(s) asks us to think through the ever-ongoing, unfinished work of conscientização. Freire stressed the idea that pedagogues must be humble, that we must remain conscious of our many limitations and make such limits aspects of our pedagogy. Kumashiro (2009) advocates for a similar approach, asking us to put front and center the very things we don't want in our teaching. That is, we should engage openly with our students or others we are working with when we are not living out our convictions. We do so because we know we are unfinished and incomplete, and this incompleteness is the condition for feelings of hope in the face of overwhelming dehumanization and structural oppression. It would surely be hopeless if we were actually in possession of the step-by-step manual that would guide us through each stage of revolutionary struggle. When we trick ourselves into thinking such guides could, should, or do exist, we are not remaining humble in Freire's sense, and we are also not allowing for any sense of hope.

Hope is not naïve, but only when it is predicated on material conditions as they exist—our hopes are conditional and must seek to transform the level that produces these conditions. As we hope for greater solidarities, we can look to the possibilities inherent in the concept of proletarian subjectivity put forward here as a source for ways to continue to imagine more just and more humanizing pedagogies. Perhaps the greatest lesson we can learn from engaging Marx in the 21st century then is the radical sense of possibility that animates not only his work, but also his students as they/we have worked to read his ideas into fields and areas that Marx himself could never have dreamed of. That there will always be more to do, and that the work of humanization is never finished might lead some to feelings of despair, but such feelings should be resisted. It is only because there is always more to do that such work remains imaginable, and this spirit of radical imagination is conditioned by hope: for proletarian subjectivity to enable greater solidarities and a more fully human experience for the whole of humanity.

## Bibliography

Apple, Michael W. (2002) *Official Knowledge: Democratic Education in a Conservative Age*. New York: Routledge.
Bureau of Labor Statistics Data (2018) "Unemployment Rate—Black or African American." July 7, 2018. Retrieved July 29, 2018. https://data.bls.gov/timeseries/LNS 14000006.
Casey, Zachary A. (2016) *A Pedagogy of Anticapitalist Antiracism: Whiteness, Neoliberalism, and Resistance in Education*. Albany, NY: State University of New York Press, 2016.
Crenshaw, Kimberlé Williams (1992) "Race, Gender, and Sexual Harassment." *Southern California Law Review* 65: 1467–1470.
Eagleton, Terry (2011) *Why Marx Was Right*. New Haven: Yale University Press.
Ebert, Teresa L. and Zavarzadeh, Mas'ud (2007) *Class in Culture*. Boulder, CO: Paradigm Pub.
Freire, Paulo (1998) *Pedagogy of Freedom: Ethics, Democracy and Civic Courage*. New York: Rowman & Littlefield, Incorporated.
Freire, Paulo (2000) *Pedagogy of the Oppressed*. New York: Continuum.
Gonzalez, Norma, and Moll, Luis C. (2002) "Cruzando El Puente: Building Bridges to Funds of Knowledge." *Educational Policy* 16, no. 4: 623–641.
Kumashiro, Kevin K. (2008) *The Seduction of Common Sense: How the Right Has Framed the Debate on America's Schools*. New York: Teachers College Press.
Kumashiro, Kevin K. (2009) *Against Common Sense: Teaching and Learning Toward Social Justice*. New York: Routledge.
Ladson-Billings, Gloria (1995) "Toward a Theory of Culturally Relevant Pedagogy." *American Educational Research Journal* 32, no. 3: 465–491.
Lakoff, George (2002) *Moral Politics: How Liberals and Conservatives Think*. Chicago: University of Chicago Press.
Lakoff, George (2004) *Don't Think of an Elephant!: Know Your Values and Frame the Debate: The Essential Guide for Progressives*. White River Junction, VT: Chelsea Green Publishing.

Marx, Karl (1981) *Capital: A Critique of Political Economy.* Translated by Ben Fowkes and David Fernbach. London: Penguin Books in association with New Left Review.

Marx, Karl and Engels, Friedrich (1956) *The Holy Family.* Moscow: Foreign Languages Publishing House.

National Committee on Pay Equity (2011) "Pay Equity Information." National Committee on Pay Equity NCPE. September 2011. Retrieved April 24, 2012. http://www.pay-equity.org/info-time.html.

Rogers, Carl R. (1989) "Personal Thoughts on Teaching and Learning." In *The Carl Rogers Reader,* edited by Howard Kirschenbaum and Valerie Land Henderson. Boston: Houghton Mifflin.

Wiggins, Grant P. and McTighe, Jay (2008) *Understanding by Design.* Alexandria, VA: Association for Supervision and Curriculum Development.

CHAPTER 10

# Teaching Marx, Critical Theory, and Philosophy: Some Personal Reflections

*Douglas Kellner*

In this chapter, I will recount, first, my first teaching experience, and then my introduction to Marxism as a graduate student at Columbia University during the 1968 student uprising, followed by discussion of my introduction to Frankfurt School Critical Theory during my studies in Tubingen, Germany, during the late 1960s. Next, I tell how I was hired to teach Marxist philosophy at the University of Texas in Austin in 1973, and describe my experiences teaching Marxism and Critical Theory at UT-Austin from 1973-1995, and then at UCLA from 1995 until the present. Finally, I suggest in the era of Donald Trump and his aftermath that reading, studying, and teaching Marxism is of crucial importance and relevance.

## 1 The Columbia Uprising and My Introduction to Marxism

While a graduate student at Columbia, I received a coveted assignment to teach the famous Great Books course to college freshmen. In my first day as an instructor in 1968, I entered the classroom modestly with long-hair and blue jeans, sitting in front of a class of undergraduates, many from prep schools who had read the classics I was supposed to teach, perhaps in their original languages. I confessed to the students that I hadn't previously read many of the books, but had read Homer and Plato and the Greek dramatists, and was looking forward to working with the class to read these books together. I sat on top of the desk, provided introductory remarks and attempted to engage, sometimes successfully, the students in conversation. Later, when I read Paulo Freire's *Pedagogy of the Oppressed*, I learned that I was practicing spontaneously a proper dialogical teaching method, learning from the students as I taught, and I have followed this pedagogy ever since.

The Marx text in the Great Book program was Marx-Engels', "The Communist Manifesto" and it can indeed be read as a great literary text, as well as philosophy of history and theory of society. The dramatic opening citing "A specter that is haunting Europe" and the evocation of the specter as communism sets the world-historical significance of the text announcing a new revolutionary force and moment in history. The dramatic proclamation that the history of existing societies has been class struggle and the delineation of the two classes facing off against each other—the bourgeoisie and the proletariat—and the evocation of revolution as the lever to socialism and socialism as the goal of the existing communist political movement dramatizes the text's contemporary significance and launched Marx and Engels as revolutionary theorists who would be come to be known around the world.

In 1968, I was studying for my philosophy comprehensive exams at Columbia and teaching my first course, when a student uprising erupted, with SDS radicals occupying the President's Office, while black radicals occupied another campus building. A series of protests during 1968 combined into a series of dramatic student occupations of key buildings at Columbia University. A student activist with the Students for a Democratic Society, Bob Feldman, discovered documents indicating Columbia's institutional affiliation with the Institute for Defense Analyses (IDA) and it was also discovered that Columbia University professors were doing research for the CIA and aiding in the Vietnam war effort. There were on-going protests as well concerning Columbia's plan to take city park land bordering on Harlem and turning it into a gymnasium, in which the bottom half would be open to Harlem residents while the top half was reserved for students and members of Columbia. On April 23, 1968, students attempted to enter the main administration building, Low Memorial Library, were rebuffed, marched to the Harlem gym site, where they clashed with police, and then returned to the Columbia campus to occupy Hamilton Hall, which had both classrooms and the offices of the Columbia College Administration.

In the protests and occupation of Hamilton Hall, the SDS students were joined by members of the Student Afro Society (SAS) group. To the surprise of SDS and white students, the African American students in Hamilton told the white students to occupy another building since their agendas were different. After both groups deliberated, the SDS group and other white students decided to take over Low Library, which housed the President's office. Since the occupation closely followed the assassination of Martin Luther King, which resulted in riots throughout the country, including New York, the administration was reluctant at first to use force to evict the students and a dramatic standoff and media circus followed.

Other student groups took over other campus buildings at Columbia in one of the first and most dramatic student insurrections of the era. The Grateful Dead came on campus to give us a free concert, and one day Stokley Carmichael, R. Rap Brown, Eldridge Cleaver, and other black radical leaders came on to campus to tell us we needed to get serious and join with blacks to carry out a real revolution, and not just a campus shutdown.

In retrospect, the Columbia occupation of the President's office and other campus buildings anticipated the Occupy Movement of 2011, and helped generate a wave of campus occupations in the decades to come, continuing into the present. As I was beginning teaching in Columbia College, I joined a group of professors, some from the Great Books program in which I was teaching, as well as some of my professors from the Philosophy Department, who began meeting and immediately decided to ring the occupied buildings to protect the occupiers from getting beat up by conservative student groups of mostly jocks and frat guys who were themselves converging on the occupied building threatening to physically remove the students within.

At first, my faculty group confrontation with the right-wing students, who adopted the name "Majority Coalition," was tense, with the short-haired conservative students declaiming that they wanted to "kill the long-haired pukes" who had taken over the campus. However, the faculty and liberal students who joined our ranks quickly convinced them that the radical students had the right to protest policies with which they disagreed, and perhaps the respect that conservative students had for faculty and authority led them to step down in their threats.

After a few days of drama and accelerating media attention, in the early morning hours of April 30, 1968 the New York Police Department (NYPD) violently crushed the demonstrations, using tear gas and then attacking both Hamilton Hall and the Low Library. Ironically, Hamilton Hall was cleared peacefully as the SAS students had assembled lawyers and media observers, and a largely African American group of police officers peacefully led the African American students out of Hamilton Hall. The buildings occupied by whites however were cleared violently as hordes of police wielding clubs and threatening with guns, beat up scores of students and some faculty members who tried to stop the police assault with approximately 132 students treated for injuries while over 700 protesters were arrested.

The night of the raid, I was at home sleeping, as the faculty group organized in 12 hour shifts to protect the students. As I approached the campus in early dawn I noticed commotion and a roar of voices, hurried to the campus, and encountered my Philosophy professor Sidney Morgenbesser with a bloodied head, holding white bandages to stop the blood flow. Sidney described how the police had stormed Low Library, how he and other professors attempted to stop the police, and how they proceeded to beat up and arrest students and faculty alike.

Classes were suspended for the spring semester at Columbia in 1968, and we were happy to receive A's even though we didn't have to write final papers; many of our professors joined us in the demonstrations, so a closeness between students and professors, rare in U.S. academia at the time, emerged. Yet, one of my Professors, Paul Oskar Kristeller, said he was worried about the student demonstrations because he had seen Nazi student demonstrations previewing the rise of fascism in Germany in the 1930s, but I assured him that the Columbia students were neither fascists nor communists. Kristeller also told me that Martin Heidegger had gotten him a scholarship to study Renaissance philosophy in Italy during the Nazi period, which saved Kristeller's life because he was Jewish.

In the euphoria of the accelerating protests of 1968, we had the feeling that we were at the heart of revolutionary upheavals in the U.S. and globally when a representative from France came and told us of the French student and worker uprising that was shutting down the whole of Paris and briefly was erupting throughout France in May 1968. The gym in Morningside Park which offended the Harlem residents and black radicals was never built, Columbia severed its relations with the IDA, and many of us experienced the euphoria of radical upheaval, and were radicalized by the experience.

My philosophical allegiances at the time were primarily to Phenomenology and Existentialism, and while I was unprepared for the explosiveness and impact of the student rebellion, I became active in New Left politics, participating in major anti-war and other demonstrations of the epoch. Indeed, students all over the United States and Europe were demonstrating against the Vietnam War, taking over University buildings and even campuses, and in Paris in May '68, it appeared that a new French revolution was in the making. To help understand these events, I went back and read the works of Herbert Marcuse, and by the time of the publication of *An Essay on Liberation* (1969), I both better understood Marcuse's writings and the philosophical underpinnings of the student movement to which I was increasingly attracted and involved.

During this time, the Vietnam War was raging and many of my generation were being sent over as cannon fodder for a cause that we did not understand or support. One day around 1968 I went over to Barnard College and heard a packed lecture by Noam Chomsky. Chomsky, at the time a Professor of Philosophy at MIT, was known to philosophy students for his controversial philosophy of mind and linguistic theory, but proved himself a brilliant public lecturer, providing an entire history of post-World War II Vietnam, the National Liberation Movement that drove out the French, the raging Civil War in the country, and how the US intervened against the Communist North in support of a corrupt

South Vietnamese government, providing a sharp critique of U.S. interventionism and imperialism. I walked away with a much deeper understanding of the dynamics of Vietnam and great respect for Noam Chomsky who I would later meet and whose writings had an impact on my view of media and politics.

The next year in 1969, there was an abortive attempt at a replay of the 1968 demonstrations which quickly dissipated and some of the disillusioned SDS members formed the Weather Underground which became notorious after some bombings in which their leaders literally went underground. During the student occupation of Columbia, we organized reading groups where some professors, graduate students like myself, and others proposed courses organized around topics or books, and I organized a reading group focusing on *One-Dimensional Man*. I remember sitting outdoors on the lawn at Columbia with a small group of students, including Nancy and Steve Fraser (Nancy became famous later as a leading Feminist-Marxist philosopher and a close comrade of mine, and her then husband Steve became a successful editor for a big publishing house). Anyway, the close reading and passionate discussion of the text *One-Dimensional Man* sealed the deal convincing me that Marcuse had the most radical and pertinent critique of contemporary US culture and society of the era that best captured its dynamics.

At Columbia in May 1969, I heard Herbert Marcuse lecture one evening, and talked with him for the first time the next day during a reception in the Philosophy Department. We were asking Marcuse about Heidegger and his study with him, and what he thought of Heidegger today. Marcuse joked that he heard Heidegger was chiseling his philosophy in stone in Germany, highlighting what he took as the reactionary and archaic nature of Heidegger's thought which he expounded upon for a whole. We then asked him about Adorno, and he replied that "Theodore W. Adorno is one of the most important thinkers of our time," and expounded upon some of Adorno's ideas. None of the philosophy professors showed up, and at one point Marcuse asked me and other graduate students to escort him to the West End Bar where earlier Alan Ginsberg and the Beat poets hung out, and where at the time my fellow graduate students also ate, drank, and discussed philosophy, politics, and other issues of the day.

As we crossed the campus in front of the Philosophy Department, some major militants in the Weather Underground approached me and said "we want to rap with Marcuse." So I asked Herbert and he agreed, and we all sat down on the grass, and one of the Weather Underground dudes explained that they planned to burn down the office of a Columbia Professor who was doing research for the US government that facilitated certain heinous practices in the Vietnam war. Almost immediately, Herbert said that he thought this was not a good idea, that it would probably backfire and bring on major repression, and argued that the University should be used as a site to recruit and train revolutionaries, going on to say that the University was a relative utopia in U.S. society where one could read and study, develop critiques of US capitalism and imperialism, could organize radical groups, and prepare for the revolution. He was quite passionate and convincing on this point and after a brief discussion, the Weather Dudes got up, thanked Marcuse for his advice and got up to leave. As they were parting, Marcuse joked, "Now if you were planning to burn down a bank, I might not be so negative" — and shortly thereafter, the Bank of America in Santa Barbara was burned down, the subject of a Newsreel documentary, and the Weather Underground took credit.

My philosophical studies at Columbia were increasingly focused on continental philosophy, and this interest led me to apply and accept a scholarship to study in Germany, a venture I prolonged for two years, before spending a year in France and then beginning a philosophy teaching career at the University of Texas, Austin, in 1973.

## 2   Adventures in Continental Philosophy

In 1969, I left Columbia to write my dissertation on "Heidegger's Concept of Authenticity" (Kellner 1973) with the support of a German government fellowship (DAAD). I chose to pursue this project at the University of Tubingen, in the small southwestern German town where Hegel, Hölderlin, Schelling, and other luminaries had studied, and which had a reputation as an excellent place to study a broad range of German philosophical traditions. Tubingen was permeated with the spirit of '60s radicalism and I bought pirate editions (*Raubdruck*) at the University Mensa of Karl Korsch's writings on Marxism, Georg Lukacs' *History and Class Consciousness*, Max Horkheimer and T.W. Adorno's *Dialectic of Enlightenment*, and other texts of the Frankfurt school. I also became involved in a Critical Theory study group, and sat in on Ernst Bloch's seminars, which alternated between seminars on the great philosophers, and ones on topics such as imperialism, fascism, and other political topics. From Bloch, among other things, I learned that philosophy was highly political and that politics required philosophical analysis and critique.

Near the end of my research on Heidegger, I picked up Adorno's *Jargon der Eigentlichkeit*, and discovered some early essays by Marcuse on his philosophy teacher Heidegger, which carried out a sharp critique of Heidegger's thought and which proposed a synthesis of phenomenological Existentialism and Marxism, of Heidegger and Marx, to overcome the respective limitations in these traditions. I found Marcuse's critiques of Heidegger convincing and his proposed amalgamation of Heidegger and Marx fascinating. I also thoroughly investigated Heidegger's relation to National Socialism and thus was not surprised by the later revelations in the Farias, Ott and other volumes on Heidegger's Nazism.

I was thus rapidly moving toward the Critical Theory of the Frankfurt School, a move intensified by a year in Paris. After two years in Germany, I had more or less completed my dissertation on Heidegger and received a good grounding in German philosophy. I was eager to improve my knowledge of French, and to immerse myself in French philosophy and culture. During a thirteen month sojourn in Paris during 1971-1972, subsidized by my paper route savings, I accordingly devoted myself to French language and philosophy, and also drafted the first version of a book on Herbert Marcuse whose work continued to interest me (Kellner 1984).

While in Paris, I meant an Algerian philosophy student, and he took me to hear the lectures of Levi-Strauss, Foucault, Deleuze, and Lyotard, inspiring me to read their recent works, as well as the texts of Baudrillard, Derrida, and other French thinkers currently in vogue. Listening to Foucault's lectures was like being in Church, as he intently read from lecture notes in a hushed darkened auditorium. Levi-Strauss was more lively and was very friendly when another French acquaintance took me to his office to meet him; Levi-Strauss had lived in the U.S. and spoke charming English and was happy to discuss his work with a young American philosopher who was moving more toward poststructuralism as many of the new French theorists were moving away from the structuralism of Levi-Strauss, Althusser, and others in favor of more complex theories of language, meaning, social institutions, and power.

One of those poststructuralist philosophers, Gilles Deleuze, was highly animated and used the blackboard to scribble out his main concepts; I later saw him perform his fabled sketching of rhizomatic proliferating categories (avoiding mere dualisms) between modern analytical thought and rhizomatic thought on a blackboard at a conference at Columbia in 1975. Deleuze was accompanied at the Columbia Semio(texte) conference by his writing partner Felix Guattari who was gaining renown in France for his work at the La Boarde experimental psychiatric clinic which was attempting to abolish doctor/ patient relations in favor of group therapy, while advancing radical ideas that "madness" was a social construct. Deleuze and Guattari had published the first volume of their critique of psychoanalysis *Anti-Oedipus: Capitalism and Schizophrenia* in 1972 and were becoming fashionable in avant-garde theoretical circles in the U.S.

While in Paris in the early 1970s, I also went out to the new University at Vincennes to hear Jean-Francois Lyotard lecture, who would become famous for his *The Postmodern Condition* (1978), which was one of the first books to popularize the concept of the postmodern. Lyotard was an extremely engaging lecturer, coming out in blue jeans, lighting up a cigarette, bantering with students about current political events, and then launching into a lecture on Kant or another philosophical theme, usually without notes, and allowing students to discuss the texts, rather rare in France at the time.

I initially read Jacques Derrida, who would become globally influential in the 1980s as the father of deconstruction, as a curious version of Heideggerian philosophy, and read Foucault, Baudrillard, and Lyotard as supplementing the Frankfurt School in developing a critical philosophy and social theory for the contemporary era. I saw similar attempts to develop syntheses of Marx, Freud, and critical philosophy in both contemporary German and French thought, and did not see the differences as sharp as they appeared to many in the feverish debates about French postmodern theory that erupted in the 1980s. Since I had been introduced to radical French theory at about the same time that I had been introduced to German critical theory, and was reading texts from both traditions, I was interested in how they fit together and supplemented each other, creating a contemporary critical and radical theory. Both so-called Frankfurt School German theorists and the French postmodern theorists provided critiques of capitalism, critiques of culture and media, a critique of modernity, and critiques of modern theory. So when later a split emerged between postmodernism and French theory contrasted to German theory, I had no part of this schism because my philosophical experiences suggested that these traditions could be articulated together, which I was doing at the time and would continue to do all my life. Thus, for me it was not a choice of the Germans or French, but of drawing on both traditions to develop new philosophical syntheses and critique of the contemporary era.

In December 1972, I offered myself for sale for a position in continental philosophy at the American Philosophical Society (APA) job market, and sold myself to the University of Texas at Austin, where I labored in the area of continental philosophy for some 24 years. I remember traveling to Boston with a group of other philosophy graduate students and sleeping on the floor in a room where someone could afford to foot the bill. I had only a couple of prearranged interviews so had to hustle to try to organize a job interview.

At a "smoker" (i.e. a mass gathering of philosophy professors and graduate students), I saw a name tag on a flamboyant looking man with the name tag "Douglas Browning, University of Texas-Austin." I knew that Texas had a job in continental philosophy so I cornered Browning, told him of my Ph.D. dissertation on Heidegger, that I had studied at Columbia, and then Tubingen and Paris, and knew a broad range of continental philosophies and would like a job in Texas. He sized me up and put me on the schedule for a 9:00 a.m. interview the next day.

I had the first interview of the day in the Texas suite, and I could see that the group of interviewers was just waking up and drinking cups of black coffee, so I joined in and bantered about Boston Celtics basketball, UT football, and other trivialities until the interview began. I noticed one prominent figure as Ed Allaire, a maven of analytic philosophy, extremely hostile to the continentals, who had taught at the University of Iowa where my brother had studied for a couple of years, and noted to Ed that my brother had enjoyed his philosophy lectures. When I presented my dissertation in the interview I did so in the language of analytic philosophy so it sounded like I was a down to earth continental theorist.

Curiously, UT-Austin's position was specifically for someone to teach Marxist philosophy, as some "know your enemy" conservative had funded and managed to get the philosophy department to offer one of the few philosophy department courses on Marxism in the country. The previous holders of this position had been fired after several years, and it was clear that the Department was not seeking a red-flag waving Marxist, so when asked whether I would be willing to teach a course on Marxism, I replied in the affirmative, saying that although most of my work had been in Existentialism, Phenomenology, Hegel, and contemporary German and French philosophy, I was interested in Marx and would be pleased to teach the course. Shortly thereafter, I was offered a position as Assistant Professor of Philosophy at the University of Texas at Austin, starting in Fall 1973 for a salary of $12,000.

## 3 Teaching Marxism at UT-Austin

My study in Europe had indeed provided a good grounding in the Marxian and continental philosophy traditions, and made the Texas offer attractive, so although I received a couple of other offers I decided to go to Texas. This choice was fortunate, as Texas had a strong tradition in continental philosophy and a pluralistic department that allowed a broad range of different types of philosophical inquiry (although an anti-continental philosophy police squad would emerge and become hegemonic in the mid-1990s, ending this phase of my philosophical adventures).

Austin was extremely exotic to someone who had spent much of his life growing up in West and East Coast suburbs and had more recently been studying and living in major urban centers like New York and Paris. Texas was publicizing itself as the Third Coast, and Austin had a growing reputation as a major (counter)cultural and music scene. When I received the offer, I called up two friends from the world of Marxist and continental philosophy, Dick Howard and Bob Stone, both of whom had studied in Austin and both of whom spoke highly of the city and cultural scene. Both strongly recommended that I take the job and assured me that I would love Austin (they were right).

From the time I arrived in Austin in the Fall of 1973 until my leaving in the mid-1990s, I taught both undergraduate and graduate courses in Marxism and Critical theory. As noted, I was actually hired to teach courses in Marxism and taught an undergrad course Introduction to Marxist Philosophy my first semester at UT. I used the *Marx-Engels Reader* edited by Robert Tucker and would continue using new editions of the text throughout my sojourn in Austin. My approach was largely contextual and historical, although each lecture focused on key ideas and their relevance for political analysis and practice. I would begin with the early Marx in the context of the aftermath of the French revolution and Marx's study of Hegel, Feuerbach, and the ideas of the French Revolution. I was especially taken by Marx's *Economic and Philosophic Notebooks of 1844* which I believed contained the first sketch of his revolutionary synthesis of German idealism, French materialism, and utopian socialism.

In addition Marx's analysis of alienated labor in the *Manuscripts* brilliantly described my two summers during college working for Cinch Manufacturing in Chicago, one summer working in the mail room, and another as night janitor (my uncle was corporate lawyer for the company and got me the job). While I could spend some time reading Plato's dialogues at night after all the supervisors went home, during the day I was forced to do busywork because of all the supervisors prowling around and I experienced that labor under capitalism was indeed external, controlled, specialized, repetitive, and soul-crushing, if one found oneself on a factory floor or in an office where one was literally a wage slave.

As noted above, around that time, I determined that I would get a Ph.D. in philosophy and be a philosophy professor as the least alienating job I could imagine and one that actually seemed cool. It was the 1960s and philosophy was seen as a desirable head trip, consciousness-raising was the rage, and a dizzying array of new philosophical ideas were in the air. Hence, although my uncle tried to talk me into going to Michigan Law School, expenses paid, and joining his law firm in Chicago, and while my next door neighbor plied me with a stack of Barry Goldwater books and urged me to take a position with the AT&T Junior Executive Program, instead I decided I would go for getting a job in Philosophy.

These personal stories helped illuminate my teaching of Marxism and critical theory at UT, and invariably students would tell harrowing stories of how they, family members, relatives, or friends were screwed over by capital. In money conscious and capital dominant Texas, Marx's theses concerning the logic of capital ruling bourgeois society were not hard to illustrate and I and my students recounted copious tales of how capital ruled Texas. Once I went to a philosophy conference for my first trip to Dallas and my group chose a popular Italian restaurant with a long line waiting to get into the restaurant. We finally approached the front and a couple of dudes with flashy faux cowboy clothes and over-dressed women pushed in front of us, and a fat waddling fuck pulled out a hundred dollar bill out of a wallet, put it in the shirt pocket of the waiter, and was quickly ushered to the next table. Being a brash newcomer, I told my group that in New York this would never have happened, and a Texas gentleman behind me informed the group that: "Son, in Texas we have a saying that Money Talks and Bullshit Walks."

After spending about half of the semester on *The Marx-Engels Reader*, supplemented by a biography of Marx or contemporary book on Marxism, that I would rotate from time to time, I would assign varied readers and texts from the history of Marxism so that students could get a sampling of classics like Lenin, Kautsky, Bernstein, Mao, Luxembourg, and Che Guevara. I would also assign from time to time a reader on Western Marxism or the *Critical Theory Reader* that Steve Bronner and I co-edited (1989). Finally, I might end the semester with Herbert Marcuse's *One-Dimensional Man* (1964) or a Marxist text on contemporary society.

My pedagogy in teaching Marxist philosophy to undergraduates was somewhat different from my proto-Freirean teaching the Great Books at Columbia. I assigned readings from *The Marx-Engels Reader* every class, would provide the historical, intellectual and political context for the readings and then would go through the key ideas. As there were often 80-100 students in the class I would pass out notes before class with the key ideas, stand lecturing, and then encourage questions and discussion. At first, the students were reticent, but as the class evolved, discussions got intense and often I would sit on top of a desk in the front row to more dialogically engage the students.

Once every year or two, I could teach a graduate seminar and often taught one on classics of Marxism, critical theory or Marcuse. In the 1980s, I also taught graduate seminars, and even undergraduate lecture courses on post-structuralism and French theory and British Cultural Studies. Graduate seminars had at least twenty students and big undergrad lectures could contain 80-100 students, so I needed to present complex critical ideas in a way relatable to undergrad and grad students at Texas.

In the graduate seminars, I would hand out notes with context and key ideas, make an opening lecture, encourage discussion, and then have student presentations and discussions. This way I could elicit more student participation. My office was just across from the UT-Philosophy seminar room and I noted that some professors droned on two hours or more as the students passively sat and took in the discourse, and I resolved to do my best to always keep students actively engaged and to encourage discussion and student voice.

Upon returning from three years abroad studying in Europe, I first encountered a relatively new journal dedicated to radical theory called *Telos*, and I was happy to learn that a group of people in the U.S. were interested in the same continental theories that I'd been studying in Europe. Consequently, I wrote *Telos*' editor Paul Piccone, told him of my interests and he immediately asked me to translate and write an Introduction to Herbert Marcuse's "On the Philosophical Foundation of the Concept of Labor." I did so, and it was published in *Telos* 16 (Summer 1973) and constituted my first publication. At about the same time, I met the editors of *New German Critique*, which was involved in a similar publishing venture with *Telos* and at the time seemed to be connected. I published "The Frankfurt School Revisited: A Critique of Martin Jay's *The Dialectical Imagination*" in *New German Critique* 4 (Winter 1974), a long review article that laid out my take on the Frankfurt School and differentiated my reading of critical theory from Jay, who is said to have muttered "Marxist asshole" when he read my critical review, which highlighted the neo-Marxian roots of Frankfurt School theory and which claimed Jay downplayed their Marxism. Later, I became friendly with Jay and realized what a groundbreaking achievement his introduction to the Frankfurt School had been, and have constantly consulted and referenced his book in future scholarship, while realizing how unfair my critique had been, driven by an excessive zeal to do Marxist ideology critique of dominant ideologies.

In the following year, I published "The Latest Sartre: Reflections on *On a raison de se revolter*" in *Telos* 22 (Winter 1974-5), and "Korsch's Revolutionary Historicism" in *Telos* 26 (Winter 1975-76), which fleshed out some material used in my first book *Karl Korsch: Revolutionary Theory*, published by the University of Texas Press in 1977. While I had been working on my book on Herbert Marcuse since the early 1970s, I had decided I would not complete the book until Marcuse passed away so I could do an overview of his entire life and work. In the meantime, I continued my Marcusean studies, supplemented by work on Karl Korsch, at the time one of the best-known representatives, along with Georg Lukacs, of so-called "Western Marxism" of the 1920s. A Soviet bureaucrat coined the term "Western Marxism" to disparage the highly Hegelian and philosophical versions of Marxism that were emerging in Western Europe, but it was soon adopted by thinkers like Lukacs and Korsch to describe a more independent and critical Marxism from the party and "scientific" Marxism of the Second and Third Internationals. Perry Anderson (1976) interprets the turn from economic and political analysis to cultural theory as a symptom of the defeat of Western Marxism after the crushing of the European revolutionary movements of the 1920s and the rise of fascism. Yet, theorists like Lukacs, Bloch, Marcuse, Benjamin, and Adorno were intellectuals who had deep and abiding interest in social and cultural phenomena, and so it is rather natural that they would bring these interests into Marxism.

In one of his most influential works *History and Class Consciousness* (1972a [1923]), Lukacs argued that the Marxian vision of totality and its focus on the primacy of the commodity and economic production provided the best methodological tools to critically analyze contemporary capitalist society and discover forces that would overthrow it in the revolutionary proletariat. Lukacs asserted that adopting the standpoint of the working class enabled one to see how capitalist society produced *reification*, the transformation of human beings into things, in all dimensions of society from the labor process to cultural production and even sexual relations. For Lukacs, all domains of society, culture, and even intimate relations were pervaded with economic imperatives and became subject to laws of the economy. The proletariat, Lukacs believed, was in a privileged position to grasp societal reification and to organize to overcome it, becoming, in an ultra-Hegelian formulation, the "subject-object" of history. Adopting an orthodox communist position, Lukacs alleged that working class revolution and socialism were the solutions to the problems of bourgeois society and became a life-long adherent to the communist movement.

In Germany, following the abortive German revolution of 1918, political activist and theorist Karl Korsch also developed a Hegelian and critical version of Marxism. In *Marxism and Philosophy* (1971 [1923]), Korsch argued that Marxism should be interpreted as a critical and dialectical theory, providing tools to criticize bourgeois theory and society and the forces to transform it. For Korsch, the unity of theory and practice was the criterion for authentic Marxism, and he interpreted Marxism as the revolutionary theory of the working class movement and developed a concept of "practical socialism." In his later work, *Karl*

*Marx* (1938), Korsch asserted that the principle of historical specificity was a key criterion of Marxian theory, maintaining that Marxism provided a historically specific critique of capitalist society and alternatives to it.

While Korsch's two major books were available in English, a large number of his essays were untranslated and the complexities of his life and tumultuous relations to German Social democracy, communism, and his turn to ultra-left radicalism was largely unknown (Dick Howard and Karl Karel published a book on the tradition of Western Marxism in 1972 titled *The Unknown Dimension*). I found a lot of Korsch's later work published in English in the University of Texas Library which had an astonishing collection of leftwing journals from the 20th century, thanks to the donation of a "know your enemy" conservative who donated significant funds to buy Marxist literature for the library. There was a Karl Korsch archive in Hannover and I also went there to collect material and met with Michael Buckmiller who had published in German a collection of Korsch's work and a biographical-political study of his life, which I would draw upon in the Introduction to *Karl Korsch: Revolutionary Theory*.

I had met at the time an editor Iris Tillman Hill who worked for the University of Texas Press and scheduled a meeting with me to discuss what texts and thinkers Texas might publish in a series of books on Marxism that they were developing. I suggested Korsch and she told me to write up a prospectus for the book and quickly guided it through the Press review process and so I published my first book in 1977 with a minimum of hassle (it would prove more difficult to publish my second book on Herbert Marcuse as I will relate below). The Korsch book was well-received as part of a growing number of studies on Western Marxism, but as the years have gone by, Korsch is now largely forgotten and I never returned to Korsch scholarship as my work turned toward Marcuse, Marx, the Frankfurt School, and related critical theorists.

In other initial journal articles of the 1970s, I paid homage to Ernst Bloch, my philosophy professor in Tubingen, with an article co-authored by one of my University of Texas philosophy students Harry O'Hara, "Utopia and Marxism in Ernst Bloch," published in *New German Critique* 9 (Fall 1976), producing the first of many studies that I would co-author with students and colleagues. While exploring the field of American philosophy, I made contact with the Radical Philosophers Group and published on "Adorno's Social Theory" in their *Radical Philosophers Newsjournal* 5 (Winter 1976).

Although initially I followed *Telos* very closely, I became one of many who became alienated from its editor and publisher Paul Piccone. Initially, I had started out closer to Paul than many people who later split with him. As noted, I published my first article in *Telos*, and invited Piccone to Austin when I started teaching there, so he came and gave a presentation. Then he invited me to St. Louis at Washington University where he taught, and thus I got to know him on a personal level. In St. Louis, Piccone took me over to the house of Alvin Gouldner, a distinguished sociologist who was publishing a new journal *Theory and Society* that would become one of the major journals of the day. Gouldner initially ferociously challenged me on my views of Marx and Marxism (something he would soon be writing about), and as I intelligently defended my position, he became friendly and asked me to contribute to his new journal, which I said I would be happy to do, and soon after was put on his editorial board.

While initially I liked and got along well with Piccone, he became increasingly crazy and increasingly rightwing, and many in the Telos group were provoked by his behavior and broke with him, including myself. Eventually, Piccone and *Telos* went so far to the right that Perry Anderson once joked to me that *Telos* was representing left-Reaganism (in anti-Soviet Cold War tirades, attacks on Marxism, support of US troops and nuclear weapons in Europe, etc), an astute observation by one of the major historians of Western Marxism.

In retrospect, I had piled up an enormous amount of cultural capital during my three years in Germany and France that enabled me to write a series of articles, reviews, and books on both the Frankfurt School and contemporary French thought over the next two decades. My books on critical theory include *Herbert Marcuse and the Crisis of Marxism* (1984), *Critical Theory, Marxism, and Modernity* (1989), and (with Stephen Bronner) *A Critical Theory Reader* (1989). My books *Karl Korsch: Revolutionary Theory* (1977), *Passion and Rebellion: The Expressionist Heritage* (1983), co-edited with Stephen Bronner, *Postmodernism/ Jameson/ Critique* (1989) and the many articles that I have written on Marx and Marxism were nourished during my two years in Germany and subsequent research trips. My books *Jean Baudrillard: From Marxism to Postmodernism and Beyond* (1989) *Baudrillard: A Critical Reader* (1994), as were two books with Steven Best, *Postmodern Theory: Critical Interrogations* (1991), *The Postmodern Turn* (1997), all were made possible by the work that I did on French theory during a year in France and subsequent return trips to France and Germany during my summer vacations during the Austin years.

In terms of my personal relations in the philosophy department at UT-Austin, I found a broad range of continental philosophers and others representing philosophical pluralism in the UT philosophy department, so I found this a congenial environment. MY UT-Austin adventures came to an end, however, in the mid-1990s when George W. Bush became Governor of Texas and a rightwing cabal took over the UT-Philosophy Department. Austin had been a great place to live with a vibrant counterculture and political culture, and for decades the University of Texas had been an excellent location to teach. But as the University became more rightwing during the Bush years, many of us saw the (w)righting-on-the-wall, saw Austin and UT drowning in a sewer of corruption and mediocrity that distinguished Bush family politics and the rightwing Republicans who had taken over Texas, and decided to move on, leaving Texas to Karl Rove, George W. Bush, and their rightwing cronies.

### 4  UCLA Adventures: Marcuse, Cultural Studies, and the Philosophy of Education

Fortunately, a job at UCLA materialized and I joined the UCLA Graduate School of Education and Information Studies in 1997, along with Sandra Harding, who I had long known from radical philosophy circles and which gave us the nucleus of a strong philosophy cohort at UCLA (we later formed a group with John McCumber, Philosophers Outside of Philosophy, which continues to be active). Ironically, many of those who I consider the top philosophers of my generation have left philosophy departments, raising some serious questions about the contemporary institutional status of philosophy. On the whole, it appears that contemporary American philosophy has fallen into a state of paralysis in which few new ideas or thinkers emerge. While the dominant analytical philosophy suffers from theoretical sclerosis, a hardening of the categories, and undergoing a slow public and academic death, the situation of continental philosophy is also dispiriting. In the 1980s, it looked as though contemporary philosophy was entering a fruitful state of pluralism with a blossoming of continental philosophy, mutating into "Theory," crossing over into every discipline from literary theory to sociology. On the philosophical frontlines, there was also a reappropriation of Dewey and pragmatism, of other strands of American philosophy, as well as the move into new fields such as feminism, African American and Latino philosophy, philosophy of technology, environmental philosophy, philosophical media studies, and philosophy of electronic culture, communication, and social networking.

These trends continue within the broader philosophical-intellectual world, but often not in philosophy departments, and they have been pushed to the margins of the academic discipline of philosophy. Most distressing, not only has reaction and retrenchment set in with analytic philosophy, but continental philosophy has been segregating itself into circles in which specific philosophers are revered as the Voice of Truth, leading to cult-like circles of devotees. Thus the onto-theological dimension of philosophy that Derrida decried has its Renaissance in schools of contemporary philosophy. Living philosophy, however, is always synthesis, always in motion, always taking in the novel, absorbing challenging ideas, trends, and theories, constantly developing and reshaping philosophy, in dialogue with other disciplines and contemporary culture and experiences.

During my almost two decades of service at UCLA as George F. Kneller Chair in the Philosophy of Education, I have taught an Introduction to Philosophy of Education that initially adopted the Great Books and historical approach that I followed at Columbia. My first seminar, I started with Plato's *Republic* but found it took at least three weeks to cover and in a ten-week quarter that didn't allow me to cover key material. I then resolved to teach Philo of Ed in the era of modernity starting with Rousseau's *Emile*, followed by Mary Wollstonecraft's *Declaration of the Rights of Women*, John Dewey's *Democracy and Education*, and Paulo Freire's *Pedagogy of the Oppressed*. I also resolved to assign a novel in every seminar and choose Toni Morrison's *The Bluest Eye*, which has continued to work well up to the present as it brings in media, family, and environment as forces of pedagogy and deals in a central way with gender, race, and class in education.

As with my UT philosophy seminars, I would open with an introductory and contextual lecture, do a close reading of the opening of the text and then have student presentations and discussions. The quasi-official pedagogy of the UCLA Graduate School of Education and Information Studies was Freirean so students were prepared and eager to make presentations and in some cases to engage in discussion. As the years went on, however, I found the Great Books method increasingly unviable as it was clear the students weren't reading many of the books unless they were making presentations so I reluctantly cut down the readings assigned from key classical texts, added texts on Latinos and education, Asian education, multicultural education, and from radical thinkers such as Herbert Marcuse, Ivan Illich, Gloria Anzahldua, bell hooks, and others since many of the students were of color and were international students.

Further, I taught courses focused on researching the relevance of media and new technologies to education, politics, and everyday life, as well as continuing work in philosophy, social theory, and cultural studies. In education from the mid-1990s to the present, I have been especially concerned to expand the notion of literacy to include media literacy and multiple technoliteracies. By the mid-1990s, it was clear to me that our culture was a media culture, and that the media were becoming increasingly powerful instruments of socialization, political indoctrination, and sources of meanings and identities as cable and satellite television mushroomed, talk radio and channels of broadcasting expanded as the Internet absorbed video, audio, and the culture of image and spectacle, and as new media and new technologies continued to proliferate.

I had long been an advocate of media literacy, once receiving a grant during the Carter presidencies in the 1970s to teach media literacy to teachers in the state of Texas, followed by a program in the 1980s where I taught media literacy in lower income high schools in the Mississippi Delta area. For months, I taught workshops on helping teachers provide curricula that would educate their students to critically read and decode media messages, including representations of gender, class, sexuality, and race to help students and educators discern racist, sexist, homophobic, classist, and other negative representations in the media, while also looking for positive images, meanings, role models, and programming. At Texas, I devised a course on Philosophy of Culture and Communication which introduced theories of media, cultural studies, and taught critical media literacy which aimed at promoting knowledge of media ownership and programming, taught textual analysis, and developed theories of media power and alternative progressive uses of media for politics, pedagogy, and social transformation. At UCLA, I transformed this course into an Introduction to Cultural Studies seminar that uses my book *Media Culture* and a Blackwell reader *Media and Cultural Studies: KeyWorks*, co-edited with Gigi Durham (2001, second edition 2012), which brings together key texts in contemporary approaches to media culture and communication ranging from Roland Barthes and Guy Debord to recent studies of YouTube, Facebook, and social networking.

In the cultural studies seminar I organized the class around topics like key concepts and methods of cultural studies, and themes like race, gender, class, sexuality, and other dimensions of media cultural text. Reading the media critically involved detecting racism, classism, sexism, homophobia, and other biases in media texts, as well as highlighting stronger and more positive images of people of color, women, men, gays and lesbians, class, and other features of media representations and identities. Here students were even more eager participants in presentations and discussion as media and internet culture was a culture they were deeply involved and immersed in and thus presented perspectives not available in many academic texts.

In the cultural studies seminar, I would begin with Marxist ideology critique as developed by the Frankfurt School and British Cultural Studies, and discuss how Stuart Hall and British Cultural studies expanded the concept of ideology to encompass gender, race, and sexuality (1980), as well as class which was the focus of the Marxian critique of ideology. I introduced Marx and Gramsci's (1971) notion of hegemony and argued that since the 1960s hegemony in the US had revolved around battles between liberals and conservatives, with more radical social movements taking on issues like the environment, gender, class, and race inequality, gun violence and other hot-button issues.

My argument, as laid out in my 1995 book *Media Culture,* was that popular film, television, music, and other forms of media culture articulated liberal positions or competing conservative issues on political issues such the war and military, the state, corporations, key social issues, and, of course, presented often conflicting representations of gender, race, class, and sexuality, either promoting biased representations or more positive ones. Of course, many media representations and narratives were contradictory, but reading media critically—and thus gaining critical media literacy, was crucial to be an active engaged consumer or producer of media.

Consequently, to conclude, I would argue in the contemporary moment of Donald Trump and his aftermath that reading, studying, and teaching Marxism is of crucial importance and relevance. Marx provides a theory of capitalism that contextualizes the infrastructure of the existing system of US society that Donald Trump and his cabinet of billionaires and other ruling class cronies represent. Everyday, Trump provides an aggressive version of the dominant ideology, highlighting the importance of Marx's notion of ideology and ideology critique. Trump also represents the culture industry that the Frankfurt school sharply attacked, and embodies the authoritarian personality that has also been a target of neo-Marxist critique. Trump's fascist tendencies disclose the continuing relevance of the Marxian theory of socialism and revolution.

Returning to Trump and capitalism, I should point out that there are, however, problems in seeing Trump as a pure embodiment of capitalism, as to a large extent Trump is a con artist and, as has often been argued, Trump is more a P.T. Barnum, a carnival entertainer, than a Rockefeller and industrial capitalist of the sort Marx described. Likewise, we are in a historical moment when we are forced to ask if the president of the United States is a criminal as in August 2018 Trump's lawyer and fixer Michael Cohen was indicted on eight criminal charges included tax fraud, false statements to a bank, and campaign finance fraud, while Paul Manafort, one of Trump's campaign managers, was convicted the same week of five counts of tax fraud, two counts of bank fraud and one count of failure to disclose a foreign bank account. Moreover, the next day, it was revealed that Allen Weisselberg, the longtime chief financial officer of the Trump Organization, was given immunity to testify in investigations that might go after Trump.

So we'll see if Trump was the sort of capitalist/bourgeois scoundrel that Marx described in his journalism and historical studies such as *The 18th Brumaire of*

*Louis Napoleon.* Marx presented Louis Napoleon as a usurper who attempted to overthrow the gains of the French Revolutions and recent 1848 revolution and described Louis Napoleon in terms that could be used to describe Trump as when Marx writes that Louis Napoleon "throws the entire bourgeois economy into confusion, lays hand on everything that seemed inviolable to the revolution of 1848, makes some tolerant of revolution, others desirous of revolution, and produces actual anarchy in the name of order, while at the same time he divests the whole state machine of its halo, profanes it and makes it at once loathsome and ridiculous" (Karl Marx, *The 18th Brumaire of Louis Napoleon*, cited in *The Marx-Engels Reader* p. 617).

## Bibliography

Best, Steven and Kellner, Douglas (1991) *Postmodern Theory: Critical Interrogations*, co-authored with Steven Best. London and New York: Macmillan and Guilford Press.

Best, Steven and Kellner, Douglas (1997) *The Postmodern Turn*, co-authored with Steven Best. New York and London: Guilford Press and Routledge.

Bronner, Stephen Eric and Douglas Kellner (eds.) (1980) *Critical Theory and Society. A Reader*, co-edited London and New York: Metheun/Routledge.

Gramsci, Antonio (1971) *Selections from the Prison Notebooks of Antonio Gramsci*. Edited by Q. Hoare and G. Nowell Smith. New York: International Publishers.

Hall, Stuart., et al (1980) *Culture, Media, Language*. New York: Routledge.

Horkheimer, Max and Adorno, T.W. (1972 [1947]), *Dialectic of Enlightenment*. New York: Herder and Herder.

Howard, Dick and Klare, Karl (1972) *The Hidden Dimension. European Marxism Since Lenin*. New York: Basic Books.

Kellner, Douglas (1973) *Heidegger's Concept of Authenticity*. Ph.D. Dissertation, Columbia University, 1973 on-line at https://pages.gseis.ucla.edu/faculty/kellner/Heidegger.pdf (accessed September 14, 2017).

Kellner, Douglas (1977) editor. *Karl Korsch: Revolutionary Theory*. Austin, Texas: University of Texas Press.

Kellner, Douglas (1984) *Herbert Marcuse and the Crisis of Marxism*. Berkeley and London: University of California Press (USA) and Macmillan Press (England).

Kellner, Douglas (1989a) *Critical Theory, Marxism, and Modernity*. Cambridge, UK and Baltimore, Md.: Polity Press and John Hopkins University Press, 1989.

Kellner, Douglas (1989b) *Jean Baudrillard: From Marxism to Postmodernism and Beyond*. Cambridge, UK and Palo Alto, Cal.: Polity Press and Stanford University Press.

Kellner, Douglas (*1994) Editor. *Baudrillard. A Critical Reader*, edited with Introduction. Malden, Mass. and Oxford, UK: Blackwell.

Kellner, Douglas (1995) Media Culture. Cultural Studies, Identity and Politics Between the Modern and the Postmodern. London and New York: Routledge.
Korsch, Karl ([1923]1971) *Marxism and Philosophy*. New York: Monthly Review Press.
Korsch, Karl ([1936] 2007) *Karl Marx*. Chicago: Haymarket Books.
Lukacs, Georg (1971a), (1971), *History and Class Consciousness.* Cambridge, Mass: MIT Press.
Marcuse, Herbert (1964) *One-Dimensional Man.* Boston: Beacon Press.
Marcuse, Herbert (1969) *An Essay on Liberatiomn* Boston: Beacon Press.
Tucker, Robert (ed.) (1978) *The Marx-Engels Reader*. New York: Norton.

CODA

# Inspiring Action: Rethinking the Public Function of Pedagogy

### 1      Class(room) Politics

A dominant and misguided narrative, predominantly though not exclusively in the United States, maintains that academia represents a bastion of the left. It mistakenly holds that universities and college campuses function as monolithic bulwarks of left-liberalism, socialism, Marxism, and other forms of contrapuntal ideology such as anarchism. This narrative is only partially true, and nearly completely misleading. For while certain enclaves of academic life are dominated by various forms of left and left-leaning worldviews, academia, as a whole, is actually dominated by liberals of a more specifically mainstream, not actually "left," sensibility. Liberals—not socialists, Marxists, or anarchists—set the tone in most academic settings that are increasingly beholden to neoliberal, corporate interests and influence. It is thus wrong to characterize higher education as decidedly leftist, much less far-left.

That being said, academia is, in general, one of the most hospitable places for those on the left to express their views meaningfully and in ways that have a social impact. Although, in many ways academia is just another kind of workplace that reflects the diversity of political perspectives within a society—and where radical viewpoints need to be asserted in struggle against prevailing, and typically more conservative, ones for them to gain any semblance of a foothold, even temporarily. The academic setting represents a milieu in which many American students first encounter serious, sustained leftist positions, however diverse and dispersed those positions may be. With effective pedagogy, it is the first time that students might come to associate the left with a careful, probing thought-process that has weighed the options and seriously considered various alternatives, both descriptively and normatively. In other words, the college classroom is often the first-time students are exposed to leftist perspectives as analytical or methodological approaches to knowledge production, and not merely as judgments or conclusions rooted solely in predetermined values or partisanship. Mainstream American society does not foster a conversation broadly hospitable to the left; both the legacy of the 1950s and the imprimatur of the Reagan (counter)Revolution have succeeded in casting it as decided un-American and indeed dangerous to the American way of life—and, if that were even true, assuming that that is automatically a bad thing (which speaks to the value-ladenness of the ostensibly neutral foundations of much of academic work). Yet aside from independent journalism, such as *Democracy Now!* and *Truthout*, the academic setting counts among the most hospitable places for a leftist commentary to express itself and to be taken seriously in contemporary American society. The pieces included in this volume exemplify the sustained, thought-provoking analysis that the classroom allows, free from the kind of stereotyping that shuts down critical insight and alternative intellectual frameworks.

The merits of rigorously critiquing mainstream American complacency and its imperial history lie in its ability to awaken students to the sexist, racist, classist, capitalistic values embedded in their experience of the everyday. Given that the classroom brings together a variety of people from different ethnic, cultural, religious, and socio-economic backgrounds, it operates as the ideal setting in which this awakening might occur; viewed from this angle, it is preferable to homeschooling, for the context of the classroom is itself pedagogically charged. Engaging those pedagogical practices that open students' eyes to Althusser's "interpellation," Erich Fromm's "social character," Antonio Gramsci's "hegemony" can produce a crucial moment in students' education, bestowing on them the analytic tools with which to reinterpret American commonplaces and to perceive their ingrained power relations. These concepts refer to the mechanism by which the material aspects of society – the wage structure, the scope and quality of social services, the distribution of wealth and class dynamics – and the ideological reinforcement of the ideas that underpin those relations are (re)produced over time and thus result not only in the (re)production of basic social structures and relations of production and consumption, but also to the ideology, the culture, and the mindset that defines American society. At both the high school and higher education levels, students can experience a life-changing epiphany regarding the politics of their surrounding society, especially when facilitated by critical-pedagogical strategies.

When the academic setting itself is appropriated by a neoliberal framework beholden to corporate culture, a college education becomes little more than a means to get a (better) job. It is our task to teach students, and to remind our colleagues, that viewing higher education in this instrumental way represents a relatively new concept in the history of education. We firmly believe that the primary purpose of education is not to get a better job (which may occur as a by-product), but to train students' minds so that they become informed critical thinkers who are culturally literate, politically savvy, and confident regarding their ability to change society in concert with others. Education should neither blindly serve the socio-cultural and economic elites nor sustain rigorous distinctions between "high" and "low" cultures; to be an educated person should not simply guarantee a good salary and facilitate sophisticated conversation disconnected from everyday life. Rather, education should empower students to be critically aware and socially engaged. It should cause them to see connections between what they study and what they routinely experience via what Foucault terms the "capillaries of power." In sum, it should inspire them to do things beyond the classroom, to make a difference and demand to be heard and heeded.

All that being said, with all the above nuance, we imagine still, if Tucker Carlson or any of the buffoons at Fox News, *Breitbart*, or *The Daily Caller* picked up this volume, they would undoubtedly see it as an object case of how radical Marxist liberal Democrats hate America and want to brainwash children. The merits of aggressively criticizing the US and its continuing imperial history aside (of which the list would be lengthy), one of the fundamental premises of all the various strands of critical pedagogy—rooted as they are, however distantly, in Marxism—is that traditional pedagogy and mainstream educational form and content are already, more or less, brainwashing children and therefore explicitly shaping the kinds of adults they become.

As the authors' contributions in this volume make clear, the classroom, the school, the university are all already political. We are not calling for politicizing the classroom. We are variously calling for teachers and professors to *alter*-politicize it—or, we are at least attempting to think through and articulate the ways that we can. Pedagogy is typically understood as how you teach, not what you teach. Critical pedagogy rejects this distinction, as Marxism rejects the distinction between theory and practice. As such critical pedagogy, at its best, is Marxian praxis, even when drawing on traditions that well-exceed (and are even somewhat critical of some versions of) Marxism to do so.

While some university and college teachers are just teachers, many (when they have the time) are both teachers and scholars, pedagogues and researchers. It is this dynamic, in relation to the various arguments made in the preceding chapters, put in the broader context of the public, social, and even possibly common[1] role of academia, that this conclusion focuses, proceeding to discuss the time and professional constraints on academic activists, academic freedom and political correctness, and the complex and often contentious (when not outrightly antagonistic) relationship between the scholarly community and radical activists and organizers among other related topics where appropriate.

---

1 For more on the concept of the common and commonwealth, see: Michael Hardt and Antonio Negri's *Commonwealth* (2009).

## 2    The Politics of the Profession: What's Our Job?

While much of this volume is rightly focused on the politics of the classroom and the relationship between classroom pedagogy and the wider world, we cannot forget that high school and university campuses are themselves highly politicized arenas. And in many but not all cases, they operate in a quite conservative capitalistic setting which, despite the advantages of tenure, sometimes limit professors' engagement with society. Indeed, a solid research agenda and publishing record are more crucial to securing tenure than is political activism. Thus, contrary to the opinion of many outside the academic arena, teachers and professors tend to be extremely busy people. The absent-minded professor is often absent-minded not because of some inherent carelessness or a continued focus on erudite abstractions, but simply because she or he is busy. To sustain a robust scholarly agenda alongside serious classroom teaching indeed represents a tall order that curtails radical activism and impedes engagement with society at large. While classroom teaching certainly allows academics to have a lasting and profound impact on society, their involvement with politics as traditionally understood necessarily becomes curtailed.

    Yet in order for teachers and professors to have a lasting impact via their control of the classroom requires that they themselves have the benefits of tenure. The job stability that tenure represents is what ostensibly allows them the freedom to speak out against positions taken by academic administrations, lawmakers, and indeed anyone with cultural capital; it emboldens academics to articulate the controversial, contrapuntal positions that a democratic society should protect. At the university level, tenure offers the professoriate the ability to conduct scholarship, mold academic programs, and be involved in university politics without fear of reprisal from department chairs, deans, presidents, chancellors, and other officials. It thus represents a crucial component of the academic profession as anyone who opposes the mainstream may engage critically without the threat of unemployment looming on the horizon.

    Nevertheless, the institution of tenure is currently under threat. While the University of Wisconsin recently abolished it completely, bills proposing its abolition have been under discussion in Iowa and Missouri. At the same time increasing numbers of temporary or adjunct faculty teach on university campuses: over 50% of university courses are taught by temporary faculty with little to no say in university governance and who lack the protection of collective bargaining. Moreover, given that they are usually not given benefits and are paid extremely low wages, non-tenure track faculty represent a cheap and easy way for universities to save money while ensuring that their classes are taught.

Reports of adjunct faculty sleeping in their cars and picking up second jobs at grocery stores, or even as prostitutes, are not unheard of; yet those eager for an academic life must continue working on their research and publishing if they ever want to move out of this vicious cycle. Adjuncts are continually encouraged to keep working while tenured faculty often fail to fight back against their university's attempts to corrode the system of tenure. The clout of labor unions on campuses thus becomes a crucial venue for protecting the integrity of the academic life.

The need to protect the academic freedom of the left is especially important, because, in general, they are the ones more likely pushing forward agendas of greater substantive (not merely descriptive) inclusivity and positive freedom—as opposed to those on the far right, perspectives which are terrifyingly becoming more mainstream, pursue policies that enhance the regressive exclusivity of higher education and knowledge production.

To advance knowledge, to pass along that knowledge and the attendant skills related to the fields we work and teach in to our students as well as the broader public: this is the public function of academics. Teaching not only transmits information but also trains students to embrace critical thinking skills and to think creatively. As such it hopefully instills the love of learning in them, which in any democracy constitutes a necessary public service that ensures the reproduction and the advancement of our society. Yet the politics of university education are not entirely "democratic" in the United States today. Firstly, a university education in America is highly inaccessible due to its cost; this throws into question its public function given that those from poor or working-class backgrounds are disadvantaged despite well-meaning, though incomplete, efforts to increase the diversity of the academy around identity categories like gender, race, ethnicity, and sexual orientation. These efforts are incomplete as they relate to class, especially in regard to hiring in higher education (socioeconomic-based affirmative action policies are a bit more robust for students than faculty and staff). While there are no extant comprehensive studies on the subject, our experience tells us that those from working-class and/or impoverished backgrounds are generally the most underrepresented "identity" in academia. While racial, gender, and sexuality diversity is crucial, if only to stamp out the enduring racism, xenophobia, and cisheteropatriarchy that maintains white, cis-straight male dominance in higher education, it is equally important to ask why class is systematically excluded from discussions (and more egregiously, policies) around diversity in hiring in higher education. Second and as alluded to earlier, the university's place in our society is under attack; for the threats to tenure and the colonization of university life by corporate interests undermine the university's traditional commitment to free thinking. Indeed, the continued existence and public function of the university is itself under threat.

Yet we believe that the classroom represents an important site of engagement that can raise awareness about this issue and train students to think against the grain. We need to fight for our universities—for a model of a university that is humane, just, egalitarian, and engaged. This needs to be part of our public function, and our ability to find joy in what we do and impart the value of sustained, critical reflection helps convey this message to our students. Given that our classrooms are inherently political, we either unquestioningly reproduce the mainstream neoliberal intellectual space that we already inhabit, or we demonstrate the great value in leftist pedagogy today.

Indeed, the university today does not always foster intellectual growth. Our classrooms and campuses are not intellectually safe spaces for radical thinking or action. Neoliberal capitalism is taking aim at our classrooms as well, with more and more classes being moved online seeking to produce measurable, quantifiable goals while assuring students that their education will translate into job skills. We are constantly encouraged to use simplifying technologies into the classroom and to present learning in terms of a technological fix. Anyone on a faculty listserv has likely received push-advertisements from Top Hat or some other educational technology service company inquiring as to whether we want to use a "tool" in our classrooms (and rest assured, your university has already paid for it!). Campuses are thus becomingly increasingly inhospitable to faculty who are interested in deploying critical and radical pedagogies that eschew the profit-making technologies of the higher education industry—which in-turn makes campuses increasingly unsafe for the intellectual development of students. Of course, technology can enhance learning and accommodate the learning process. Yet when "teaching" becomes reducible to having expensive equipment on hand, and when "learning" becomes tantamount to accessing a computer program, our society is in danger of losing the critical distance on itself that the essays contained in this volume have sought to validate.

The contemporary liberal notion of tolerance, rooted as it is in John Stuart Mill's nineteenth century political philosophy, is a kind of teleology. Mill (1989) argues that progress is the telos of tolerance and freedom, that giving expression to contrasting opinions and unpopular ideas will ensure a forward-thinking society. Yet if in the "marketplace of ideas" it is the marketplace that wins out over ideas, then a neoliberal paradigm has cunningly established itself as the champion of democratic ideals. Our job as professors who are committed to safeguarding the leftist tradition and the canon of critical theory is to guard against this paradigm. Our job is to educate students regarding the contemporary pertinence of Marxist thought – both orthodox and revisionist – as it speaks directly to the concerns of the twenty-first century. The aim of this volume has been to underscore that pertinence today and to demonstrate the ongoing relevance of leftist critique despite the success of countervailing forces, or indeed perhaps because of them.

Our classrooms are already political. We either unquestioningly reproduce the limited conservative-liberal intellectual space that maintains the unjust society we continue to live within—psycho-social, and deeply political, parameters that continue to allow millions to suffer and die unnecessary every year, to say nothing for the ecocide which defines the capitalocene—or we politicize them differently. We support the status quo through maintaining the current politicization of the classroom, or we *alter*-politicize the classroom in service of transformative justice, democracy, and equality.

## 3   Unsafe Spaces

Our classrooms and campuses are not safe spaces, at least not for radical thinking or action. They are not safe for campus staff workers, students, or faculty. We must resist the increased dominance of capitalistic norms and "values" in education. We must resist the adjacent and intersecting forces of cisheteropatriarchy (systemic chauvinism, [cishetero]sexism, and [cishetero]misogyny), racism, and classism. These forces are not in retreat. They are advancing and too often winning. Some have suggested, though not as many as one might think from the characterizations offered by the corporate media, that banning right-wing speakers and instituting extreme anti-harassment, anti-discrimination, and microaggression/safe-space policies is the best route for the time being.

Those of us on the left in academia should support rigorous anti-harassment and anti-discrimination policies that are transparent and democratically accountable, but we must be wary. We must be wary because neither our politics nor our universities are fundamentally democratic—to say nothing of their opacity. No-platforming (the denial of speaking platforms to those deemed to engaged in hateful, overtly discriminatory or even exclusionary rhetoric) is practiced variously throughout European universities. It has done very little, if anything, to stifle the rise of far-right politics. In the US, one need only look at the recent cases of university responses to far-right hate campaigns against Steven Salaita, George Ciccariello-Maher, James Livingston, and Marc Lamont Hill to see how policies of this kind can be weaponized against left-leaning professors. We must be wary. Any policy that is designed to exclude far-right ideas, even if effective in the short-term, are likely to be written in a general way, such that in the future (or the present) these policies can be deployed against left-wing speakers, scholars, and teachers. Hating the rich, white supremacists, and/or sexists are each technically forms of hate, after all (however morally, politically, and logically superior these forms of hate are). University policies typical in these areas are not usually, if ever, nuanced enough to exclude these perversions (and we should also be wary of assuming that liberal "allies" intend these policies to only apply to the far-right).

As Herbert Marcuse (1969) suggested, we run into a problem with tolerance when the good ideas—the emancipatory, positive freedom-increasing ideas—are losing again and again. Undemocratic university policies, likely to be draconian and unnuanced, are not ideal avenues to fight the rise of fascism and the endurance of classist racist cisheteropatriarchy. Organizing is our best alternative. This means both as workers on campus and, intersectionally, beyond campus. To put it bluntly, we should be in the streets with our students; we should be bringing the streets into our classrooms.

Universities and educational environments around the world should be safe for all—all those willing to accept the inclusion and basic dignity of all people. This does not mean that students should go unchallenged in the classroom. In fact, the project of building a truly safe world for all demands that aggressive attempts be made to facilitate students' unlearning of some of the most egregiously harmful things they've previously learned. This should be done in a fair and compassionate manner, but no student has the right to enter into a classroom and have their views remain unchallenged. No one, neither faculty nor students, have a right to remain intellectually comfortable. Physically comfortable? Absolutely, without question. Comfortable and secure in the knowledge that they will be graded on transparent and equitable standards of evaluation, not on whether they agree politically with an instructor? Absolutely, without question. At the same time, in the same way that no biology professor would or should assess the rejection of evolution or the acceptance of the superiority of a particular race on an exam or student paper, there are certain views that are so beyond the realm of knowledge that they have no place in a university classroom or on a university campus. It is not inherently unfair to suggest that there are more of these kinds of views, nearly by definition, on the right-wing of the political spectrum than on the left.

This will strike many as a hopelessly biased and self-serving position. After all, one could reasonably (though not undeniably accurately) argue that history has shown near equal failure of supposed left political projects as it has right political projects. There is quite a bit of a difference between building a political project on false hope in undemocratic central planning of an economy and the intentional extermination and/or subjugation of entire peoples. Being a proponent of central planning is not the same as being a virulent racist. Supporting central, or democratic, planning does not necessarily demand that the voices defending the free market or wage labor exploitation be silenced. Racists, on the other hand, believe that the voices of people of color are not to be taken seriously, at the very least, and often there are violent implications beyond that basic premise. Historical failures to build an inclusive economy should be scrutinized, especially when there are serious doubts as to whether these goals were ever seriously attempted in most of the historical examples typically offered as failures of socialism. Right-wing views should be studied as well, but the problems emerge when students (and not few enough faculty) defend these views in the classroom, in meetings, or really anywhere. How can other students feel (or be) safe when another student or faculty member is openly espousing racist, sexist, or aggressively classist views? They cannot, and that should be unacceptable. The looming question is: what is the recourse? This is a question the left needs to have much better answers to. Banning speakers through undemocratic processes may feel good now, but it does not do much to actually build egalitarian democracy.

The good news for those skeptical or hesitant to apply this with regard to the teaching of specific content, which to be clear is not exactly what has been suggested here, teaching students one specific set of view points or demanding that they regurgitate left-wing perspectives on things is not only unnecessary, it is not an effective way to get students to come to those conclusions (and in a lot of ways would undermine the unlimited democratic ethos that is at the heart of socialist politics and economics). Engaging with our students critically; assisting them in the development of their capacities to question the status quo and the systems of power and injustice that permeate all our lives is far more effective. Part of that demands that we assign heterodox literatures and develop unconventional assignments. This is part of teaching, and teaching in a genuinely fair manner.

Teaching to the status quo deprives students of real learning and intellectual development opportunities. It limits the public function of pedagogy in even a superficially democratic society—all the more problematic when that ostensible democracy is actually an imperial plutocracy. Now, if teaching students how to effectively engage in democratic forms of knowledge production and social criticism is a kind of brainwashing, then yes, precisely that kind of brainwashing is being advocated for—but not the requirement to accept a certain political or intellectual perspective. Again, not only would that be hypocritical, it is not the most effective way to move students to the left politically.

Our campuses must be safe for faculty to push against the boundaries put up against these practices of imperial plutocracy and neoliberal bureaucratization; they must be safe for students to have the opportunity to learn from and against them, even if, still, in the end, they come away maintaining more moderate or even conservative political viewpoints.

Though politics is not biology, it is worth reminding ourselves again that in a biology class not all perspectives are equally valid. And while social science does not have facts like biology does, this is a far cry from suggesting that all viewpoints should be acceptable in the social sciences. This kind of delineation does not mean there is a specific way that we should deal with students who hold right-wing, capitalistic, or otherwise anti-democratic views. Demanding their agreement surely will not work. Demanding students tell you what you want to hear is a deeply cynical and deeply conservative approach to pedagogy and belies everything the left should stand for. Real teaching, real radical or critical pedagogy demands much more.

The starting point for thinking more broadly, critically, and even radically about our pedagogical function in society, is that our campuses must be undeniably safe for students, workers, and faculty. They should be intellectually unsafe for racists, capitalists, sexists, and bigots of all kinds. They should be unsafe for corporatization and corporate influence. They should be unsafe for business models and inapplicable quantitative evaluation. They should be unwelcoming to, at the very least, and hopefully politically unsafe, for ICE and Border Patrol.

## 4 Beyond the Class(room): On Activism and Organizing

Why are academics and college campuses so reviled by so much of society? It is because campuses are undeniably elite spaces that produce consistently condescending faculty and, not rarely enough, graduates. Universities remain unequitable and unequally accessible, especially in the US. They remain largely bastions of privilege and detached navel-gazing (and, much worse, profit-gazing). Academics, even those who place themselves on the left, are rarely activists. They rarely, though there are enough exceptions to this to make it far less true than is generally thought, put themselves in more horizontal spaces with non-academics. For the most part, likely having a lot to do with the income/class position of many tenured or tenure-track faculty[2], academics

---

2 Though untenured and temporary faculty (i.e., adjuncts) are likely just (un)engaged as their more secure and better paid colleagues, it is unfair to criticize them for their lack of engagement given the onerous teaching loads and low pay those in these positions receive.

are more often than not agents of the status quo. Even a lot of critical scholars keep their criticism within the walls of the classroom or within the covers of the journals they publish in (and further hidden behind the paywalls of most academic journals and steep price points of most academic monographs).

While this conclusion certainly betrays some specific notions of a public pedagogy and role for the teacher-scholar-activist, there are likely a multitude of ways this can be done effectively in the current conjuncture. To say quite literally the very least, we need to do better—and we can do better, but only if we organize and struggle together in various ways. This need not be exclusively through conventional labor organizing and solidaristic support for others engaged in labor organizing. It need not always be organized protest. We are smart people, and, if we care enough to try, we can figure out strategies to develop a praxis of radical-critical public pedagogy suitable to the contemporary moment and beyond.

Beyond that, academics with politics that resonate with the range of politics represented in this volume need to do a better job of working with social movements and radical organizations in humble, committed, and non-condescending ways. It is a truism that an injury to one is an injury to all, and when we fight we win, but for good reasons. We need to support one another on campus and beyond. Though we should maintain support and time for genuinely critical scholarly analysis and research of all kinds, the contemporary moment demands more. It demands that we put our principles and our words into action.

## Bibliography

Marcuse, H. (1969) Repressive Tolerance. *A Critique of Pure Tolerance*. Boston: Beacon Press.

Mill, J.S. (1989) On Liberty. *On Liberty and Other Writings*. Ed. Stefan Collini. Cambridge: Cambridge University Press.

# Index

abstraction   56, 59, 153, 158, 174, 227
Adorno, Theodor   135, 140, 144–146, 150–151, 156, 162, 207, 215
alienation   82, 90, 93–94, 95, 95n, 96, 98, 99, 150, 167
American Dream   5, 9, 131, 133, 136–137
anticapitalist antiracism   10, 109, 187, 187n, 188–189, 193–200
Aschoff, Nicole   119–120, 121n

banking education   153–154, 169, 176, 194–195
Barrett, Michele   105n, 106–108, 112, 112n, 113–118
base   96, 134
Baudrillard, Jean   25, 133
Berlant, Lauren   137, 139
Black Lives Matter   2, 138, 141
*Blade*   96
Brexit   62
Brown, Wendy   27, 104, 129
*Buffy the Vampire Slayer*   94, 97

Cabral, Amílcar   6, 16, 37–38, 38n, 41, 149
Campbell, Joseph   177
*Capital*   7, 20n, 35, 57–58, 72, 91, 135, 152
capitalism   2, 8, 30, 33–36, 40, 55–56, 61–62, 67–69, 72–73, 76–77, 79–86, 90, 91n, 92–93, 95–98, 103–116, 116n, 119–127, 143–152, 157–158, 166, 188–200, 208–212, 221
  global capitalism   7–9, 17, 24–27, 29n, 49–53, 181
  neoliberal capitalism   50–54, 60–62, 229
Castro, Fidel   66–67, 69–71, 73, 75
challenges of teaching Marxism   90–91, 41, 66
Chomsky, Noam   84n, 206–207
class   2, 6, 10, 16, 18, 21–22, 22n, 25–26, 26n, 31, 38, 40, 48–62, 72, 98, 104, 106–107, 143–144–146, 147n, 151–160, 191–193, 199, 214–221, 225, 233
  class conflict   90, 93–94, 98–99
  class consciousness   33, 38, 96
  class-in-itself   58–59

middle class   1–2, 72, 128, 161, 167, 188
working class   1, 4, 26, 30–37, 50–51, 58–62, 93, 96–97, 113, 148, 151, 198, 204, 215, 228
Clinton, Hillary   119n, 120
Columbia University   20n, 203–209, 211, 213, 219
community   7, 38, 66, 75, 110–111, 128, 139, 174, 178–80, 190, 197, 226
comparative politics (CP)   6, 15, 19–22, 24, 27, 29, 35, 40
conscientization   10, 171–173, 189, 200
constructivism   23, 27n, 48, 52, 55
co-optation   8, 104, 119, 122–123, 128, 136
corporatization   86, 165, 170, 233
  corporate university   143–145, 147, 160–161, 179
courage   9–10, 164–166, 172, 177, 179–180, 182–183
Crenshaw, Kimberle   187
critical pedagogy   2n, 3, 6, 9–10, 105, 109, 143–148, 150–156, 188, 199, 226, 233
critical self-reflection   144–150, 155–156, 160
critical theory   1–2, 2n, 4, 6, 10, 55, 203, 208–214, 217–219, 230
cruel optimism   137
Cuban Revolution   69, 170

De Certeau, Michel   165
dead labor   92–93
dependency theory   7, 21, 48–49, 56, 59–60
determinism   29, 108n, 188
dialogic cultural synthesis   149, 154
*Dracula*   8, 89, 90n, 92–97
Dussel, Enrique   175

Ebert, Teresa   188, 191–193, 198
Ehrenreich, Barbara   108
end of history   6, 15, 18, 24, 27, 29, 41, 152, 171
Engels, Friedrich   6, 17, 26, 33n, 67, 69, 72, 74, 76n, 83, 93, 96–97, 106–107, 110, 111n, 127, 147n, 203–207
enlightenment (also Enlightenment)   2, 28, 35–36, 41, 135, 148, 152

essentialism 105n, 191, 198
Eurocentrism 1, 16, 18, 27–36, 39–41, 72, 191
exile 7, 9–10, 34, 66, 164–167, 169–171, 173, 175, 183

false consciousness 67n, 90, 93, 96–99, 188, 193
Feenberg, Andrew 134
feminism 2n, 6, 23, 29, 103, 111, 114, 117–119, 121, 144–147, 154, 159, 171, 187, 218
    femininity 103, 105, 109, 112, 113n, 114–117, 120–122
    feminist standpoint theory 9, 143, 156–157, 160
    Marxist feminism 106–112, 143, 207
    neoliberal feminism 8, 103–104, 119–120, 122
    socialist feminism 8, 103, 105–112, 116n, 117n, 118–120
framing (frames) 7, 188, 193, 197–200
Freire, Paulo 3, 9–10, 144–151, 153–155, 161–177, 180–182, 188–189, 193–196, 199–200
Friedan, Betty 119
Fromm, Erich 78n, 225

gender 2–4, 16m, 18, 31, 98, 103–109, 111, 112n, 113–120, 121n, 122, 148, 154, 158–161, 193, 200, 219–221, 228
    gender-neutral 8
global supply chain 60–61
Goulart, João 168
Gramscian 48–49, 54–56
*Grundrisse* 92

Harding, Sandra 157, 171, 218
Heidegger, Martin 206–211
hooks, bell 3, 102–103, 105, 111–112, 116, 219
Horkheimer, Max 135, 150, 208
human nature 67, 73–79, 81–82, 94
hyperreal 133, 137

identity politics 62, 143, 147, 151, 153
ideology 1–10, 15–19, 24–31, 35, 39, 41, 50–55, 62, 66–68, 78–86, 96, 107, 112, 120–122, 127–132, 143–148, 153, 160, 165–173, 176–177, 214, 220–225
imperialism 28, 30–31, 34–35, 37, 60, 207–208

indigenous people 18, 38–39
inequality 18, 41, 61, 82–83, 104, 143–148, 151–152, 156–162, 221
international relations (IR) 6, 10, 15, 19–24, 27, 29–31, 40, 48–49, 51–56, 164–167, 173–174, 176–178, 180–183
intersectionality 3, 8, 10, 16, 18, 27, 104, 187–188

Jay, Martin 214

Kant, Immanuel 74–75, 210
Korsch, Karl 208, 214–217
Kumashiro, Kevin 198, 199–201

labor theory of value 50
Ladson-Billings, Gloria 196, 201
Lakoff, George 198, 201
living labor 92, 93
Lukács, Georg 75n, 157, 208, 215

mansplaining 113n, 122
Marcuse, Herbert 3, 6, 8–9, 129, 132–136, 138–141, 206–209, 213–218
    false needs 128, 132, 133, 137
    Great Refusal 6, 8, 9, 127, 128, 133, 137, 141
    repressive desublimation 8, 9, 135, 140, 141
Mariátegui, José 6, 16, 37–39, 41
Marx, Karl 1–8, 10, 13–28, 30–34, 37, 39–42, 66n, 67, 69, 71, 74, 83, 95, 95n, 109–110, 147, 147n, 150–196, 211–213, 220, 224, 226, 230
    as utopian thinker 82, 127
    confronting students' ideas about 67, 69–70, 73–74, 82, 86, 89–91, 93, 99, 127, 200–201, 213
    criticism of British rule in India 30, 33–35
    criticism of Indian caste system 34n
    critique of imperialism 30–31, 34–35
    critique of religion 96
    Eagleton, Terry 41, 67n
    "Eighteenth Brumaire of Louis Napolean" 92, 221–222
    materialist history and stages of development 69, 75, 75n, 78n
    non-European writings 30, 36, 39, 40

on post-scarcity, post-revolution society  80–83
pre-capitalist societies  34, 37
relevance to feminism and critique of patriarchy  102–123, 143–162
surplus value  72, 74n, 84n
"The Holy Family"  187
theory of revolution and revolutionary consciousness  99, 148, 196–197
"Wage Labour and Capital"  94
Marxism  3–7, 9–10, 15–18, 23–24, 24n, 30, 30n, 31, 31n, 32, 32n, 36, 38, 40, 48–63, 67–75, 75n, 83–85, 90–91, 107–111, 143, 148–149, 151–154, 157–159, 161, 167, 172, 188–189, 192, 194, 196, 198, 203, 209, 211–217, 221, 224–226
  in Latin America  39n
  Korsch, Karl  208, 215, 218
  Western Marxism  213, 215–217
Masculinity  8, 103–106, 109, 112–114, 115–117, 118–120, 122–123
Merleau-Ponty, Maurice  174, 180
Miami, Florida, USA  4, 6–7, 66–68, 68n, 74–75, 75n, 79, 79n, 82–87
Million Woman March  138, 141
Mitchell, Juliet  114
"More factor"  131

narrative  5, 8, 30, 51, 67, 69n, 70n, 93, 97, 104, 172, 174, 182, 221, 224
Nazism  209
needs, true and false  82–83, 128, 132–133, 136, 188, 199
neoliberalism  4, 17, 50–51, 103–104, 106n, 122, 122n, 143, 148, 151, 170, 187n
*New German Critique*  214, 216
New Left  206

Occupy Movement  1, 138, 141, 205
one-dimensionality  134, 138
Open Door School  54

parrhesia  165, 178–179
patriarchy  8, 103, 107–108, 108n, 111, 187–189
  cisheteropatriarchy  228, 230–231
pedagogy, *see* critical pedagogy
phenomenology  167, 206, 211
Piccone, Paul  214, 216–217
places-to-be  175

political activism  137, 139, 164, 227
positivism  157
postcolonialism  16, 18, 29–30, 30n, 32n
postmodernism xii  2n, 29, 48, 148, 157, 210, 217
Power, Nina  120
praxis  4, 6, 25, 59, 86, 138, 147, 149–150, 153n, 161, 175, 188–189, 191, 193, 198–199
proletarian subjectivity  6, 10, 187–189, 192–196, 196–201, 215
property law  143, 146, 155–156, 161

race  2, 2n, 3, 16, 18, 31, 33, 74, 104, 147–149, 154, 157–159, 161, 193, 219–221, 228, 231
realism  7, 23, 48, 52–54
reflexivity  9–10, 164–166, 171, 173, 177, 178–181
repressive desublimation  8, 9, 135, 140–141
revolution  10, 18, 22, 25–26, 32–35, 38, 69, 72, 83, 83n, 86, 99, 102, 109, 122n, 127–128, 141, 143, 146–149, 151, 153–156, 160, 168–170, 176, 189, 194, 196, 200, 203–204, 206, 212, 214–217, 221–224
Rogers, Carl  195
ruthless criticism  144, 148, 150, 156

Said, Edward  164
scientific neutrality  24, 25
sectarianism  189–192
slavery  18, 33, 33n, 34
socialism  21, 24n, 38–39, 66n, 68–69, 80, 82, 204, 209, 212, 215, 224, 232
species-being  78, 78n
Standing Rock  138
Student Afro Society  204
Students for a Democratic Society  204
superstructure  77, 96
surplus value  26, 49–51, 55–59, 60–62, 72–73, 84, 84n, 90, 95, 144, 158, 161
syncopation  8, 127, 137, 139

tactics  168
Tahir Square  138, 141
technē  134
"The Communist Manifesto"  20, 41, 72, 89, 93, 96–97, 203
the Great Refusal  127–128, 137, 141
transnational capitalist class  54, 56
*True Blood*  90, 93, 96n, 97, 99n
Trump, Donald  203, 221

Turkle, Sherry   131–132
*Twilight*   8, 90, 90n, 93–94, 97

unequal exchange   49
U.S. Civil War   33
USAID   168

vampires   6, 8, 89–90, 90n, 92n, 93–94, 96n, 98, 99n
*Van Helsing*   94–95, 97
Vietnam War   204, 206–207

"Wage Labour and Capital"   94
white supremacy   187–188, 190, 197
World Social Forum   138, 141
world systems theory   7, 48–49, 50–53, 56, 59, 143

Zavarzadeh, Mas'ud   188, 191–193, 198
zombies   29, 98

www.ingramcontent.com/pod-product-compliance
Lightning Source LLC
Chambersburg PA
CBHW070920030426
42336CB00014BA/2467